Sociolinguistics

Language in Society

GENERAL EDITOR
Peter Trudgill, Chair of English
Linguistics, University of Fribourg

ADVISORY EDITORS
J. K. Chambers, Professor of Linguistics,
University of Toronto

Ralph Fasold, Professor of Linguistics,
Georgetown University

William Labov, Professor of Linguistics,
University of Pennsylvania

Lesley Milroy, Professor of Linguistics,
University of Michigan, Ann Arbor

Sociolinguistics

Method and Interpretation

Lesley Milroy and Matthew Gordon

Blackwell
Publishing

350 Main Street, Malden, MA 02148-5018, USA
108 Cowley Road, Oxford OX4 1JF, UK
550 Swanston Street, Carlton South, Melbourne, Victoria 3053, Australia
Kurfürstendamm 57, 10707 Berlin, Germany

Some material in this book was originally published in Lesley Milroy,
*Observing and Analysing Natural Language:
A Critical Account of Sociolinguistic Method* (Blackwell, 1987).

First published 2003 by Blackwell Publishing Ltd

Library of Congress Cataloging-in-Publication Data

Milroy, Lesley.
  Sociolinguistics : method and interpretation / Lesley Milroy and Matthew Gordon.
    p.   cm. — (Language in society ; 34)
Includes bibliographical references and index.
  ISBN 0-631-22224-3 (alk. paper) — ISBN 0-631-22225-1 (pbk. : alk. paper)
  1. Sociolinguistics. I. Gordon, Matthew. II. Title. III. Series: Language in
society (Oxford, England) ; 34.

  P40 .M544 2003
  306.44—dc21

                                                                    2002007988

A catalogue record for this title is available from the British Library.

Set in 10.5/12pt Ehrhardt
by Graphicraft Limited, Hong Kong
Printed and bound in the United Kingdom
by MPG Books Ltd, Bodmin, Cornwall

For further information on
Blackwell Publishing, visit our website:
http://www.blackwellpublishing.com

Contents

3 Data Collection 49

4 Language Variation and the Social World: Issues in Analysis and Interpretation 88

List of Figures

List of Tables

Series Editor's Preface

In Lesley Milroy's *Observing and Analysing Natural Language*, published earlier in this series, there was distilled, as I said at the time, the collective wisdom of the first generation of sociolinguists about how to *do* sociolinguistics. This wisdom included, most of all, that of Lesley Milroy herself, who was one of the best practitioners of this form of linguistics there had ever been. Here was an author who really knew what she was talking about because, in her own pioneering work, she had confronted and overcome many of the thorniest practical and theoretical problems that the field had had to offer. Like most other people teaching sociolinguistics, I had often been approached by students who were excited about work they had read in sociolinguistics, who wanted to carry out work of this type themselves, but who had no idea how to set about doing it. Lesley Milroy's book was therefore a godsend; it was a book to refer such students to with gratitude and with confidence that their questions would be answered.

Many things have changed since that very welcome publication. Sociolinguistics has acquired new concepts, new problems, new concerns, new methodologies, new theories, and new analytical tools. One thing has not changed, however. Lesley Milroy remains one of the best practitioners of sociolinguistics there has ever been. In this new book, therefore, we have once more an expert, insightful, exciting and up-to-date guide to sociolinguistic methodology and interpretation that will be invaluable to all those concerned with the carrying out of sociolinguistic fieldwork, and the meaningful analysis of the data obtained through such fieldwork. Lesley Milroy and Matthew Gordon deal with the history of sociolinguistic methodology, modern methods in fieldwork and data collection, recent approaches to the handling of data, and the relevance of social categories, social relationships and social practices. Once again, we know which book to refer our students to with gratitude and confidence.

Peter Trudgill

Preface

Over the past decade and a half the field of sociolinguistics has experienced remarkable growth which is marked not simply by the continuing attraction of new scholars to the field but more importantly by the expanding range of approaches now practiced by sociolinguists. Evidence of the expanding interests of sociolinguistic researchers can be seen in the kinds of linguistic phenomena they investigate, the data they consider, the analytical tools they employ to uncover patterning, and the linguistic and social theories they draw upon to interpret their results. This book seeks to provide readers with a sense of the range of this research.

While questions of method constitute a major focus of our discussion, the book is not intended to be a handbook or an inventory of techniques, although it certainly is designed to be of practical value to anyone interested in studying the ways people use language in various social contexts. Sociolinguistic method is discussed in terms of its relationship to theory, in the belief that if this link is not acknowledged, *interpretation* of research results may ultimately be difficult and unsatisfying. Some apparently innocuous methods – which are in fact associated with a specific theoretical paradigm – can often conceal important underlying assumptions. Methodological problems and principles will therefore be discussed not only in practical terms, but in terms of the assumptions underlying the chosen method and the theoretical goal of the research. An account of method divorced from theory is not considered to be helpful, desirable, or even possible.

The origins of this book lie in Lesley Milroy's *Observing and Analysing Natural Language* (*OANL*) which first appeared in 1987. While the general orientation of that work has been maintained, and some of its material has been reproduced here, the tremendous expansion of the field has necessitated that the original work be substantially revised and updated for the current project. A good deal of new material has also been included to treat issues that have since emerged as significant (see, for example, the discussions of instrumental techniques for analyzing phonological variation (section 6.3.2) and the treatment of style-shifting as a strategic maneuver (section 8.3)). The additional perspective provided by the co-author, Matthew Gordon, serves to distinguish further the current work from *OANL*.

The basic structure of the book partly follows that of *OANL*. Chapter 1 offers a theoretical introduction to the general framework of variationist sociolinguistics, and is followed in chapters 2 and 3 by a discussion of study design and methods of data collection. Chapters 4 and 5 explore issues related to the social dimensions of language variation, and chapters 6 and 7 focus on linguistic issues, discussing various aspects of data analysis and interpretation related to phonological variation, and grammatical variation. Finally, style-switching and code-switching are examined in chapter 8.

Acknowledgments

A great many people have contributed in various ways to making this book a reality, and we gratefully acknowledge their help and influence. First of all we are indebted to our colleagues and students at the University of Michigan and the University of Missouri for providing moral support and an intellectually stimulating environment. Various conversations with Charles Boberg, Dave Britain, Jack Chambers, Gerry Docherty, Penny Eckert, Naomi Nagy, Robin Queen, Natalie Schilling-Estes, Peter Trudgill, and Dominic Watt have been particularly helpful and, of course, our debt to William Labov is apparent throughout the book. We also wish to thank Vicki Carstens, Aidan Coveney, Paul Foulkes, Janet Fuller, Jim Milroy, Acrisio Pires, and Robin Queen for their thoughtful comments on various chapters. We are particularly indebted to Keith Walters who read and commented on the manuscript in its entirety, and to Bridget Anderson and Jennifer Nguyen for their assistance in preparing the text for publication. Jennifer also undertook the task of compiling the index.

The authors and publisher gratefully acknowledge the following for permission to reproduce copyright material:

Figure 6.5 from B. M. Horvath, *Variation in Australian English: The Sociolects of Sydney.* © 1985 by Cambridge University Press;

Figures 7.1 and 7.2 from T. Nevalainen, "Making the best use of 'bad' data: Evidence for sociolinguistic variation in Early Modern English," in *Neuphililogische Mitteilungen.* © 1999;

Figure 8.1 from A. Bell, "Language Style as Audience Design," *Language in Society* 31 (2). © 1984 by Cambridge University Press;

Table 4.1 from J. K. Chambers and P. Trudgill (eds.), *Dialectology* (2nd edn.). © 1998 by Cambridge University Press;

Table 4.4 from S. Dubois and B. M. Horvarth, "Let's Tink about Dat: Interdental Fricatives in Cajun English," *Language Variation and Change* 10 (3). © 1998 by Cambridge University Press;

Table 8.3 from P. Eckert, "Style and Social Meaning," in P. Eckert and J. Rickford (eds.), *Style and Sociolinguistic Variation.* © 2001 by Cambridge University Press;

The Panjabi excerpt and translation on p. 211, from V. Chana and S. Romaine, "Evaluative reactions to Panjabi-English code-switching," in *Journal of Multilingual and Multicultural Development* 5. © 1984 by Multilingual Matters.

Lesley Milroy would also like to thank the US National Endowment for the Humanities and the College of Languages, Science and the Arts at the University of Michigan for financial support during the process of writing this book.

1

Sociolinguistics: Models and Methods

1.1 Data and Theory

This book focuses primarily on the methods and theories underlying the quantitative paradigm of sociolinguistic research pioneered by William Labov, with the goal of providing a resource for investigators who are setting up a research project, large or small. This tradition of research is sometimes called *variationist*, to distinguish it from other sociolinguistic subfields. We consider in subsequent chapters data collection, analytic procedures, and interpretation of results, with continuing attention to the theories and assumptions underlying research practice. Like all fields of enquiry, variationist theory has developed a distinctive orientation to its object of investigation (i.e., human language), and a distinctive set of research questions which, while not always explicitly articulated, provide the characteristic focus of those investigations. Variationists do not of course operate independently of other branches of linguistic science, nor indeed of other kinds of socio-linguistics. Furthermore, their orientation, and sometimes the assumptions underlying their theories, are often best understood with reference to historical antecedents.

Mindful of these observations, we have approached the task of writing this book with the conviction that effective researchers need to develop an awareness of the assumptions underlying practice in their fields, so that they may, if necessary or appropriate, coherently query those assumptions. They also need to develop an ongoing awareness of the relationships between their own fields and others – and of the historical antecedents that have shaped their field – sometimes by providing a framework against which practitioners react. A clear example of such a reaction is the critical stance of Labov's early work to what Chambers (1995) describes as *the axiom of categoricity* – the traditional assumption in linguistics that language structure should be treated as invariant. In accordance with this principle, variability has often been dismissed as unstructured and thus of little theoretical value, but Labov's classic sociolinguistic studies in Martha's Vineyard (1963) and New York City (1966) demonstrated that the trajectories of specific linguistic changes could be inferred from the observation of patterns of variation in contemporary speech communities (see further section 2.5 below). He thus reacted quite radically not only against the axiom of categoricity but against the Saussurian dichotomy, fundamental to structural linguists, which held that the synchronic study of language states was an endeavor entirely separate from the diachronic study of language change. Labov also reacted in these influential early works against the methods and assumptions of contemporary dialectological research – a field quite distinct from the mainstream linguistics of the 1960s. These intersecting reactions still inform many of the assumptions and practices that characterize variationist theory as a subfield.

In this chapter, we expand on these observations, attempting in the remainder of this section to locate the methods and assumptions of variationist theory in relation to those of adjacent fields. In section 1.2 we examine two important historical antecedents to quantitative sociolinguistics – the work of the American descriptivists and that of traditional dialectologists in both the United States and Europe – and in section 1.3 we explore further the relationship between the dialectological and variationist traditions by considering examples of projects that bridge the two approaches.

Johnstone (2000b: 1) points out that contemporary sociolinguistics comprises a great many different traditions of research which address correspondingly different sets of research questions. However, all sociolinguists share a common orientation to language data, believing that analyses of linguistic behavior must be based on empirical data. By this we mean data collected through observation, broadly defined, as opposed to data constructed on the basis of introspection. The most commonly studied data among sociolinguists are those representing speakers' performance – the way they actually use language. Still, researchers may observe elements other than language use. Sociolinguists are often interested in subjective responses to particular linguistic behaviors (e.g., a specific feature or a variety/dialect) and may observe them by eliciting evaluations of speech as is done in perceptual dialectology (see section 1.3.2). Researchers may also make use of speakers' self-reports of their usage (see, e.g., our discussion of written questionnaires in section 3.2.1). Such data can be useful in examining the effects of language ideology (see Milroy and Milroy 1999), but it is important to recognize, however, that such reports are not generally accepted by sociolinguists uncritically as "true" reflections of actual usage.

This general orientation to language data is shared with adjacent fields such as linguistic anthropology and conversation analysis (see Psathas 1995; Pomeranz and Fehr 1997). Qualitative traditions of research such as those of Gumperz (1982a) and Hymes (1972), which emerge from linguistic anthropology, have been influential from the earliest days of sociolinguistics, continuing to influence contemporary subfields such as discourse analysis (Schiffrin 1994) and interactional sociolinguistics (Gumperz 1982a; Brown and Levinson 1987). Although qualitative research characteristically does not focus on patterns of linguistic variation or employ quantitative methods (but see Schiffrin 1987 for an example of an extensive project which combines quantitative and qualitative procedures), it continues to exert an important influence on variationist theory. Particularly important is the emphasis of linguistic anthropologists on ethnographic methods of observation which attempt to uncover patterns of informal social organization in speech communities, with a primary focus on speakers as social actors, rather than on abstract language patterns. This focus enables a richer and more accountable interpretation of social information than is found in much of variationist research (see further section 3.4).

Like sociolinguists in general, variationists are trained as linguists and routinely use descriptive and analytic tools that are common throughout the field of linguistics. In fact, one regularly finds in the variationist literature descriptive accounts of particular linguistic phenomena which employ standard concepts from syntactic or phonological theory. For example, Martin and Wolfram (1998) examine negative concord and other syntactic features in African American English using a Government Binding framework. Guy and Boberg (1997) offer an account of coronal stop deletion in English that draws on the obligatory contour principle – a construct borrowed from formal phonology. Nevertheless, despite sharing some analytical common ground, such accounts, and those of variationists generally, differ from the accounts of contemporary theoretical linguistics in at least two fundamental ways: (1) they involve differing orientations to data, and (2) they derive from distinct approaches to linguistic variation.

As noted above, variationists, like other sociolinguists, tend to base their analyses on observed data. Traditionally these data have often been gathered in the context of conversational interviews in which the subject (or informant) remains unaware that his or her linguistic usage is the focus of investigation (for alternatives to such methods of data collection see chapter 3 and section 7.2). This source of data clearly contrasts with those sources often used by mainstream theoretical linguists. In this tradition, investigators may rely on data that they themselves construct, drawing on their own intuitions. Alternatively, when dealing with languages which they do not command natively, the investigators may elicit forms from, or verify their own constructions with, native-speaker informants. Thus, the data arise from an explicitly metalinguistic context, one in which the investigator and any informants are thinking about language. Here the questions are of the form "Can you say X?" By contrast, the sociolinguist's questions are closer to "Do you say X?" though, since the data are usually gathered through observation rather than elicitation, such questions are not made explicit. The sociolinguist's orientation toward data is further distinguished from that of the theoretical linguist's by the former's adherence to the principle of accountability, which is discussed in the following section.

A more fundamental distinction between theoretical linguistics and variationist sociolinguistics relates to their respective approaches to variability. The principles set out by Weinreich, Labov, and Herzog (1968) are still taken as axiomatic by variationists; namely, a language system that did not display variability would not only be imaginary but dysfunctional, since structured variability is the essential property of language that fulfils important social functions and permits orderly linguistic change. Chambers (1995: 12–32; see also Chambers and Trudgill 1998: 127) has discussed the role of the *linguistic variable* as a structural unit, parallel to such units as the phoneme and noun phrase in linguistic theory. Chambers points out that, from the earliest days of structural linguistics, analysts produced descriptions and generalizations based on an underlying assumption that linguistic structure was fundamentally categorical. Following the Axiom of Categoricity, language is seen as operating with a kind of mathematical consistency. Still, it has always been known that speakers varied in their realizations of particular abstract linguistic structures (intraspeaker variation) and, furthermore, that usage varies across speakers (interspeaker variation). Thus, for example, /æ/ (the vowel of *cat* and *bad*) in many varieties of American English is realized with a range of vowel qualities from a low front monophthong [æ] to a high front diphthong [ɪə] (see Labov 1994; Gordon 2001b). It is also common for plural subjects sometimes to take singular and sometimes plural forms of the verb BE (as in *we was sleeping/we were sleeping*) (Tagliamonte and Smith 2000; see also Tagliamonte 1998). In the past many linguists (notably, Edward Sapir) have displayed sensitivity to the pervasiveness of variation. Nevertheless, the mainstream linguistic approach to the plain fact of variability has often been to exclude it from consideration in the interests of providing a coherent and elegant descriptive and theoretical account. This orientation was captured in Chomsky's oft-quoted statement that the primary concern of linguistic theory is "an ideal speaker-listener, in a completely homogeneous speech-community" (1965: 3). In this tradition variability is treated as a methodological complication: it introduces a kind of noise which obscures the important underlying invariance. The perceived peripherality of variation to theoretical matters is reinforced by a dichotomy that segments off language structure (competence) from language use (performance) and assumes many kinds of variation to be the purview of the latter (see further below).

Such an orientation to variability describes alternative realizations like [æ] versus [ɪə], or *was* versus *were* following a plural subject as either the outcome of *dialect mixing*, held to be a temporary situation of instability, or instances of *free variation*. However, as the psychologist Fischer noted "Free variation is a label, not an explanation. It does not tell us where the variants came from nor why the speakers use them in differing proportions, but is rather a way of excluding such questions from the scope of immediate enquiry" (Fischer 1958: 47–8; cited by Chambers and Trudgill 1998: 128). As their name implies, variationists view variation as central to their immediate enquiry; rather than treating, and often dismissing, variation as free, accidental, unconstrained, or temporary, variationists begin with the assumption that variation is structured and seek to uncover patterning. In truth, many theoretical linguists approach variation with similar assumptions, and treatments of variation have made their mark within theoretical linguistics from time to time. For example, Pollock (1989) used evidence of the variable position of infinitival verbs in French and in English to propose a radical revision of sentence structure which resulted in major changes to mainstream syntactic theory. Similarly, Diesing (1992) presented a highly influential proposal for how interpretation relates to syntactic position, based on variable word orders in German and their semantic correlates. Moreover, alternations like the English dative shift (*give the book to her* vs. *give her the book*) and the variable position of objects in verb particle constructions (*turn off the light* vs. *turn the light off*) are also time-honored topics of study within the generative paradigm.

Nevertheless, one obvious difference between treatments of variability within the generative tradition and within sociolinguistics is that the latter make reference to social (i.e., extralinguistic) as well as linguistic information in specifying the constraints on variability. Thus, frequencies of particular variants are constrained not only by different linguistic contexts (type of following consonant in the case of (æ); type of grammatical subject in the case of (BE PAST)) but also by social characteristics of the speaker such as gender, age or status and the kind of social context (interview talk vs. peer interaction, for example) in which language samples are embedded.

A somewhat more subtle distinction between generative and variationist approaches to variability stems from the emergence of the linguistic variable as a structural unit. Chambers (1995) elaborates in some detail the significance of this development for the sociolinguistic enterprise and for linguistic theory more generally. Examples of underlying linguistic variables would thus be (æ) or (BE PAST), as mentioned above. Variants which realized those abstract variables would include, respectively, [æ] and [ɪə] (and countless intermediate forms) and *was* and *were*. A major goal of the variationist enterprise is to specify and order the constraints which lead to one choice rather than another. The linguistic variable works in terms not of categorical use, but of greater or less frequency of one variant than another, so marking the abandonment of the axiom of categoricity. However, like other structural linguistic units, it is understood as an abstraction underlying actual realizations (see further section 6.5 below).

Chambers suggests that the abandonment of the axiom of categoricity renders variationist theories irreconcilable with those of contemporary generative linguistics, since the latter paradigm abstracts away from variability while variationists treat it as central. It is worth considering for a moment some reasons for Chambers's rather pessimistic verdict. First, the constructs of mainstream generative linguistics have become more rather than less abstract over the years. Sidnell (2000) notes the continuing relevance of Givón's (1979) critique, namely that the abstraction that was originally devised as a point of methodological convenience has become progressively more prominent. Thus the focus is no longer on the detailed linguistic rules of early generative theory, but on the specification of broad principles and parameters constraining the form of universal grammars (Cook and Newson 1996). For this reason, the hope for fruitful collaboration between different traditions of linguistic research expressed by Labov (1975) has become less likely to be realized in the intervening quarter century. Labov's (1996) examination of problems in the use of intuitions (introspective judgments of grammatical well-formedness), either of the analyst or of the individual whose dialect is being studied, is both an update of and sequel to his 1975 monograph. In the course of this more recent article, he contrasts the approaches of variationists and generativists, and examines the roles of intuition and observation in deriving valid linguistic generalizations. While he finds many points of overlap between the two traditions, the optimistic hopes of collaboration expressed in his 1975 paper are noticeably absent.

Second, the distinction between *competence* and *performance*, first expounded by Chomsky in 1965, remains problematic to all sociolinguists. A speaker's competence is the underlying ability to produce and interpret well-formed sentences in a given language and to distinguish well-formed from ill-formed strings. The specifics of such competence are generally established by eliciting intuitions (or using the analyst's own intuitions) of grammaticality. Performance, on the other hand, covers not only the manifestation of competence on actual occasions of language use, but the effects of memory, perception, and attention on language behavior. In 1986, Chomsky revised the competence/performance dichotomy, preferring a distinction between I(nternal) and (E)xternal language. As Sidnell (2000) points out, this change in terminology involved no significant alteration in the underlying abstraction except a slight change of focus on what constitutes E-language. While generativists are interested exclusively in competence/I-language and have not elaborated any coherent theory of performance/E-language, the distinction is problematic to sociolinguists, most obviously because it treats language as intrinsically asocial (see, again, Labov 1996 for a wide-ranging discussion of the issues). Much systematically variable language behavior is treated globally as performance/E-language, along with the linguistic effects of memory and attention. For variationists, not only is variation essential and intrinsic to human language, but the detail of systematic, socially embedded variable behavior is the key to an understanding of the dynamics of language change. In an account of variability of pronominal reference in Spanish, Cameron (1996) aligns himself with Prince (1988), arguing specifically for an enlarged conception of competence to include memory and attention phenomena.

In the early days of sociolinguistics Hymes (1972) pointed out that Chomsky's competence was only one kind of linguistic competence. Not only did competent speakers produce and interpret well-formed sentences, but they also used varieties of language from a systematically structured community repertoire to perform social actions in contextually appropriate ways that were meaningful to other members. They also recognized particular utterances as ironic, teasing, serious, etc. (Hymes 1972, 1974). Any socially informed linguistics concurs with Hymes in conceiving of knowledge "with a view to its fundamental role in communication between socially located actors in continuously changing human societies" (Sidnell 2000: 41).

While these rather fundamental incompatibilities need to be acknowledged, it is important not to exaggerate the impenetrability of the boundaries between sociolinguistics and theoretical (usually generative) linguistics or to further polarize the two research traditions. On the generative side, Henry (1995) has produced an account of dialect acquisition in Belfast, Northern Ireland within a principles and parameters framework, which takes account not only of variability but is based largely on observed data (see also Wilson and Henry 1998). Prince (1988) has argued for a much enlarged concept of competence that takes account of observed and naturalistic language data. Schütze (1996) provides a critique of the role of intuition in syntax research, arguing for a radical rethinking of its empirical base. Conversely, variationists regularly work with frameworks developed by theoretical linguists. For example, Cornips (1998) examines syntactic variation within a principles and parameters framework; Nagy and Reynolds (1997), Guy (1997), and Zubritskaya (1997) work with Optimality Theory from theoretical phonology; and Docherty et al. (1997) examine the descriptive adequacy of theoretical accounts of glottalization phenomena from a variationist perspective.

We conclude this review of the interrelationships between linguistics, sociolinguistics, and cognate disciplines with some comments on the orientation of variationist theory toward the social dimension of language behavior. Gumperz (1982a) has pointed out that although Labov rejects Saussurian and Chomskyan assumptions of uniformity in grammatical systems, he shares with other linguists an interest in understanding the general character of grammars, believing these to be affected by the social characteristics of human groups. Our discussion so far has in fact assumed this orientation by locating variationist theory as a subdiscipline of linguistics. However, Gumperz then argues that the relatively abstract approach associated with Labov's theoretical goal entails a neglect of the speaker as participant in interaction, and that quite different methods are needed to investigate issues arising from the ability of speakers to interact, such as the co-occurrence (or otherwise) of their judgments in the interpretation of discourse: "A speaker-oriented approach to conversation . . . focuses directly on the strategies that govern the actor's use of lexical, grammatical, sociolinguistic and other knowledge in the production and interpretation of messages in context" (Gumperz 1982a: 35). Labov himself has contrasted in a similar way two alternative approaches to linguistic variation: one can start by examining linguistic forms (variables) and their distribution, or by examining speakers and the kind of behavior appropriate to different situations. Labov prefers the first type of framework because it gives a better idea of the *system* as a whole, although it is not capable of yielding optimal information about *speakers* (Labov 1966: 209).

The distinction drawn here between the properties of a variable system and the behaviors of the speaker is an important one that still gives rise to tension in the field. It embodies the chief distinction between qualitative and quantitative, interactional and variationist traditions of sociolinguistic research, the former type being influentially exemplified by Brown and Levinson (1987). Johnstone (2000b) has recently provided a clear account of the methods, goals and assumptions of qualitative sociolinguistics. Over the years, Labov's work has become increasingly oriented to the linguistic system rather than to the speaker, attempting primarily to specify universal patterns of change in vowel systems (Labov 1991, 1994) and to map out the large-scale spatial distributions of these systems (see further section 1.3.2; Labov, Ash, and Boberg, forthcoming). These analyses make little if any reference to social information or to the behaviors of speakers. A more generally unsophisticated treatment, or even neglect, of social factors by variationists has given rise to criticism not only by linguistic anthropologists but by variationists themselves (see, for example, Rickford 1999; Eckert 2000). As we will see in chapter 5, Eckert and others have recently argued strongly for a more socially sophisticated approach to language variation that systematically takes into account the behaviors and motivations of speakers. The chief point we make here, however, is the continuing relevance of the distinction articulated by both Gumperz and Labov between an approach that primarily addresses the properties of variable linguistic systems and one that primarily addresses the behaviors of speakers in their speech communities.

1.2　Earlier Approaches to Linguistic Description

1.2.1　The American descriptivists

The American linguists, commonly known as "structuralists" or "descriptivists," placed a high premium on the development and practice of a rigorous and accountable set of field and analytic methods. In this section we outline the characteristics of their approach and philosophy only insofar as they are particularly relevant to the central concerns of this book. For fuller accounts, the reader is referred to Lepschy (1982), Hymes and Fought (1980), Robins (1967), and Sampson (1980).

The concern with method in mainstream American linguistics from the early decades of the twentieth century until the emergence of Chomsky's generative grammar is largely attributable to a desire to describe as rapidly and efficiently as possible a large number of dying native American languages. Gumperz (1982a: 12) contrasts the atmosphere of empiricism at that time in America, where scholars were concerned with working in the field, with that in Europe, where they worked in offices. He apparently sees contemporary sociolinguistics as a continuation of this empirical tradition. Following the line of reasoning elaborated by Bloomfield (1926; 1933), the accreditation of a *scientific* status to linguistics was associated with the development of rigorous methods of description. American linguists strove to obtain objectivity by developing accountable procedures for inductively deriving linguistic generalizations from observable data, and an important methodological principle springing from this concern was that the phonological, morphological, syntactic and semantic patterns of a language should be analyzed separately. They should, moreover, be analyzed in that order so that the analyst could remain in touch with the "observable" part of language – the sequence of sound segments with which the description began.

A similar concern with accountability to the data subsequently became the hallmark of variationist work; Labov's *principle of accountability* extends the general philosophy of accountability to a specifiable procedure which is the cornerstone of quantitative method (see further section 6.1). In this respect his views resemble those of earlier American linguists but differ sharply from those of Chomsky and others working within the generative paradigm. Replacing induction with a hypothetico–deductive mode of reasoning, the generativists argued that no corpus of data, however large, can usefully serve as a basis for linguistic generalizations since any corpus is a partial and accidental collection of utterances (Chomsky 1965: 15). Chomsky's general point about the inadequacy of corpora as the *only* source of information is surely correct, but in practice seems uncontroversial since intuition and introspection (either of the investigator or more usually of the informant) have always been used by linguists, including sociolinguists, who work in the field. Voegelin and Harris (1951) discuss the relative roles of observation and intuition (of the informant) as data-gathering procedures, and the same theme is revisited by Rickford (1987). Johnstone (2000b: 71–9) discusses at some length the role of intuition and introspection in sociolinguistic research. Although Chomsky seems to be attacking a straw man in his critique of corpus-based research, the effect of his remarks has been a shift of focus from observation to introspection, and a corresponding removal from mainstream linguistics of the need to be accountable to an independently collected body of data.

Despite this major paradigm shift in linguistics, American descriptivist methods still provide the basis for procedures of data collection and analysis in the field. The extensive studies of Australian languages by Robert Dixon and his associates are obvious examples, as are the continuing efforts of linguists working on the indigenous languages of the Americas (see Mithun 1996 for a review). Rather less obviously, structuralist methods – the most influential of which are outlined below – have been developed in various ways for use in quantitative sociolinguistic work (see particularly Labov 1984).

To get a sense of descriptivists' methods, we can consider their approach to establishing which sounds were contrastive – a procedure that they considered to be the major task of a phonological analysis:

> We take an utterance recorded as DEF. We now consult an utterance composed of the segments of DA′F where A′ is a repetition of a segment A in an utterance which we had represented as ABC. If our informant accepts DA′F as a repetition of DEF . . . and if we are similarly able to obtain E′BC (E′ being a repetition of E) as equivalent to ABC, then we say that A and E . . . are mutually substitutable (or equivalent) as free variants of each other . . . If we fail in these tests we say that A is different from E and not substitutable for it. *The test of segment substitutability is the action of the native speaker: his use of it or his acceptance of our use of it.* (Harris 1951: 31 – our italics)

In the absence of any alternative framework capable of application to a substantial body of data, linguists studying unknown languages still need to establish contrastivity in a similar way (see Healey 1974: 8 for a New Guinea example). And so do variationists; but one respect in which they have advanced the substitution method is by querying the assumption of objectivity in pair testing and showing that native speaker judgments of "same" and "different" do not necessarily correspond in a straightforward way with independently observed phonological patterns (see section 6.5; Milroy and Harris 1980). Harris's painstaking account in the above quotation gives an idea of the care with which the descriptivists formulated their "discovery procedures" as they were called – this basic method of substituting one element for another being viewed as the equivalent in linguistics to the controlled experiment of the physical sciences. Most importantly, it permitted replicability.

The descriptivists pursued similar techniques in their analysis of the *syntactic* patterns of an unknown language. The main aim was to assign words to classes on purely distributional grounds, using syntactic frames (parallel to Harris's phonological frame DEF) to present a range of items that were candidates for membership of a particular category. In most cases, particularly for investigators of North American languages, the examination of syntax and other higher-level linguistic elements was aided by the recording of texts containing longer stretches of connected speech (Mithun 2001: 35). Field linguists continue to rely on both direct elicitation and texts as complementary sources of data (Mithun 2001; Payne 1997). It is also important to note the central role of native-speaker consultants in the transcription and analysis of texts. In fact, Payne suggests that working through a text with a consultant can provide a fruitful context for eliciting data. The linguist can ask, in reference to a passage in the text, "Can different word orders be employed? What would the speaker have meant if he/she had said ACB instead of ABC?" (Payne 1997: 369). Thus, syntactic analyses in this tradition may still rely on the intuitions of native speakers even when they incorporate data from independently collected texts.

As in the case of phonological pairs tests, sociolinguists and others who gather data in the field have reported that speaker judgments do not always accord well with the results of independent observation, and are more likely to reflect stereotypical attitudes to linguistic forms than the facts of grammatical structure. Chelliah (2001) describes how some of the speakers of Meithei, a Tibeto-Burman language spoken in India, rejected as ungrammatical certain constructions that she had recorded in conversational contexts. Based on their labeling of the relevant constructions as the product of "laziness," Chelliah concluded that the judgment of these speakers was influenced by their familiarity with Sanskrit-based prescriptive grammars of their language. Mithun (2001: 48) notes a range of difficulties related to the elicitation of grammaticality judgments, including the fact that consultants may reject sentences as "ungrammatical" based on pragmatic considerations or even on poor pronunciation. Based on similar concerns, Labov (1975, 1996) has cited the unreliability of speaker judgments as an argument against the uncontrolled use of introspection as a methodological tool (see also Schütze 1996).

1.2.2 Traditional dialectology

Many aspects of the geographical observation and description of language – an approach that was developed during the nineteenth and twentieth centuries – underlie the variationist methods that are discussed in the following chapters. Conversely, in recent years Labov's innovations have heavily influenced contemporary dialectology which has become revitalized after many years of relative decline. Chambers and Trudgill (1998) provide a comprehensive account of the methods of traditional dialectology ("dialect geography," in their terms) which they integrate with those of contemporary urban (i.e., variationist) and rural dialectology. The discussion in this section is limited to the methods and goals of traditional dialectology which provided a context to Labov's early work. Later developments are reviewed in section 1.3.2 below.

Generally speaking, the aim of dialectological work is to produce a geographical account of linguistic differences, the end product often taking the form of a series of maps showing the broad areal limits of the linguistic features (usually lexical or phonological) chosen for study. Boundaries (known as *isoglosses*) are plotted on a map, to show where form A gives way to form B; a *dialect boundary* is said to exist where a number of isoglosses more or less coincide. For example, Wakelin (1972: 102) illustrates the boundary between the northern and north-Midland dialect areas of England by showing eight isoglosses which mark the approximate southern limit of eight phonological features characteristic of northern English dialect speech. It is important to appreciate that the field methods of traditional dialectology were not devised to survey patterns of contemporary language use as an end in itself, but to offer a means of answering questions about the earlier history of the language within the philological tradition of the nineteenth century. The main objective was to study contemporary reflexes of older linguistic forms in their natural setting, concentrating on speakers and locations that were relatively free from external influence. Associated with this theoretical model was a view of rural life strongly colored by nineteenth-century romanticism, as noted by the influential American dialectologist Hans Kurath:

> In Europe, the practice has been to confine the survey to the speechways of the folk, and to give prominence to the oldest living generation in rural communities. A predilection for historical problems, the hope of shedding light on processes of linguistic change by observing the linguistic behavior of the folk, and admiration for the soil-bound "ethos" or "world-view" of "natural" people have been the motives and justification offered for this practice. (Kurath 1972: 13)

With these motives, Jules Gilliéron approached his linguistic survey of France (1896–1900) by seeking out older male, uneducated speakers who lived in remote rural communities. Chambers and Trudgill (1998: 29) note the selection of this type of speaker as the hallmark of traditional dialectology: "No matter how diverse the culture, how discrepant the socioeconomic climate, and how varied the topography, the majority of informants has in all cases consisted of nonmobile older rural males," for whom they adopt the acronym NORMs. Both Orton (1962: 15) and McIntosh (1952: 85) discuss the value of this type of speaker on whom it does indeed seem reasonable to concentrate if the goal is to collect evidence confirming hypothetical reconstructions of earlier forms. By the same token, however, rather different sampling procedures are needed if the survey purports to make a more general statement about patterns of language variation.

While nineteenth-century research is overwhelmingly historical in orientation, twentieth-century dialectologists working within the traditional paradigm frequently shifted theoretical goals in the direction of an attempt to describe the contemporary language. This is a particularly notable feature of early dialectology in the United States, the achievements of which are described by Carver (1987). Thus, Hans Kurath, appointed director in 1929 of a proposed Linguistic Atlas of the United States and Canada, sought to adapt the traditional model by selecting subjects at three educational levels, each notionally categorized as "old-fashioned" and "modern" types. Kurath (1972: 11) comments: "Until recently, large-scale surveys have been deliberately restricted to folk speech, especially to that of the countryside . . . In *The Linguistic Atlas of the United States* all population centers of any size were regularly included and, in principle, all social levels are represented." Proportionally the resulting samples still favored the traditional type of speakers, but it is nevertheless significant that people representing higher educational and socioeconomic levels were included. In fact, as Bailey (1996) points out, even in the nineteenth century the American Dialect Society was much more inclined than its English counterpart to recognize urban dialects as falling within the domain of investigation. An example of this wider focus is Babbitt's (1896) account of the urban dialect of New York City. At this time, British urban speech was thought to be unworthy of serious study (Bailey 1996: 71–2).

A tendency in more recent British studies to shift the theoretical goal is evident from McIntosh's comment that the Scottish survey will concentrate on older (or, as he calls them, "resistant") speakers *"only in the first instance"* (1952: 86). Orton, on the other hand, while aware of the sensitivity of patterns of language use to factors such as status, age, sex of speaker, and situational context, is nevertheless quite clear in his view that these facts are irrelevant, since his objective is to locate for the *Survey of English Dialects* speakers who can provide samples of traditional dialect speech (Orton 1962: 15). In a sense Orton's apparent recalcitrance is quite justified. As the examples discussed below (section 1.3.1) illustrate, established dialectological methods of the mid-twentieth century were fundamentally incapable of producing a realistic account of contemporary language variation. Indeed, one of the major points made by Labov in his early (1966) comments on the

work of the dialectologists is that such an account necessitates radical altera-
tions to the traditional method; minor adaptations are insufficient.

Moving on from the question of strategies of speaker selection to methods
of data collection in traditional dialectology, the two major techniques are
on-the-spot transcription of responses to a questionnaire elicited by a trained
fieldworker and the postal questionnaire (see Chambers and Trudgill 1998:
21–4). The technique of on-the-spot transcription (particularly phonetic
transcription) adapted in various ways, has provided the major model for
later work. For more than half a century on-the-spot transcription has been
supplemented or replaced by audio recordings – a development that has
made possible close study of larger stretches of spontaneous spoken language rather than isolated lexical items (see chapter 3). However, in general,
those twentieth-century dialectological projects (for example, the *Survey of
English Dialects*), which work within an only slightly modified framework
of the traditional paradigm, have not fully exploited the technological
advances that have increasingly facilitated the study of spontaneous speech.
Often the tape-recorder is used simply as a support for the fieldworker, who
proceeds otherwise in much the same way as his or her nineteenth-century
equivalent.

The postal questionnaire is an older technique, pioneered in Germany
by Georg Wenker in 1876. More recently it has been used by McIntosh
(1952) in Scotland and Le Page (1954) in the Caribbean; see also Le Page
and Tabouret-Keller (1985: 83). McIntosh notes the obvious advantage of
the method: that it provides an economic means of collecting large volumes
of data. Nevertheless, the technique has its limitations and raises questions
about the reliability of self-reported data (see further section 3.2.1). Questionnaires are still widely used where there is a need to collect quickly a
large amount of easily processable data; examples include the Adult Language Use Survey of the Linguistic Minorities Project in Britain (1985)
and Amuda's (1986) study of Yoruba/English code-switching patterns in
Nigeria. The adaptability of the postal questionnaire as an instrument for
sociolinguistic research has been illustrated by Chambers's Golden Horseshoe project in Canada (see section 3.2.1; Chambers 1998b). Some researchers
have even taken the postal questionnaire into the digital age by utilizing the
Internet in gathering responses (von Schneidemesser 1996; Murray, Frazer,
and Simon 1996; Murray and Simon 1999).

Some of the difficulties associated with self-reported data are alluded to
by Le Page (1957, 1958). His procedure in the *Linguistic Survey of the British
Caribbean* was to send a questionnaire containing the following instructions
to schoolteachers, who were asked to locate suitable respondents:

> It is essential that the answers given to each question should not be those
> which the school teacher or other helper (whom we will call the *Interrogator*)

can supply from his own vocabulary, which will have been considerably enlarged and influenced by his education and travel, but those which a local *Informant* supplies without undue prompting. You are therefore requested to select as an *informant* somebody, preferably middle-aged and not too well educated, who has lived in your area for the greater part of his or her life, and has had comparatively little contact with other places. The *Informant* will have to be a person whom you know is willing to talk to you unaffectedly in the language he would use to his own family; somebody who will not be trying to impress you with his knowledge of white-talk all the time or of what is said by other people in other places. It would be useful to explain to the informant that you only want the words and phrases exactly as they would be used by the ordinary unsophisticated people of this community. Men or women who work or live in daily contact with people from other countries or other walks of life should not be used as informants. In an agricultural village, select an elderly labourer, in a fishing village a fisherman but not somebody who goes to sell goods in a distant market or somebody who works as a domestic servant. (Le Page 1954: 2)

Le Page identifies here a number of problems that are not associated exclusively with the use of a questionnaire, but are quite general in linguistic fieldwork and were not addressed by traditional dialectological methods. First, the effect of social or occupational mobility on language use is noted; second, the natural effect of style-shifting in inhibiting the use of everyday language as opposed to more formal varieties is hinted at; and finally the effect of "white-talk" on attitudes to vernacular usage is noted, together with the consequence that an informant will often claim to use forms considered to be of higher status than his or her normal usage. All of these problems of eliciting samples of low-status vernacular speech in contexts where negative social values are attached to it have subsequently received considerable attention from investigators working within Labov's framework. Indeed, for many years Le Page worked partly within this framework, although he has been critical of some aspects of it (see McEntegart and Le Page 1982; Le Page and Tabouret-Keller 1985).

1.3 Adaptations of the Traditional Model

Until the mid-1960s, the general framework offered by the traditional dialectological model was widely used for descriptions of language variation largely because it was the only coherent one available at that time. In the following sections we look at various attempts to adapt it for purposes other than those for which it was originally intended, and discuss some of the problems and successes encountered.

1.3.1   Between paradigms: Early urban studies

We noted in section 1.2.2 that the goals and methods of traditional dialectology were motivated by the historical preoccupations of nineteenth-century philology. With the emergence of structural linguistics in Europe and the United States in the early decades of the twentieth century, the links between dialectology and mainstream linguistic science disappeared, and dialectology developed for a time more or less independently of linguistics. Chambers and Trudgill (1998: ch. 3) discuss developments which attempt to restore that link. Of these the most influential is the structural dialectology associated with Weinreich, Labov's mentor (Weinreich 1954), and Moulton, the Germanic dialectologist (Moulton 1960). Structural dialectology addressed the tendency of dialectologists to treat linguistic elements (particularly sounds) in isolation, rather than as parts of a system. Labov has recently reaffirmed Weinreich's influence on his students (specifically himself and the creolist, Beryl Bailey) in encouraging them "to apply the tools of linguistics to the language of everyday life and to set aside the barriers between linguistic analysis and dialectology" (Labov 1998: 111). Since a full account of the focus of structural dialectology on phonological systems is provided by Chambers and Trudgill, we do no more here than note its continuing influence. The focus of Labov's recent work on whole vowel systems (noted in section 1.1 above) appears to reflect the influence of structural dialectology, as does his continuing interest in the dynamics of vocalic chain-shifting, mergers, and splits (Labov 1994).

We turn now to a very different kind of problem associated with traditional dialectology – the practice of selecting the conservative, rural type of speakers termed NORMs by Chambers and Trudgill and (particularly in Britain) ignoring city dwellers. We look briefly at some early urban studies which nevertheless retained salient characteristics of the traditional model. One of the most pervasive assumptions underlying the traditional dialectological method is that a particular form of a dialect – usually represented by the speech of a conservative, socially marginal speaker – is in some sense the "genuine" or "pure" form. The main difference between early and more recent (variationist) urban studies is that by employing the concept of the linguistic variable the latter examine *alternative* linguistic forms, seeing this alternation as a significant property of language rather than admitting the concept of the "pure" or "genuine" dialect. This difference in the conception of what constitutes a dialect has important implications for subject selection procedures.

A fine example of a thorough traditional study of an urban dialect is Viereck's *Phonematische Analyse des Dialects von Gateshead-upon-Tyne* [sic] (1966), a substantial and clear synchronic phonological account which includes a discussion of the relation between Received Pronunciation and "local standards" (an idea derived from H. C. Wyld). Viereck considers in some detail how dialect forms might interact with RP forms to produce such urban varieties as that of Gateshead, a city adjacent to Newcastle on the southern bank of the River Tyne (see section 5.3 below where this issue is addressed somewhat differently in contemporary Tyneside as an example of the process of dialect leveling). Although Gateshead's population is given as 100,000 and consists of males and females of all ages and various social statuses, Viereck's description is based on the speech of 12 men, all retired manual workers, whose average age is 76. This does not seem to be a reasonable basis for a systematic description of an urban dialect.

Gregg's work in Larne, Co. Antrim, Northern Ireland (1964) resembles Viereck's study in its orientation to phonological structure and its interest in the emergence of local urban standards. Gregg relates his findings in Larne to data on the local Ulster-Scots dialect, noting that while Larne speakers have a similar phoneme inventory to rural hinterland speakers, they characteristically reorganize it in such a way that the available phonemic contrasts appear in different lexical sets. This kind of systemic difference is what Wells (1982) describes as a difference in phonological incidence. Although Gregg's account is linguistically sophisticated, it is also clearly traditional in orientation insofar as it is preoccupied with the "genuine" speech of Larne as opposed to speech in which influence from nearby Belfast can be detected.

Similar comments might be made about Sivertsen's *Cockney Phonology* (1960), a study of the working-class dialect of London. While recognizing that there are various kinds of Cockney which vary according to style and social location of speaker, Sivertsen is explicitly interested in what she describes as "rough Cockney." Her work is based mainly on the speech of four elderly female speakers from Bethnal Green, selected for their relative social isolation, low social status, and lack of education. This is a substantial and clear description which also includes a number of observations on matters that became quite central in later variationist work – for example, gender-related differences in language. Sivertsen nevertheless retains the traditional preoccupation with the "pure" form of the dialect – in her view most reliably obtained from uneducated, elderly, low-status speakers.

The best of these early urban studies, of which we have discussed only a few examples here, provide valuable sources of data on the phonologies of urban dialects (see further Kurath 1972: 184ff) but they present two main problems.

First, certain assumptions are inherent in the preoccupation with "genuine" dialect, the most obvious being that young speakers, by virtue of access to education and modern communications networks, are more likely to be influenced by the standard. This assumption has not in general been borne out by observation. An early example of a contrary finding is provided by

Hurford's (1967), investigation of the language of three generations of a London family. Hurford shows that Cockney features are advancing among the youngest speakers at the expense of RP features.

A very large number of quantitative studies suggest that the kind of age grading in language noted by Hurford is in fact rather general, to the extent that researchers now expect to find the most progressive form of an urban vernacular among adolescent speakers and may therefore focus on that age group (see, for example, Cheshire 1982; Eckert 2000; Kerswill 1996). Furthermore, if traditional features recede, they are not usually replaced by forms that could be considered "standard" (Trudgill 1988; Kerswill and Williams 2000). The apparently common-sense assumptions inherent in the older urban studies are found on closer investigation to be false.

The second problem with these studies is their lack of representativeness. For example, London is one of the largest cities in the world and has, at least since the sixteenth century been linguistically very heterogeneous (Nevalainen 2000b). Even if we confine our interest to working-class speech from the low-status East End of the city, we are still talking about a pool of hundreds of thousands of people. It therefore seems inappropriate to limit the description to a single type of speaker without acknowledgment or justification. If this criticism is accepted, sampling procedures emerge as salient. At much the same time as Labov was developing in New York City the sampling procedures that subsequently became widely used by variationists, others attempted to tackle the sampling problem while still working broadly within a traditional framework. A brief outline of three such attempts will help to contextualize Labov's more radical methods, which are discussed in chapter 2.

In his study of Chicago, Pederson (1965) expanded greatly the traditional system for classifying subjects socially in order to represent more accurately the diversity in the population. Instead of the three-way distinction used in the linguistic atlas projects (see section 1.2.2), Pederson categorized his speakers into 10 types based on their education and another 11 types based on their socioeconomic status. He sampled the speech of 136 people from across these categories. Moreover, his sample attempted to represent some of the ethnic diversity of the city and included African Americans, Hispanics, and whites of various European descents. Unfortunately, this rich demographic detail is never correlated systematically with the linguistic data. In his discussion of phonological variation, Pederson often notes forms as having been used by particular speakers and attempts generalizations about the types of speakers offering a certain pronunciation. It is nevertheless difficult to assess the validity of any suggested patterns since they seem to be based on casual observations rather than a systematic comparison of groups.

Similar difficulties are found with Houck's survey in Leeds, England. This work was intended to provide a model for the study of urban dialects generally (Houck 1968). Using a sophisticated two-stage sampling procedure, he ended up with a sample of 115, representing a 75 percent success rate, which is very high for a linguistic survey (see further section 2.2.1). Unfortunately, however, Houck gave little indication in his published work of how the speech of his 115 subjects was handled; the intention seems to have been to set up a phonological system using minimal pairs elicited by means of sentence frames (cf. section 1.2.1). Thus, although he succeeded in obtaining a large amount of representative data, he was unable to find a way of handling it. Houck's work, like Pederson's, is suggestive of the tension between the need for accountable sampling procedures and the demands on the analyst's time and energy of analyzing large amounts of linguistic data. We return to this issue later (sections 2.2.3 and 3.5).

Heath's survey (1980) of the urban dialect of Cannock, Staffordshire, England, carried out in the late 1960s, is characterized by an equally rigorous approach to sampling. Eighty speakers are divided into five groups, in accordance with the amount of influence upon their speech of the "extremes" of Received Pronunciation (RP) on the one hand and Cannock urban dialect on the other. The influence of traditional assumptions on Heath's approach – as on that of the other researchers whose urban dialectological work has been considered in this section – is evident in frequent references to the "pure" Cannock speaker.

In subsequent chapters, we discuss methods of data collection and analysis that do not rely on the concept of the "pure" dialect speaker but allow the contemporary language to be modeled in a somewhat more realistic way than was possible by adapting traditional methodology. For although there is much that is valuable and innovatory in Heath's work, he was not able to model the *systematic* character of interspeaker variation The major contribution of Labov's methods was that in explicitly recognizing such patterns they provided a means of describing the language of a much broader range of speaker groups, without forcing the investigator to argue (or imply) that the language of one particular group was in some sense more "genuine" than that of others. In the final section of this chapter we consider research that has borrowed aspects of Labov's methods for describing linguistic variation. We see this work as exemplifying a growing union between dialectology and sociolinguistics or at least between some of the practitioners of each field.

1.3.2   Bridging paradigms: Adaptations of traditional dialectology

One acknowledged deficiency of traditional dialectology is its difficulty in dealing with variable forms and especially in representing variability among the sample populations. An isogloss drawn on a map to illustrate the geographical extent of a given form suggests that people on one side of the line use that form while people on the other side use an alternative form. In doing so, the isogloss can mask variability within the regions (i.e., the use of both forms on either side of the line). For this reason, many dialectologists seemed hesitant about drawing isoglosses and preferred maps showing the distribution of forms with symbols representing individual communities (see, e.g., Kurath 1949). Even this approach is problematic as it masks variation within communities and within individual speakers.

More recently, dialectologists have turned to various quantitative methods to address these problems. For example, Carver (1987) adopts the notion of isoglossal layering as a means of representing the complexity of dialect boundaries. Carver's work is based exclusively on lexical data taken mainly from the Dictionary of American Regional English (DARE) project. His approach treats dialect boundaries as more incremental and distinguishes "core" regions from secondary and tertiary ones. These distinctions are based on the number of regional features in use in an area. So, for example, Carver examined 61 features associated with the traditional Lower South dialect region in the US. Certainly, we do not expect to find all 61 features in a given community, and in fact the highest number recorded for a single location was 37. Carver designated the core layer of the Lower South to include those communities having between 17 and 37 of the features. A secondary layer extended to those areas in which at least 10 features were found, and a tertiary layer to those with between one and nine of the features. This layering approach reflects the fluidity of dialect divisions more accurately than do simple isoglosses. Moreover, by considering relatively large numbers of features and employing objective criteria for drawing boundaries (i.e., numerical cut-offs), Carver does appear to remove much of the subjectivity involved in determining dialect divisions and let the data speak for themselves. Nevertheless, as Kretzschmar (1996) observes, this approach remains highly subjective as demonstrated by the fact that Carver selected the data he examined from hundreds of available features without offering any objective evidence that the chosen variables are more signficant as dialect markers than those he rejected.

Central to the increased interest in quantitative methods among dialectologists have been advances in computer technology which make every step in the process quicker and easier from analyzing the data statistically to plotting results on maps. Such technology has reinvigorated the field, and a wide range of new approaches have appeared (see, e.g., Kretzschmar, Schneider, and Johnson 1989; Girard and Larmouth, 1993). A leading figure in this area has been William Kretzschmar, Jr., who directed the creation of a computerized database of the materials from the Linguistic Atlas of the Middle and South Atlantic States (LAMSAS). Among other advantages, this database facilitates the representation of variability. In an illustration of this, Kretzschmar (1996) presents "probability maps" for selected lexical and phonological features. To generate these maps, the LAMSAS survey area, which covers 1,162 communities and stretches from northern Florida to New York state, has been divided into sections of roughly 200 square miles. Each of these sections is shaded to represent the probability that a given form will occur in that area. The shading distinguishes four percentage degrees of probability: 75–100, 50–74, 25–49, and 0–24. In this way, the maps attempt to provide a more textured view of usage than the traditional representations that make only the binary distinction between use and non-use of a given feature. Of course, when viewing such maps, one must bear in mind that the usage being represented is that of the socially restricted set of speakers sampled for the linguistic atlas projects.

With its acknowledgment of the complex nature of language variation and its innovative use of quantitative methods to explore this variation, current dialectological research, such as that of Kretzschmar, bridges the gap between dialect geography and variationist sociolinguistics. The same might be said about recent work in "Perceptual Dialectology" though this approach has a rather distinct focus. Research in this area examines dialect divisions not on the basis of actual usage but rather on the basis of popular perceptions of linguistic differences (see, e.g., Preston 1989, 1999). It is, therefore, fundamentally a study of people's attitudes and beliefs. Sociolinguists have long recognized the role of such perceptions in shaping usage. In his description of the "social motivation" of the sound change he documented on Martha's Vineyard, Labov (1963) seeks support for his conclusions by looking at the islanders' attitudes toward the mainland and newcomers to the island. Whereas Labov examined general attitudes toward island life and correlated these with linguistic patterns, the subject matter of research in perceptual dialectology is confined to direct examinations of attitudes toward language.

As a final example of the growing union of dialectology and sociolinguistics, we note the Telsur (TELephone SURvey) project directed by William Labov. The objective of this research is a phonological survey of the speech of the United States and Canada. Such broad geographical coverage is achieved by sampling two speakers from hundreds of locations. In larger metropolitan areas, as many as six speakers might be sampled. In favoring breadth across communities over depth within communities, this project has much in common with traditional dialect geography. This resemblance is strengthened by the presentation of the results in atlas form: *The Atlas of North American English* (Labov, Ash, and Boberg, forthcoming). On the other hand, the Telsur project investigates urban speech, whereas the emphasis for dialect geographers was typically rural. Moreover, the linguistic features examined by Labov and his colleagues involve ongoing changes in sound systems rather than historical retentions like those discussed in more traditional studies. The methods for gathering and analyzing the data also distinguish this project from the early linguistic atlases. As the name implies, the survey is conducted through telephone interviews rather than face-to-face fieldwork. The interviews are recorded so that instrumental acoustic analysis can be performed, and, in fact, the results are typically framed in these acoustic terms. For example, a feature such as the fronting of a given vowel will be listed as present in a region if those speakers show formant frequencies (F2) above a certain threshold (see chapter 6 for discussion of acoustic data). In the United Kingdom, scholars are similarly adopting methods which blur the distinction between dialect geography and sociolinguistics. Upton and Llamas (1999) and Kerswill, Llamas, and Upton (1999) describe a wide range of procedures that are currently being developed in a large-scale survey of language variation in the British Isles.

These examples illustrate how two formerly distinct fields – dialect geography and sociolinguistics – have come to learn from each other. As a result, the traditional distinctions have begun to erode, though important differences of orientation remain. One of the most important of these differences pertains to the relationship between data and theory. As Kretzschmar and Schneider explain (1996: 14), dialect geographers operate under a principle of "data first, theories later" which suggests a separation between the collection and presentation of speech data and the theoretical structures employed to make sense of them. As will be developed in the following chapters, such a separation is not practiced or even desired in sociolinguistics, where the methods of investigating language are at every stage bound up with theoretical concerns.

2

Locating and Selecting Subjects

2.1 Introductory

One of the defining characteristics of sociolinguistic research is its commitment to the examination of language that is actually produced by speakers (as opposed to the potential language of their "competence"). An acknowledgment of the inherent variability of language follows directly from this commitment since any investigator who examines actual usage is quickly faced with enormous variation. Individuals vary in the extent to which they use particular features, and speak noticeably differently according to situational context.

Before modern sociolinguistic methods were developed, even dialectologists, the linguists best equipped to deal with usage differences, struggled with the facts of variation. The limitations of traditional approaches became particularly apparent in the study of complex urban communities. In Cannock, for example, Heath simply remarked that speakers dropped *h* "inconsistently" (1980: 51). As discussed earlier (section 1.3.1), such difficulties stem in part from a preoccupation with the notion of a "pure" dialect. Consistency is quite elusive when sought in the idiolect of the "ideal" dialect speaker. Radically different methods were required to uncover the regularity in interpersonal and intrapersonal linguistic variability that typifies every community.

These methods were first developed by William Labov (1966) and have since been adapted by researchers investigating speech communities around the globe. As described in the previous chapter, a belief in the social and linguistic functionality of variation is central to this approach. In order to uncover sociolinguistic patterning amidst the variation, the investigator must acquire sufficient types and quantities of language data, and must also take into account the social context in which the data are gathered. Thus, the investigation needs to be broad enough to include different types of language (used by the same speaker) as well as different types of speakers. Various methods of collecting data are treated in chapter 3, and we examine issues related to intraspeaker or stylistic variation in chapter 8. In this chapter we focus on the prior step of identifying the pool of subjects from which data will be gathered. The purpose of this chapter is to discuss principles of speaker selection or *sampling* in such a way as to bring out the relationship between research design and research objectives. Sampling is one area in which the methodologies commonly practiced have developed quite dramatically since Labov's pioneering work, and our discussion also addresses changes in the way variationists have treated sampling issues over the past three decades.

2.2   Representativeness

2.2.1   Some general principles

Any social scientific study that draws conclusions about a large group when only selected members of that group have been observed must be concerned with representativeness. Indeed, the strength of the conclusions one can draw depends on how accurately the sample represents the larger population. Thus, a researcher who examines the speech of a group of young, working–class men in a given city may be able to generalize about speakers of this type (though not necessarily so), but certainly could not claim the findings to be representative of the entire city, or even of the city's young people, or its working class, or its men. By the same token, if the data examined come from a particular context of speaking, such as reading aloud or addressing children, then the researcher must be cautious in making any generalizations about usage in other contexts. We return to this latter concern in chapter 8; our discussion here focuses on issues related to speaker samples.

The key to achieving a representative account of the language of a group of speakers is the avoidance of bias. Selecting speakers of a particular subgroup is an obvious source of bias if the goal is to describe the population in general. Imagine, for example, an investigator who is interested in language use among adolescents and whose target population is the student body of a particular school. The investigator might enlist the help of a teacher or administrator in identifying likely participants for the study, but the resulting sample would run the risk of being biased in favor of "good" (i.e., academically successful) students. A representative sample would need to consider a much wider range of subjects (see sections 2.3 and 3.4 for the discussion of Penelope Eckert's study of a Detroit-area high school).

Unfortunately, many sources of bias are not so readily predictable. Linguistic usage varies along a remarkable array of social dimensions, any of which may introduce bias into a sample. Indeed, achieving representativeness is most challenging when studying a highly diverse population such as is typically found in urban settings. For this reason, the issue was of great concern in many of the early sociolinguistic studies of urban speech, and these researchers employed sampling methods designed to eliminate as much bias as possible.

In New York City, Labov attempted to attain representativeness for his Lower East Side survey by taking his subjects from a previously constructed *random sample* of the population. The guiding principle of random sampling is that anyone within the sample frame has an equal chance of being selected. A *sample frame* is any list which enumerates the relevant population, simple examples being electoral registers and telephone directories. Any sample frame is likely to be biased in some way; for example, an electoral register excludes all persons under voting age and those not registered – but where this kind of bias is known, it can be taken into account. The sample is drawn by some mechanical procedure such as assigning random numbers to the names on a list or selecting every *n*th individual from the frame.

The New York City sample, itself a subsample derived from a larger sample constructed for sociological research, originally comprised 340 individuals. But, as in all randomly selected sets of linguistic subjects, many of these were not interviewed for reasons such as death, illness, change of residence, non-local origin or simply refusal to cooperate. Labov's ultimate description was based mainly on 88 speakers – just over one quarter of the original random sample. As Davis (1990: 6) and others have observed, the resulting New York City sample was not random by statistical definitions. Difficulties of this kind soon led researchers to query both the wisdom and the validity of a laborious sampling procedure which in the end might not measure up to the standards demanded by disciplines outside linguistics; the main objections were discussed by Romaine (1980). Briefly, they are first that linguistic samples are usually too small to ensure representativeness in the strict statistical sense. By this we mean that the findings based on the subjects studied can be extrapolated to the population as a whole within measurable and statistically specifiable confidence limits (Moser and Kalton 1971; Woods, Fletcher, and Hughes 1986). A second (and related) problem is the difficulty of replacing people selected for the original sample who are eventually excluded for one reason or another. Among this group would be anyone who declines to participate – a situation likely to introduce bias if the refusals have the effect of disproportionately excluding particular subgroups. The investigator must attempt to replace unavailable members with people who have similar characteristics in order to achieve representativeness in the remaining sample.

Although Labov's sample was not statistically representative in the sense that its relationship to the population can be precisely specified, his procedure was undoubtedly a great advance over earlier dialectological methods as he neither concentrated on a particular group of speakers nor claimed that any particular type of speech was "typical" of New York City. A realistic discussion of sociolinguistic sampling must then distinguish strict statistical representativeness from this rather weaker kind of representativeness attained in most linguistic surveys. Certainly, it is by no means clear that strict representativeness would necessarily give greater insights into sociolinguistic structure. Weighing the costs of achieving statistical representativeness against the limited additional benefits it might provide, investigators today rarely practice strict random sampling, preferring instead some form of judgment sampling (see section 2.3 below and Chambers 1995: 38–41).

Deciding how the sample will be drawn is just one issue the researcher must face in designing a variationist survey. Gillian Sankoff (1980a) details three different kinds of decisions that the researcher must make about sampling procedures:

1   Defining the sampling universe. That is, to delineate, at least roughly, the boundaries of the group or community in which one is interested. An adequate sample frame to investigate group members may then be sought.
2   Assessing the relevant dimensions of variation within the community. This involves constructing stratification for the sample. Thus, we must ask whether ethnicity, gender, or social class of speaker might affect the kind of language used. Most studies so far have shown that to a very great extent they do, as does situational context.
3   Determining the sample size.

Each of these tasks can present considerable methodological challenges as we discuss below.

2.2.2   Defining the sampling universe

Delineating the boundaries of the community in which we are interested has not usually been discussed as a problem. Typically the universe of people from which the sample will be drawn is easily defined (e.g., residents of a particular locale, members of a particular social group, etc.). Researchers should be aware, however, of the ways in which the definition they employ may affect their results.

Consider, for example, Labov's decision to reject from his sampling universe a large number of randomly selected persons because they were not "native speakers" of the dialect or of the language. In view of the number of immigrants in New York City, it seems reasonable to ask whether it is desirable to exclude such speakers. Even if we allow that it is legitimate to confine our attention to native speakers, work by Payne (1980) and Trudgill (1983, 1986) shows that the *definition* of a native speaker is problematic in a manner critical for sociolinguistic analysis; native speakers cannot be picked out easily just by listening to their accents. Payne's work suggests that children whose parents come from different dialect groups may never acquire the structural patterns of the dialect spoken by the community into which they are born (see further section 2.4). Similarly, Trudgill (1983: 10) points out that some people have lived all their lives in Norwich without acquiring a Norwich accent.

Horvath's (1985) study of the English spoken in Sydney addressed the significance of how the sample universe is defined. Her sample did not exclude in advance persons for whom English is a second language. This decision turned out to be theoretically important, since ethnic minority speakers seem to be leading linguistic changes that are affecting the entire Sydney speech community. However, the decision was also methodologically very far-reaching, since the range of data obtained required methods of analysis radically different from those of Labov. The Sydney study (which is discussed further in sections 2.5 and 6.6.3) shows clearly how decisions made at the sampling stage have implications for data analysis and interpretation.

There is an important logistical dimension to the issue of defining the sample universe: the researcher must know how to access the target population. The case of the Linguistic Minorities Project, based in London, illustrates some potential challenges that researchers might face in identifying the population to be investigated. The general goal of this project was to study various aspects of the language of non-English speakers in England and Wales, and one part was the Adult Language Use Survey, which attempted to describe the languages used by 11 linguistic minority groups in three cities. The major problem of concern here lay in the provision of a sample frame, since it was extremely difficult for the researchers to discover the location of minority speakers, or even to discover how many individuals constituted the sampling universe. Minority groups of immigrant origin in Britain, as in many other countries, are geographically and socially distributed throughout the population in a non-random manner. This means that random selection from a sample frame such as an electoral register will be both inadequate and inefficient; the national census (which has in the past avoided questions on ethnicity) cannot provide a sample frame. In the event, the researchers used two methods of constructing sample frames, neither of which was entirely satisfactory.

The first was the use of *ethnic name analysis*. A sample frame was constructed by enumerating distinctive ethnic names extracted from electoral registers, and various systematic and random methods of selecting speakers from the resulting list were then employed. The second was the use of *community lists* of minority language speakers, obtained from the communities themselves. This method was used, for example, to delineate a sampling universe of Italian speakers in Coventry and London, where exhaustive lists of minority community Italian speakers were available. Ethnic name analysis had proved to be unsuitable for this group for two reasons: first, the names of most Italian speakers did not appear on electoral registers; second, most Italian names are not especially distinctive indicators of ethnicity. Readers are referred to the report of the Linguistic Minorities Project (1985) for a fuller account.

The general point is that difficulties in delineating the sampling universe are likely to be critical for researchers studying minority populations. These difficulties may influence other decisions about speaker selection procedures. In this case, for example, the researchers felt that since they did not know the size or the location of the target population, they should attempt to attain as far as possible the goal of statistically representative sampling.

2.2.3   Stratification and sample size

Once the sampling universe is determined, one may decide on the size and structure of the sample to be taken. Samples for linguistic studies tend to be much smaller than those found with other types of surveys. As a general social-scientific guideline, Neuman (1997: 222) suggests that a sample of 300 would be appropriate for a small population (under 1,000) while a large population (over 150,000) could be accurately represented by a sample of 1,500. Even the most ambitious linguistic surveys fall well short of these figures.

Nevertheless, it has been argued that large samples tend not to be as necessary for linguistic surveys as for other surveys. Labov (1966: 180–1) suggested that linguistic usage is more homogeneous than many other phenomena studied by surveys – such as, for example, dietary preferences or voting intentions – because it is not so subject to conscious manipulation. Sankoff has offered a more functional account:

> If people within a speech community indeed understand each other with a high degree of efficiency, this tends to place a limit on the extent of possible variation, and imposes a regularity (necessary for effective communication) not found to the same extent in other kinds of social behavior. The literature, as well as our own experience, would suggest that even for quite complex

communities samples of more than about 150 individuals tend to be redundant, bringing increasing data-handling problems with diminishing analytical returns. It is crucial, however, that the sample be well chosen, and representative of all social subsections about which one wishes to generalize. (Sankoff 1980a: 51–2)

As these comments suggest, practical considerations also play a role in determining sample size. It is clear that the very demanding kind of data handling involved in any linguistic study limits the number of subjects that can be included, and many of the landmark variationist studies were based on samples that are quite small by general social-scientific standards. Labov's generalizations in New York City were based on 88 speakers; and Trudgill's in Norwich on 60 (Trudgill 1974). Shuy, Wolfram and Riley (1968) carried out a total of 702 interviews from 254 families in Detroit, using a most carefully constructed random sampling procedure (based on schools) to attain strict statistical representativeness. However, the data-handling problems encountered in linguistic work meant that in the end only a fraction of the data was selected for detailed analysis (60 speakers, on the basis of their general suitability). Thus, there appears to be a point at which careful sampling actually becomes counterproductive.

The need to consider the relevant social dimensions of variation has clear consequences in terms of sample size. If the sample is to be representative of a society that contains persons of different social statuses, different ages and both sexes, we will be obliged, if we want to make generalizations about any of these subgroups, to subdivide an already small sample. If we adopt a stratified type of sampling in order to be sure of picking up individuals representing, say, four status groups, both sexes and four age groups, we will need to fill 32 cells. If we elect to fill each cell with four speakers, we will need a sample of 128. This is already larger than many sociolinguistic samples, and will in itself create a very large amount of data and necessitate much time-consuming analysis; but if we add one other variable – such as "ethnic group of speaker" – we potentially double or triple the number of cells. Alternatively, if we keep our original sample size of 128, we arrive at cells containing two speakers. This has the unfortunate consequence that generalizations on the language of, for example, working-class male speakers of a particular age and ethnic group are based rather insecurely on just two speakers. In practice, many surveys have fewer than four speakers in each cell and smaller samples than our notional 128 as the examples in the previous paragraph indicate.

In conclusion, it seems that practical considerations partly dictate sample size. Stratified samples such as Labov's and Trudgill's were criticized because generalizations about a group such as "upper-middle-class women" were based on a very small number of speakers. However, the only solutions to this problem are to increase the size of the sample or decrease the number of social dimensions by which the pool is stratified. Neither of these options will appeal to most researchers. This may explain in part why investigators in the last two decades have tended to reject strict random sampling in favor of more efficient approaches, since obtaining a balanced, stratified sample is more difficult when random procedures are employed.

2.3   Quota and Judgment Sampling

It was suggested above (section 2.2.1) that the important feature of Labov's sampling procedure is not its statistical sophistication, but the fact that it provides a basis for a description of urban speech which does not concentrate on any particular group of speakers, or claim that any particular type of speech is "genuine." Since Labov's pioneering efforts, variationist studies have stayed true to that goal though they have in most cases abandoned formal random sampling procedures in favor of *quota* sampling. The principle underlying this approach is that the researcher identifies in advance the types of speakers to be studied and then seeks out a quota of speakers who fit the specified categories. In contrast to the mechanical procedures involved in random sampling, quota samples rely on the investigator's judgment in determining the structure of the sample and even in selecting the subjects that fill the quotas. For this reason, the approach is often called judgment sampling. A good quota/judgment sample needs to be based on some kind of defensible theoretical framework; in other words, the researcher needs to be able to demonstrate that his or her judgment is rational and well-motivated.

Macaulay's study of Glasgow speech, using 54 speakers, is an early example of a city-wide survey that used judgment sampling: "On the judgement of a member of the Education Department a total of seventeen schools . . . was selected as being representative of the schools in Glasgow" (Macaulay 1977: 20). Although this sample can be criticized even within its own lights as a judgment sample, it is successful in revealing important patterns of variation in Glasgow and in providing the basis for a description that is not confined to a particular subgroup of the population. Thus, although one must be cautious of claiming representativeness, Macaulay's study shows that it is possible to make useful generalizations about linguistic variation in a city without becoming involved in the practical difficulties of combining strict random sampling with linguistic analysis.

Both Romaine (1978) and Reid (1978) based their studies of the language of Edinburgh children on schools that were selected on the basis of the social and demographic characteristics of the schools' catchment areas. This information was derived from the 1971 Census of Population. Since

Romaine's aim was to examine aspects of the language of working-class children, she selected a school from an area that ranked low in terms of various demographic characteristics enumerated in the Census such as housing, education, employment and health. Reid, on the other hand, selected one school near the top of a rank-ordered list, one near the bottom, and a private (i.e., fee-paying) school; the purpose of his study was to compare and contrast aspects of the language of children from different social groups.

The methods of Romaine and Reid seem to be quite appropriate to the purposes of their studies, which were essentially to focus on the linguistic characteristics of specifiable and well-defined social groups; indeed, it is difficult to imagine that any kind of random procedure would have been of value in these cases. But what is important about the composition of these judgment samples is that they are defensible on the basis of specifiable sociological and demographic criteria – those underlying the design of the 1971 Census. Romaine remarks that Macaulay's judgment sample in Glasgow is not based on such objectively specifiable criteria but on the subjective assessment of an Inspector of Education (Romaine 1980: 170). It could indeed be the case that the subjective assessment of the expert whom Macaulay consulted corresponded closely to a rank-order of schools derived from the Census – but that is not the point. Precisely *because* it was based on subjective assessment, the composition of Macaulay's sample is open to legitimate challenge by any individual who feels prepared and qualified to make a rival assessment. The same problem does not arise with a judgment sample selected on the basis of objectively defensible criteria.

When the relevant social categories are not readily specifiable by demographic criteria, a much greater responsibility falls to the investigator. What is required is a thorough knowledge of the community that typically comes from long-term participant observation or other ethnographic methods. As Eckert (2000: 69) describes, "Rather than testing hypotheses against predetermined categories, ethnography is, among other things, a search for local categories. Thus while survey fieldwork focuses on filling in a sample, ethnographic fieldwork focuses on finding out what is worth sampling." Eckert spent two years as a participant observer in a suburban Detroit high school (see sections 3.4 and 5.2.1 for further discussion of this study). She developed an understanding of the social structure of the school and a closeness with the students she was studying, and her experience allowed her to construct a judgment sample based on "local categories." In selecting the 69 speakers she used in her sample from among the 200 she had interviewed, Eckert certainly relied in part on her own subjective assessments. Nevertheless, the reliability of her judgments is hard to challenge given her extensive knowledge of the community, as is evident from her detailed and comprehensive analysis. Moreover, this knowledge allowed her to construct a sample reflecting social categories identified by the subjects themselves.

In filling the quotas for a judgment sample, researchers often adopt a "snowball" technique. This approach utilizes the social networks of participants in the study to recruit potential new participants. It is thus sometimes known as network sampling (Hammersley and Atkinson 1995: 135). The researcher simply asks the subject to recommend other people who might be willing to participate in the study. Gordon (2001b) found this approach to be very effective in filling out the quotas in his study of small towns in Michigan (see further section 2.4). Among its advantages, the technique serves to reduce the rate at which potential subjects decline to participate. The reason for this can be seen in the way new subjects are contacted. For example, in speaking with a potential participant Gordon mentioned the name of that person's friend and noted that the friend had recommended him or her as a good candidate for the study. In this way, the investigator approaches a new subject not as a complete outsider but more in the role of a "friend of a friend" (see further section 3.5.1).

Snowball sampling has been most profitably adopted by researchers examining social network as an analytical construct. In a network study, sampling operates in a fundamentally different way. Whereas other studies (including most of those discussed in this chapter) take as their starting point the isolated individual who is assumed to represent a particular age, social class, or gender, the network study seeks to examine a pre-existing social group. This distinction has profound implications for the interpretation of observed variation which we explore in chapter 5. Moreover, the network approach offers the practical advantage of providing a set of procedures for studying small groups where speakers are not discriminable in terms of any kind of social class index – as, for example, the Eastern US island communities investigated by Wolfram, Hazen and Schilling-Estes (1999). Other cases might include minority ethnic groups, immigrants, rural populations, or populations in non-industrialized societies. Examples of network studies are those of Labov in Harlem, who examined the language of young black males (Labov 1972a); Cheshire in Reading, who studied groups of working-class adolescents who met in adventure playgrounds (Cheshire 1982); Bortoni-Ricardo in Brasilia, who studied the language of rural immigrants to Brazlandia, a satellite town of Brasilia (Bortoni-Ricardo 1985); Lippi-Green (1989) in the remote Austrian village of Grossdorf; and James and Lesley Milroy in Belfast, who studied two generations in three Belfast working-class communities (see section 3.5 and Milroy and Milroy 1978; Milroy 1987).

The research discussed in this section and in the next illustrates how sociolinguistic variation can be fruitfully surveyed using speaker samples whose construction entails some degree of judgment on the part of the investigator. Certainly there may be situations in which concerns about attaining representativeness may lead the investigator to employ some form of random selection, as was the case with the Linguistic Minorities Project

Adult Language Use Survey where the boundaries of the sample universe were difficult to define. However, in most cases judgment sampling is more appropriate for linguistic work. Indeed, Chambers (1995: 41) suggests that this view has become the consensus in the field.

2.4 Research Objectives and Sampling: Some Examples

In this section we discuss rather directly the relationship between research objectives and methods of speaker selection; the questions asked determine where the researchers look to answer them. Many of the early urban studies focused their attention on the role of social class as a factor in linguistic variation, and their samples were stratified accordingly. We illustrate here the relationship between goal and method by considering examples of studies that ask rather different questions.

Many researchers, especially in the United States, have investigated the sociolinguistic reflexes of ethnic identity. Kirk Hazen explores the role of ethnicity as a social force in his study of Warren County, North Carolina (Hazen 2000). While many studies of the American South approach ethnicity binarily, contrasting African Americans and whites, Hazen also considers a third ethnic group, Native Americans. He constructed a sample of 45 speakers, 15 representing each ethnic category. Because he was interested in the dynamics of social changes in the community (and the linguistic consequences of such changes), Hazen also stratified his sample according to age, though in this he was guided by his primary interest in ethnicity. He divided his sample into three age groups: "those speakers who went to segregated schools exclusively, those who were in school during the time of integration, and those who began school after integration" (2000: 9). Rather than using arbitrary chronological distinctions, this approach was based on a recognition of the importance of the integration of the public schools during the 1960s as an event shaping ethnic relations in Warren County (as elsewhere). Thus, it allows for more concrete explanations of any changes suggested by the sociolinguistic data.

An interest in the geographical diffusion of linguistic features led Gordon (2001b) to compare samples drawn from different locations. The linguistic focus of this study is a set of sound changes known as the Northern Cities Shift (see chapter 6). These changes are associated with urban speech though they are spreading to more rural areas. Gordon sought to investigate the sociolinguistic status of the Northern Cities Shift in two small towns in Michigan. The selection of the research sites was based on a number of factors including the location of the towns relative to large cities. One town was located fairly close (within 60 miles) to Detroit while the other was roughly halfway between Detroit and Chicago. Also important was the fact that both towns are located along the major highway linking those urban centers. Within each town, a sample stratified by age and gender was constructed. These categories were predicted to be relevant because the linguistic features under investigation involved changes in progress. Differences between men and women are commonly reported in studies of language change (see section 4.2), and age differences among speakers are of obvious importance in examining active changes. Rather than an age continuum, Gordon investigated a clear separation between generations by comparing adolescent speakers (aged 16–18 years) with adults of roughly their parents' age (40–55 years). In all, the sample included 32 speakers: 16 from each town divided equally for age and gender. By purposefully structuring the sample in this way, Gordon was able to examine the interactions of three important social variables (location, age, and gender) using a relatively small number of speakers. As with Hazen's project, the choice of social variables to investigate was guided by the objectives of the study.

This connection between goal and method is even more clearly illustrated by Arvilla Payne's study of children's language in the Philadelphia suburb known as King of Prussia, designed to discover "the extent to which children of various ages acquire the phonological system of a second dialect after moving from one dialect region to a new one" (Payne 1980: 143). As it was for Gordon, the choice of the research site was an important decision for Payne. The first task was to select a community where speakers of the appropriate types might be found. King of Prussia was selected for the following reasons:

> The study required (a) an area where there was one dominant dialect and many families from other dialect areas; (b) an area where children moving in had the opportunity of learning new dialect forms; and (c) a situation in which the parents' dialect had a maximal opportunity of influencing a child's language acquisition. In King of Prussia (a) the local dialect details were well known; (b) at least 50% of the population was local, and (c) the non-local dialects were known to have high or neutral prestige. (Payne 1980: 144)

Speakers within this area were next selected according to the composition of the block (each block consisting of 20 to 30 residences). Three types of block were identified, each exhibiting different neighborhood residential patterns described as *mobile*, *mixed*, and *local*, and at least four families from each block were interviewed. In all, six blocks were located (two of each type) thus yielding 24 families with a total of 108 children. Further criteria for selecting types of family were introduced, as follows:

1   Families with local-born parents and children.
2   Families with local-born children and out-of-state-born parents.
3   Families with out-of-state-born children and parents.

One imagines that Payne's major problem was not in deciding the selection method to use, but rather in identifying families in the various blocks which met these very specific requirements so that she could fill a quota that might be considered reasonable. She reports that initial contacts were made by approaching children in the streets and that church and other community leaders helped to identify and contact suitable families.

The examples discussed in this section serve to illustrate how investigators locate and select subjects in accordance with the demands of their research objectives. In the following sections we examine issues of speaker selection as they relate to two commonly studied social variables: age and social class. Our goal is to illustrate some of the questions faced by researchers trying to operationalize social categorizations related to these variables.

2.5 Sampling and Age

Since Labov's earliest work (1963, 1966) the study of linguistic change has been central to sociolinguistic research, and it is certainly one area in which the application of the variationist paradigm has been most fruitful. Using variationist methods, investigators have been able to identify and examine active language changes while they are in progress (see Labov 1994: 43–5 and Chambers 1995: 185–7 for some historical perspective on this development). This line of research has produced important insights into the mechanisms at work in language change by exploring the roles played by various social factors (see section 4.2 below). Chief among these factors is age, since establishing that a pattern of variation represents a change in progress typically requires the consideration of speakers of different generations.

Differences across generations of speakers are interpreted as evidence of language change in accordance with the *apparent time hypothesis*. This principle maintains that people of different ages can be taken as representative of different times. Thus, the speech of a 75-year-old of today represents the speech of an earlier period than does the speech of a 50-year-old or a 25-year-old. Comparing these three speakers synchronically allows the researcher to draw diachronic inferences about developments over the last 50 or so years.

David Britain (1992) used such apparent-time reasoning in his interpretation of intonational changes affecting New Zealand English. Britain examined the frequency of an intonation contour involving a sharp rise at its end (the high rise terminal) in the speech of several types of speakers. Most relevant for the present discussion, he compared speakers of three generations aged 20–29, 40–49, and 70–79. The results demonstrated a steady increase in the use of the intonation pattern across the generations; it appeared in just 1.5 percent of the utterances of the oldest group but in 3.1 percent of those of middle-aged speakers and 7.9 percent of those of the youngest group. To lend further support to his suggestion that these figures evidenced a change in progress, Britain cites a 1966 report that commented on this feature in the speech of children, particularly of Maori children (the group who showed the highest frequency use in Britain's study). This real-time record helps to establish that the rising contour pattern is fairly new – since it was associated with children in 1966 and had not been noted by earlier reports – and gives some hints of its social origins.

Britain's use of the earlier report is in keeping with Labov's advice to obtain "at least one measurement at some contrasting point in real time" (1972b: 275). Researchers commonly look to earlier dialectological descriptions as a way of providing some kind of baseline against which their current results can be interpreted. For his Martha's Vineyard study, Labov (1963) used the linguistic atlas records from the 1930s in this way. Having such an anchor in real time can be an important preventative to the misdiagnosis of apparent-time evidence. Synchronic indications of generational differences are not necessarily evidence of change in progress. Similar patterns emerge from cases of *age-grading* in which the use of a form is associated with a particular stage of life. These are stable patterns that are repeated in each generation; speakers begin to use the form around a certain age and eventually abandon it as they grow older.

Stable age-graded variables are not very common in the sociolinguistic literature, though Chambers (1995: 188–90) cites the example of the name for the last letter of the English alphabet. In southern Ontario (as elsewhere in Canada and the world) this letter is usually called *zed* except by young children who tend to use the American form *zee*. A series of surveys conducted over time shows this pattern repeating across generations. Apparently children acquire their usage by watching television shows broadcast from the US that teach the alphabet using the American form *zee*. As children grow up, however, they replace *zee* with *zed* in accordance with adult norms.

The evidence of age-grading presents an important challenge to the basic assumptions of apparent-time reasoning. In order to accept that the current speech of a 75-year-old represents that of a 15-year-old 60 years ago we apparently must posit that linguistic usage does not change over the course of one's life. The changes associated with age-grading seem to contradict this assumption. The damage to the hypothesis is not, however, fatal. First, we note that most cases of age-graded changes appear related to childhood or adolescence (see Chambers 1995: 188–93; Chambers and Trudgill 1998: 151). Moreover, age-grading seems to pertain to features that involve a high degree of social awareness and would therefore be more readily subject to conscious manipulation. Thus, the basic assumption of the apparent-time hypothesis – that an individual's speech remains stable throughout life – seems to be reasonably secure if we understand it to apply to particular types of features (those that do not attract social awareness) and to cover the course of one's adult life only.

Several studies have attempted to test the concept of apparent time empirically by comparing the trends inferred from synchronic age-stratified data with real-time observations. Bailey et al. (1991) sought confirmation that the patterns emerging from a telephone survey of Texas speech (see section 3.2.2) represented changes in progress. They compared their results with data from the Linguistic Atlas of the Gulf States (LAGS) that had been gathered some 15 years earlier and found the Atlas data to fit in well with the trends they observed in apparent time; forms judged to be innovative on the basis of synchronic data were found to be infrequent in the speech of the LAGS speakers while forms judged to be receding appeared as more frequent in the LAGS data.

Trudgill (1988) sought real-time confirmation of his Norwich results by returning to the city after a period of 15 years. In effect he extended the chronological scope of his original study by gathering comparable data from children aged 10 to 15. The new data generally confirmed the trends inferred earlier. For example, changes in progress like the centralization of /ɛ/ before /l/ (as in *bell*, *tell*) were found to be increasing in frequency among the youngest generation. Trudgill also notes several features (e.g., a labio-dental approximant variant of /r/) that have become well established in the speech of the youngest cohort despite their infrequency or complete absence from his earlier corpus. Such cases illustrate the rapidity with which linguistic changes can take hold in a community.

Neither Trudgill nor Bailey and his colleagues test directly the main assumption of the apparent-time hypothesis, because they do not compare age cohorts across the two samples they examine. In this sense, Cedergren's research on "ch-lenition" in Panamanian Spanish represents a stricter test of the apparent-time construct. This feature involves an apparent change in progress in which the standard affricate variant [ʧ] is giving way to the innovative fricative form [ʃ]. She collected data from a broad age range of speakers first in 1969 and again some 15 years later (see Cedergren 1973, 1987 or synopses by Chambers 1995: 204–6 or Labov 1994: 94–7). Thus, she was able to compare groups representing the same age cohorts at different points in their lives. Her results offer an interesting mix of support and difficulty for the apparent-time hypothesis. On the one hand, she finds the same general pattern indicating progressive use of [ʃ] across the generations. In fact, the figures for many cohorts are quite similar across the two studies. For example, speakers born in the 1920s were found to use [ʃ] at a rate of about 25 percent in both the 1969 data (when these speakers were in their forties) and the 1982 data (when they were in their late fifties and early sixties). However, the results also reveal some discrepancies across the two studies that suggest that speakers may change their usage over time. Particularly striking is the sharp rise in the use of the innovative [ʃ] that appeared in the second youngest group in each study. The group covers people in their twenties and early thirties, and their embrace of the innovative form at this stage in their lives seems motivated by their entering into the linguistic marketplace (see Chambers 1995). Nevertheless, even some of the older groups show increased use of [ʃ] over the span of the two studies, which suggests that adult speakers may alter their usage and participate in changes in progress (see also Eckert 1997).

An even more direct examination of these issues is offered by Mees and Collins (1999) who analyzed the speech of a group of young people in Cardiff, Wales, over a period of 14 years. With a focus on glottalization, a feature spreading throughout the UK (see Docherty et al. 1997), the researchers collected samples of speech from the same subjects in 1976 when the speakers were aged about 10, in 1981 when they were about 15, and in 1990 when they were about 24. These data allow them to track an individual's usage throughout these socially important "life stages" (see below). They report an interesting discrepancy within their group of working-class women: while two of these women show no significant change over time, the other two show a marked increase in their use of glottalization. In Wales and elsewhere, glottalization has recently become associated with middle-class speech, and Mees and Collins suggest that the exceptional behavior of the latter two women is related to their upward social mobility, an interpretation they support with qualitative evidence. These women appear, then, to be guided by similar motivations to those affecting the post-adolescent generations in Panama. What is most relevant to the present discussion, however, is that in both these cases speakers are shown to modify their usage over time.

In citing these examples we do not intend to suggest that apparent-time reasoning is somehow flawed and to be avoided. Rather our goal is to point out the assumptions upon which it rests and to have these cases serve as caveats about interpreting age-related differences. Much of the difficulty in dealing with such data lies in our limited understanding of the relationship between age and sociolinguistic variation – a fact that has clear relevance to the issue of sampling.

Age is a social variable which allows for a fairly straightforward classification of speakers. Unlike other variables, including socioeconomic status (section 2.6), age is easy to measure. However, assigning a numerical age to each subject is only a preliminary step in interpreting age-related variation. In this sense, age is very similar to gender. While speakers typically are readily classified as male or female, this simple dichotomy belies a much greater complexity of relations (see further section 4.4). Similarly, the challenge in examining age-related effects lies in determining meaningful ways of grouping and comparing subjects. Eckert (1997) recommends an approach to age that is based on life stages rather than simple chronology. As she notes, "age has significance because the individual's place in society, the community, and the family changes through time" (1997: 155). She sketches a three-way division of life stages distinguishing childhood, adolescence, and adulthood, with each involving important subdivisions. For example, an approach sensitive to life stages might want to consider working adults separately from retirees since retirement normally brings about significant changes in one's everyday experiences.

The studies discussed in the previous section illustrate some of the varying approaches to structuring samples in order to examine age-based variation. Hazen's (2000) study of the tri-ethnic community in North Carolina compares speakers from a life-stage perspective employing three categories. These categories were defined in locally significant terms relative to a seminal historical event for the community, the integration of the public schools. By contrast, Gordon's (2001b) binary division of his Michigan subjects, which contrasted adolescents and middle-aged adults, was motivated by more general life-stage differences. These two age groups were projected to offer the clearest separation in terms of their participation in the sound changes being studied. Adolescents are commonly reported to lead in the use of innovative forms, a trend apparently related to their "engagement in constructing identities in opposition to – or at least independently of – their elders" (Eckert 1997: 163). On the other hand, the speech of middle-aged adults tends to be highly conservative, often more conservative even than that of older speakers. Many variables show a U-shaped distribution in which the youngest and oldest groups behave similarly and are distinguished from middle-aged speakers (see Trudgill 1988). The explanation seems to lie with the conservatizing pressures of the linguistic marketplace, an arena in which only working-aged adults normally participate (Eckert 1997).

Not all studies examining speakers of different ages rely on categorizations motivated by the life-stage perspective. Some studies simply divide their subjects according to arbitrary age groups such as decades (i.e., those aged 20–29, those 30–39, etc.). While such an approach may demonstrate significant correlations between the social variable of age and use of linguistic variables, the researcher is put at somewhat of an analytical disadvantage. Age by itself has no explanatory value; it is only when examined in the context of its social significance as something reflecting differences in life experiences that it becomes a useful analytical construct. Age, then, is like all other social variables in that investigators seeking to examine it will be better off if they design their samples in accordance with defensible principles.

2.6 Sampling and Social Class

While age is a variable primarily of interest to researchers engaged in studies of language change or acquisition, social class has relevance to a much broader range of situations. Indeed social class is a variable which plays so prominent a role in language variation, at least in industrialized countries, that a socially accountable researcher cannot avoid considering it at least at some level of the analysis. Chambers (1995: 37) notes that the blue-collar versus white-collar distinction, which represents a major class division, is salient to most people, and his own extensive discussion of social class (a term often used synonymously with socioeconomic status) touches on a number of issues relevant to variationists. However, Rickford (1997b: 165) has recently pointed out that although quantitative sociolinguistics is widely thought to deal extensively with the relationship between social class and language variation, only a few fully fledged social class studies, mostly from the 1960s and early 1970s, have actually been carried out. Although influential early studies such as those of Labov (1966), Wolfram (1969), Trudgill (1974) and Macaulay (1977) examined the language/class relationship, researchers have not always found it as (relatively) straightforward to replicate Labov's procedure in New York City as Trudgill did in Norwich. In this section, we discuss some difficulties in handling a variable which seems at first sight to be easy to operationalize. We begin by looking briefly at the concept of social class before reviewing the way some of the major early studies employed it, and finally we discuss some of the difficulties reported by researchers in replicating this early work. These difficulties frequently spring from numerous conceptual, ideological, and interpretative complexities associated with the social class variable, which are discussed further in section 4.3.

During the period when variationists were working to develop viable field procedures, measures of socioeconomic status were indeed seen as an obvious and practical way of getting a handle on socially constrained language variation. However, criticisms of the rather unreflecting use of the social class concept characteristic of early work have been advanced not only by variationists such as Rickford (1986), Eckert (2000: 17–25), and Milroy and Milroy (1992) but by scholars in adjacent disciplines such as Woolard (1985). In fact, the nature and definition of social class has for a long time been controversial in the social sciences, with different intellectual positions often reflecting opposing ideological commitments (see further section 4.3 below).

Giddens provides a widely accepted account within a broader discussion of structures of inequality, where he distinguishes class as one of four major types of stratification system which promote inequality in society (1989:

205–73). While the other three (*slavery*, *caste*, and *estates*) depend on institutionally sanctioned inequalities, class divisions are not officially recognized. Although, as Chambers (1995: 35) has observed, sociolinguists often begin discussions of class by contrasting class with caste, the practical and conceptual difficulties which spring from the fact that class distinctions are not institutionally sanctioned are seldom explored. Importantly – and sometimes awkwardly – for a researcher who attempts to operationalize the concept, stratification by class is always accompanied by varying degrees of mobility, since an individual's class position is to some extent achieved. Where mobility is greater, as in the United States and other New World countries, class-consciousness is likely to be less salient than in the Old World countries of Europe, where it is often further reinforced by inherited rank systems. Chambers and Giddens both discuss such differences between Old World and New World concepts of class in terms that make it clear that class "means" something quite different in these different social and economic contexts. Cannadine (1998: 187) spells out major contrasts between the United States and Britain:

> . . . the prototypical classless society remains the United States of America. Undeniably there are great – and growing – inequalities of wealth and power. But these do not translate into corresponding inequalities of social prestige or social perceptions. Unlike the British, Americans do not conceive of their society hierarchically. Nor do they think of it triadically [i.e., as divided into upper, middle and lower classes] since the overwhelming majority regard themselves as middle class. And nor, therefore, do they think of their society as being fissured in one deep, fundamental way. (Or if they do it is on the grounds of race, not class.) By comparison with England, Americans are not interested in the language of class, or in the models of society which in Britain that language describes. The result, as Lord Beaverbrook once remarked, is that in the new world, unlike the old, the only difference between the rich and the poor is that the rich have more money. This remains a shrewd insight.

While some of these views are certainly open to debate, Cannadine usefully highlights a frequently noted difference in class consciousness between Britain and the United States. This is surely relevant to variationists, as language variation is associated with social categories only insofar as the categories identified by the researcher are meaningful to social actors. (We will return to this point in chapters 4 and 5.) Cannadine also touches on another relevant issue: the distinction between class as a system for promoting inequality in society (see again Giddens 1989, above), and the social perceptions of prestige which arise from the operation of the system. Halsey's influential account of social change in Britain in the course of the twentieth century (1995) is helpful in explicitly distinguishing *class* and *status* as economic and evaluative concepts respectively. Halsey analyzes structures of inequality in Britain as having three dimensions, namely *class*, *status*, and *party*, through which power and advantage are distributed. The distinction between class and status is particularly relevant to variationists:

> Classes – for example professional people or factory workers – are formed socially out of the division of labor. They make up more or less cohesive and socially conscious groups from those occupational groups and their families which share similar work and market situations. Status is formed out of the no less fundamental tendency of human beings to attach positive and negative values to human attributes, and to distribute respect or honour and contempt or derogation accordingly: status groups, for example peers of the realm or vagrants, form as social networks of those who share similar social prestige or life-style. Parties form out of the organised pursuit of social objectives . . . In short, classes belong to the economic, status groups to the social, and parties to the political structure of society. (Halsey 1995: 31)

The relevance of class/status will become apparent shortly as we discuss some difficulties reported by variationists in analyzing language variation with reference to an undeconstructed concept of social class. Descriptions like Halsey's of social classes as loose but more or less conscious and cohesive social groups are found in many places in the sociological and historical literature. Thompson (1963) elaborates further on the wide range of cultural differences between such groups which is encompassed by a broad conception of class: "When we speak of *a* class we are thinking of a very loosely defined body of people who share the same congeries of interests, social experiences, traditions and value-systems, who have a *disposition to behave* as a class, to define themselves in their actions and in their consciousness in relation to other groups of people in class ways" (Thompson 1963: 939). It is this kind of grouping of persons into loosely defined bodies intersubjectively perceived as occupying positions relative to each other that linguists have tried to capture quantitatively by means of a *social class index score*.

Chambers (1995: 42) provides an account of social class indices – an instrument widely used in many kinds of social scientific research. Typically, they consist of ordered rankings based on occupations that have been assigned by randomly sampled participants to reflect relative social standing. The indices that Chambers cites are derived from Canadian evaluations with, for example, lawyers and biological scientists at the top (index score 75.41) and janitors and cleaners near the bottom (28.22). Chambers reports similar rankings in other industrialized nations. Sometimes variationists have used occupation alone as an indicator of class, as did Macaulay in Glasgow, where he employed the British Registrar General's rankings. Research in Arabic-speaking and other Middle Eastern countries characteristically uses education alone as an indicator, apparently because access to elite language codes is directly dependent upon educational level (Al-Wer 1997; Abd-El-Jawad 1987; Abu-Haidar 1989; Jahangiri and Hudson 1982). However, Haeri (1997) follows Labov (1966) in creating a composite index in her study of gender and class in Cairo, and investigators in western societies such as Trudgill (1974) and Shuy, Wolfram, and Riley (1968) also used such composite indices. Where this is done, indicators may also be weighted to reflect the investigator's perception of their relative importance in indicating advantage.

Haeri used the four indicators of parent's occupation, speaker's education, neighborhood, and occupation, arranged in order of relative importance. These were used to distinguish four social classes ranging from lower-middle class to upper class. In New York City, Labov used the three indicators of education, occupation, and income to distinguish ten classes ranging from low-paid laborers with minimal education through to well-educated professionals and business people. For analytic purposes these were grouped into four strata lower class, working class, lower-middle class, and upper-middle class. Trudgill in Norwich used a more complicated index constructed from occupation, income, education, type of housing, locality, and father's occupation. Speakers' positions on these scales were used to construct five social classes: lower-working, middle-working, upper-working, lower-middle, middle-middle. Shuy, Wolfram, and Riley in Detroit distinguished four social classes (upper-middle, lower-middle, upper-working, and lower-working). Unlike Labov and Trudgill, they weighted their indicators, each speaker's score for occupation being multiplied by 9, for residence by 6 and for education by 5. The resulting composite index reflected their view of the relative importance of these indicators in the system of stratification.

Different indicators are, then, perceived as important by different investigators; moreover, perception of their *relative* importance seems to vary, not only between distinctively different cultures, but even within, for example, the United States. This arbitrariness appears to be a consequence of the very diffuse range of cultural and social phenomena (as noted by Halsey and Thompson) encompassed in the popular notion of social class. Cannadine's comments may lead us to consider the potentially far-reaching implications of attempting to transplant indices from one society to another – even when these are as apparently similar as Britain and the United States.

Sometimes the usefulness of social class indices seems dubious, as in much of Latin America, which is characterized by a large difference in access to power and advantage between the elite and the majority of the population (Lloyd 1979; Bortoni-Ricardo 1985). For such a society, indices carry inappropriate implications of a gradiency. A similar point might be made about the social structure in the village of Cane Walk, Guyana, where Rickford (1986) reports dissatisfaction with the social class concept that was used at that time in sociolinguistics. The major linguistically and ethnographically relevant social distinction in Cane Walk is a binary one, between the estate class, consisting of field workers on the sugar estate, and a heterogeneous non-estate class, consisting of foreman, drivers, shopowners, skilled trades-men and others. As well as asking how social class should be employed to uncover patterns of language variation in Cane Walk, Rickford's discussion raises more profound questions of the kind of social class model appropriate for variationist research. These fundamentally interpretive issues are dis-cussed in chapter 4.

Let us return now to Halsey's distinction between class (an economic concept) and status (an evaluative one). The particular relevance of the evaluative domain to sociolinguistic variation is reflected by the attention that variationists have always accorded, with varying degrees of explicitness, to the evaluative reactions of hearers. While much sociolinguistic work assumes the importance of such reactions (for example, Eckert 2000), Labov in his early work (1972b) developed a wide range of subjective reaction and self-evaluation tests. Bell (1984, 1999) incorporates social-psychological work on language attitudes into accounts of variation, while the collection by Milroy and Preston (1999) represents a sample of recent variationist work on language attitudes.

To the extent that occupational groups overlap with status groups sharing similar prestige and life-style (see again the comments of Thompson and Halsey above), class and status can be viewed as co-extensive and the distinction between them as unproblematic; that is precisely why *class* is frequently used as a general term to cover both. But practical problems arise when the interrelationship between status and class varies in different com-munities, with the result that a stratification scale which was sufficient for its purpose in, for example, New York City or Norwich, is not always easily transplanted as the following cases illustrate.

It is clear that the proportion of the population that falls into a given *class* category (as specified in Britain, for example, by the Registrar-General's occupational indices) varies from one community to another. In Britain, where a disproportionate amount of the national wealth continues to be concentrated in the south of England, comparison of the Census returns for a northern English, Northern Irish or Scottish city with those for a southern English city typically shows that in southern England a higher proportion of the population falls into the higher socioeconomic groups. One consequence of such local variation in class structure is likely to be differences in the prestige accorded to occupational elites, since a small occupational elite will be accorded relatively greater prestige. Thus, persons of the *same* class may have very different *statuses* if they live in cities with different class struc-tures; a lawyer in Belfast or Newcastle is likely to enjoy more prestige than a lawyer in Tunbridge Wells or Colchester.

A second problem is that the amount of *mobility* between occupationally defined classes varies in different places. Mobility appears to be greater (for example) in the United States and Australia than in the United Kingdom and since migration in the British Isles has traditionally been into England, is probably greater in England than in Scotland or Ireland. Macaulay (1977) reports extremely limited mobility in Glasgow, for example, as does MacAfee (1983: 26; 1994: 12).

This factor also affects the relationship between status and class. Social mobility may result in substantial mismatches between an individual's class as measured by an index score and the actual status that person holds in the community. Particularly in fast-developing modern cities with a high migrant population, interactions between the variables of status, class and ethnicity can create problems for the analyst. These difficulties, and the manner in which they were resolved, are exemplified particularly clearly by Horvath's (1985) survey of the urban dialect of Sydney, Australia – a city that has received a massive influx of immigrants in the years since World War II.

Horvath's original plan was to adapt Labov's procedures in New York City to examine patterns of language variation in a sample stratified by age, gender, class, and ethnicity. However, unlike Labov, she included non-native speakers in her target population. Because ethnic groups in Sydney were distributed non-randomly both socially and geographically, she constructed a judgment sample to ensure a reasonable spread of speaker types in preference to any kind of random selection. Following a snowball approach (section 2.3), initial contacts were asked to nominate anyone in their friendship group who might be willing to participate in the survey, the aim being to interview a fixed quota of adults and teenagers, both male and female, further categorized by social class and ethnicity. Using this general procedure the researchers continued interviewing until all the social variables were represented by up to five speakers in each cell. Care was taken to ensure that the speakers were reasonably evenly distributed geographically around Sydney.

An additional problem encountered in the early stages of the research was that class differences translated less consistently into status differences in Sydney than in New York City (Horvath 1985: 4). Moreover, the social class indices used by Labov were based on a widely used and theoretically defensible set of sociological classifications for New York. But at the time of the Sydney research (the late 1970s) only a somewhat out-of-date set of classifications by Congalton (1962, 1969) of 135 occupations was available. This scheme was not helpful in classifying subjects and many of the classification problems encountered by the survey were attributable to the mismatch between status and occupational class. The effects of this mismatch were compounded by the effects of ethnicity which are particularly noticeable in a socially mobile immigrant city like Sydney.

Horvath exemplifies one aspect of the problem in her discussion of milk-bar owners (1985: 46). Although this occupational group is classed as small business owners by the Congalton system, milk-bar owners are probably of lower status than other small business owners. The fact that they are often of immigrant origin is relevant, since in Australia as in many other places the relationship between ethnicity and status needs to be considered as well as the relationship between class and status: frequently, two persons from different ethnic groups but with similar occupations are accorded different prestige evaluations. Some milk-bar owners in Sydney run their businesses alone or with the help of their families; some live on the premises but employ assistants to work in the bar; yet others own several businesses and do not live in any of the premises. The Congalton system does not discriminate between these categories, who are of very different statuses, thus giving rise to a mismatch between status and class as defined by occupation.

However, even the availability of a more sophisticated scale (such as the Registrar-General's in the United Kingdom) would not be of much help in dealing with problems in Sydney resulting from extensive class mobility. Very frequently speakers had changed their class position since childhood – and Horvath notes that this in itself may be a fact with important sociolinguistic implications (see Chambers 1995: 52 for a discussion of the effects of mobility on patterns of variation in New York City). Commonly, immigrants have taken a downward step in both class and status on entering Australian society, but may reconstruct previous occupational positions after a period of about 20 years. In Sydney, however, the researchers assigned speakers to three categories – middle class, upper working class, and lower working class. This adaptation of the Congalton system was probably the best they could achieve, given the unavailability of a reliable account of Sydney's demography. The relationship between class and language was ultimately analyzed using Principal Components Analysis (see section 6.6.3) – a technique which permits initial analysis of the linguistic data without prior aggregation of speakers into social classes. Consequently, the chances of a number of misconceived classifications previously distorting sociolinguistic trends and patterns are much smaller than they might have been (Horvath 1985: 47).

We have noted in this section the methods of the classic early survey studies which initially approached language variation with reference to the social class index scores of speakers. Horvath's 1985 Sydney study is revealing not only for the intrinsic interest of its findings (see further chapter 4 below) but because of practical difficulties in handling class, both independently and in relation to ethnicity, which Horvath carefully documents. In fact, for some years sociolinguists have tended to work with small groups of speakers in particular urban neighborhoods or rural locales, using methods that sidestep such problems as Horvath described. Large-scale surveys are now seldom attempted, and social class indices are rarely used. In his more recent work (e.g., 1990) Labov has used occupation alone as an indicator of class, arguing, like Macaulay (1977), that this factor correlates best with linguistic variation. Citing his own recent work in a middle-class neighborhood in Toronto, Chambers notes that one-class studies are now common, as are judgment samples of speakers contrasted according to class (Chambers 1995: 39). For example, a recent project in the English cities of Newcastle upon Tyne and Derby handles the class variable by drawing a judgment sample of speakers, differentiated by age and gender, from two neighborhoods in each city which are shown by a number of social indicators to contrast markedly in life-style and in access to wealth and advantage (see Milroy et al. 1999 for details; also chapter 4 below). Poplack, Sankoff, and Miller (1988) similarly draw a class-differentiated sample in Francophone Canada from five different neighborhoods, while Eckert (2000) examines post hoc the social characteristics of the adolescents sample who are contacted using basic ethnographic methods. While such procedures cannot claim to survey the socioeconomic range covered by the samples constructed by Labov, Trudgill, or Wolfram, they address the goals of the research project by allowing the analyst to examine the effects of class on specific linguistic variables along with others such as gender, age or adolescent category.[1]

2.7   Concluding Remarks

This discussion of sampling has served to illustrate one of our central themes: the interconnectedness of theory and method. Choices about which speakers to sample are methodological decisions that must be informed by theory. These choices can have powerful consequences for the results of a study and their interpretation. Our discussion of age and social class has attempted to illustrate some of the interpretive issues raised by these two social variables around which samples are routinely structured. These variables and others are explored in more detail in chapters 4 and 5.

As with many aspects of sociolinguistic research, sampling is an area in which Labov's pioneering efforts have been greatly influential. His methods represented a break with dialectological tradition in constructing a sample that systematically considered both interspeaker and intraspeaker variation. In the decades since Labov's New York City study, researchers have developed a wide variety of sampling procedures while remaining true to the general principles. The range of sampling methods used in recent work suggests that researchers are now more relaxed than they once were about methodological issues such as whether or not their account should be technically representative or whether strict random sampling procedures should be used. This shift in attitude has come with the maturing of sociolinguistics as a field of research, and it enables researchers to select more freely from a range of methods those which, within a defensible theoretical framework, will best enable them to achieve their goals. In the following chapter we shift our focus away from methods of selecting speakers, to concentrate on different ways of obtaining from those speakers good quality data.

3

Data Collection

3.1   General Issues

Chapter 2 was concerned with locating research subjects in a manner sensitive to their social characteristics. Once the speaker sample has been identified, the question arises of how to obtain useful data. There are a variety of approaches available to sociolinguists. In choosing from among these – as with all decisions in the study design – the investigator is guided by the aims of the research. What constitutes "good data" depends on the research objectives, as do the methods for collecting such data. Decisions about data collection are crucial because patterns of language use are sensitive to various contextual factors. As a result, researchers must recognize that the manner in which they approach a speaker will affect the data available for analysis.

Traditionally, the data of primary interest to sociolinguists have been those representing the spontaneous, everyday usage of vernacular speakers. However, the status of researchers as community outsiders inevitably challenges their ability to gain access to such data. The investigator is faced with the "observer's paradox": we want to observe how people speak when they are not being observed. The problem is made more acute when tape-recordings of speech are needed for analysis, since many speakers will tend to shift away from their casual usage in situations where they are being recorded by a stranger. Sociolinguists have developed a variety of techniques for overcoming the observer's paradox, or at least for reducing its effects since the problem can never be entirely resolved. Several of these techniques are described below (section 3.3.3).

Preoccupation with the observer's paradox stems from certain beliefs about the speech variety known as "the vernacular." Just what constitutes the vernacular is not always clear (see further Hudson 1996; Milroy and Milroy 1999). Labov has described the vernacular variously as the variety

acquired in pre-adolescent years (1984: 29), and as the variety adopted by
speakers when they are monitoring their speech style least closely (1972b:
208). More recently, Eckert refers to the vernacular as "the language of
locally based communities" (2000: 17), a definition that focuses on this
variety's status in direct opposition to the supralocal standard variety. Labov,
Eckert, and others have suggested that the vernacular offers the best database for examining the processes and mechanisms of linguistic change or
the structural characteristics of a particular variety. According to this thinking, vernacular speech is seen as more regular because it is removed from
the potential influence of high-status varieties. Speakers attempting to adopt
a "correct" style of speech often make sporadic and sometimes hypercorrect
movements in the direction of the standard.

The difficulty in pursuing the vernacular, however, lies with the impossi-
bility of recognizing the quarry when it is caught. It is a fundamentally
abstract object, rather like its counterpart, the standard language. Indeed,
sociolinguists' devotion to the vernacular at times bears a striking resemblance to popular conceptions of the standard as the one, true language
(see Cameron 1995). Nevertheless, it may be theoretically useful to examine
variation in terms of the relative influences of such idealized varieties. As
long as we acknowledge the abstractions involved, we will not fall into the
trap of attempting to record the vernacular of a given speaker, defining this
as his or her most natural and unconstrained linguistic code, for it is clear
that *any* speech varies considerably in response to situational context. Hence,
the concept of an entirely natural speech event (or an entirely unnatural
one) is untenable, as several sociolinguists have pointed out.

Labov's characterization of the vernacular relates to his formulation of
stylistic variation in terms of attention paid to speech. However, Labov's
(1972a) own work on African American English illustrates some of the difficulties with such an approach since many of the vernacular verbal arts he
describes, such as "toasting" or "sounding," inevitably involve rather self-
conscious performance and can hardly be described as unmonitored speech
styles. In fact, stylistic variation is an area that has garnered a lot of attention in recent years; the whole issue has been greatly problematized. For
example, certain studies have argued that shifting between styles can be
used strategically by speakers to serve their communicative needs. Such an
argument runs counter to an earlier variationist treatment of style as purely
reactive to contextual factors such as addressee or topic. These matters are
explored further in chapter 8, but here we simply note that stylistic variation seems to be influenced by a range of factors to which investigators must
attend when using style as a methodological construct.

As sociolinguists' appreciation of the complexities involved in stylistic
variation has grown, so too has their interest in examining data from a range
of styles. Data representing spontaneous, everyday conversation can be

useful for examining a number of sociolinguistic questions, but we should not assume that they will work best in every study. The procedures for collecting and analyzing such data are extremely labor and time intensive. Furthermore, free conversation may not provide all the relevant information; for example, conversational data typically pertain only to speech production and not to perception – a deficiency that is especially significant in the study of phonemic mergers (see chapter 6 and Gordon 2001a). Recognizing such problems, researchers frequently turn to other kinds of data that may be used as a complement or even an alternative to conversational data.

Our discussion in this chapter describes several methods for gathering sociolinguistic data of various types. The focus here is on data produced for a particular research project that is, data initiated in some way by the investigator, as opposed to data produced for some other purpose. Included in this latter category are data from publicly available sources, such as written texts or media broadcasts. Data from public speech can be fruitfully applied to sociolinguistic research; for example, Hay, Jannedy, and Mendoza-Denton (1999) examined phonetic variation in the speech of Oprah Winfrey using broadcasts of her talk show. A less public style was investigated by Kiesling (1997) who used data recorded during group meetings in his study of a college fraternity (see also examples discussed by Johnstone 2000b: 111–12). While investigators may want to take advantage of opportunities to use such data, we will restrict our discussion here to data gathering in contexts that involve more control on the part of the researcher.

3.2   Survey Approaches to Data Collection

3.2.1   *Written questionnaires*

While an overwhelming majority of variationist studies examine spoken language exclusively, some recent projects have demonstrated the usefulness of written surveys in sociolinguistic research. Collecting data through written questionnaires is an established method in other social scientific fields and has a long history in dialect geography beginning with Wenker's studies of northern German dialects in the nineteenth century (see section 1.2.2; Chambers and Trudgill 1998: 15; Chambers 1998b). The manner in which sociolinguists use questionnaires differs from that of dialect geographers, not so much in the instruments used but in how they are applied. Both types of researcher may ask similar questions, but they typically ask them of rather different types of people. In keeping with their general orientation, sociolinguists strive to survey a sample that is more representative of the social diversity in a given population than the NORMs (non-mobile, older, rural, males) surveyed by dialectologists (Chambers 1994).

A good illustration of this sociolinguistic focus is found in the Golden Horseshoe project directed by J. K. Chambers. The Golden Horseshoe refers to the region of Canada along Lake Ontario that includes Toronto. This project gathers data using a postal questionnaire that is distributed through various means to respondents who fill it out and mail it back to the researchers. The questionnaire contains 76 questions that investigate the respondent's usage with regard to morpho-syntactic, lexical, and phonological variables. In addition, there are 11 questions covering demographic information including age, sex, occupation, and education (Chambers 1994). With the respondents representing a broad social range, the investigators are able to examine patterns of covariation between linguistic and social variables. In fact, much of the work (e.g., Chambers 1998b) has explored patterns of language change – patterns that would not be apparent without sampling across generations of speakers. The Golden Horseshoe work has established a model that is being emulated throughout the country so that eventually the survey will cover all of Canada. See Chambers's website: [http: //www.chass.utoronto.ca/~chambers/dialect_topography.html].

As Chambers (1994) notes, one major advantage of using written surveys is their efficiency. They allow researchers to gather data from a large number of speakers in a relatively brief amount of time. The Golden Horseshoe project surveyed over 1,000 respondents within a period of about two years (Chambers 1998b). Similarly, by enlisting their students in collecting responses, researchers for the McGill–New Hampshire–Vermont Dialect Survey secured over 1,300 respondents in just two years (Nagy 2001). However, the use of written questionnaires has often raised questions of reliability among dialect geographers and sociolinguists. Chambers (1998a) has responded to these concerns by demonstrating statistically that the data gathered in this way are no less reliable than those gathered through questionnaires administered by field workers. He suggests, in fact, that questionnaire data are *more* reliable when they are gathered through a postal survey than directly by a fieldworker due to the potential for fieldworker bias in recording responses as well as the potential bias introduced by the mere presence of a fieldworker who is unfamiliar to the respondents (the Observer's Paradox). Similar support for questionnaire techniques is offered by Tillery and Bailey (1998) and Bailey, Wikle, and Tillery (1997).

Despite their strengths, written questionnaires (like all data collection methods) have their limitations. They are an efficient instrument for surveying a large number of people, but they do not allow for in-depth examination of language use for any particular speaker or community. One obvious deficiency of questionnaires is that they generally call for categorical responses. They do not, therefore, attempt to examine intraspeaker variation. Thus, as in the Golden Horseshoe questionnaire, respondents might be asked whether they would use *sneaked* or *snuck* in the frame "The little devil ____ into the theatre" (Chambers 1998b). If one's usage varies, for example sometimes saying *sneaked* and sometimes *snuck*, this information may be difficult to capture. Phrasing questions without suggested responses – for example, "What do you call the upholstered piece of furniture that two or three people sit on in the living room?" (Chambers 1998b: 8) – allows respondents to offer multiple variants. Such responses can be valuable, but unless the respondent offers some explanation, the investigators know nothing about the relative frequency of each variant for that respondent or about any possible situational or semantic distinctions among the variants.

The categorical nature of the questions when this method is used also restricts the types of variable that can be investigated. Respondents must be able to determine their own usage and, when given choices, compare that usage with alternatives presented in the question. In the case of lexical and morpho-syntactic variables, this task is relatively straightforward, but it becomes more difficult when dealing with certain phonological variables, namely those involving subphonemic distinctions. We can illustrate this difficulty by considering two different patterns of variation involving the low back vowels in American English. In many areas of North America, the traditionally rounded back vowel /ɔ/ appears as an unrounded and lowered [ɑ]. In some cases, this development results in the merger of the two phonemes in a change known as the "*cot/caught* merger" (see, e.g., Labov 1994). In other cases, the movement of /ɔ/ is part of a pattern known as the Northern Cities Shift that involves several other changes including the fronting of /ɑ/ (see further chapter 6). An investigator might test for the appearance of the *cot/caught* merger by asking whether pairs of words like *cot* and *caught* or *Don* and *dawn* sound the same or different. While this approach is somewhat crude,[1] it might produce some useful results. On the other hand, it is hard to formulate a question to test for the appearance of the Northern Cities Shift because speakers typically are not consciously aware of vowel-systemic variations like those involved with this change. Asking, for example, whether the vowel in *caught* sounds like the vowel in *cot* is pointless since both innovative and conservative speakers (i.e., those who do and those who don't participate in the shift) are likely to answer in the negative even though phonetically these two groups of speakers sound very different.

When carried out appropriately, written surveys can provide good amounts of useful data in a fairly brief time-frame. As we have suggested in this section, they are better for addressing some matters than others. Fittingly, Chambers refers to his approach as "dialect topography" to indicate that it produces "a description of surface features" (1994: 36). In this sense, such work is seen as a first step that can "be useful in delimiting places where micro-level sociolinguistic studies might profitably be pursued" (1994: 36).

3.2.2   *Fieldworker-administered surveys*

As an alternative to having respondents fill out surveys themselves, prepared questionnaires may also be administered by fieldworkers. This
approach was the preferred method for traditional dialect geographers from
Gilliéron to Kurath to Orton (Chambers and Trudgill 1998: 15–25), and there
were practical reasons for this preference given the generally low levels of
literacy among the NORMs who served as their consultants (Chambers
1994: 37). Nevertheless, even in modern societies with mass literacy there
may be situations in which the fieldworker-administered surveys have an
advantage over other methods.

   One clear benefit to having fieldworkers collect data is that it allows for
direct observation of language use. This might be particularly useful in the
study of pronunciation variants. Returning to the examples discussed in the
previous section, both the *cot/caught* merger and the Northern Cities Shift
could be investigated fairly simply in this context. A fieldworker might
construct questions designed to elicit the pronunciation of diagnostic words
(e.g., "I catch the ball today; I ____ the ball yesterday."). More straightforwardly, the respondent might be asked to read a list of words illustrating
the variables of interest. Responses could be tape-recorded and analyzed
later, or transcribed on the spot.

   Still, direct observation of language use is not always what is being done
by fieldworkers. As is the case with written questionnaires, fieldworker-
administered surveys often gather respondents' self-reports about their
usage. They are fundamentally metalinguistic tasks in that they rely on the
respondents' ability to consider their own linguistic behavior. Unlike interviews involving free conversation (see section 3.3), it is difficult to disguise
– assuming that one wanted to do so – the purpose of a survey in which all
the questions ask what the respondents call X or how they would say Y. In
general, variationists have been skeptical about the accuracy of self-reported
data. There are well-known cases of people who, when asked directly, claim
not to use particular forms that they in fact use at less-guarded moments
during an interview. Labov's experience of the New York mother and
daughter who believed they always pronounced postvocalic /r/ illustrates
such discrepancies (1966: 470–2). Incidentally, this case also serves as a
cautionary tale for investigators who might seek to disabuse such speakers of
their inaccurate perceptions: when Labov played back the tape of their speech,
the subjects were "disheartened in a way that was painful to see" (1966: 471).

   Despite such discrepancies, we should not assume that all self-reported
data are less accurate than those collected through observation of actual usage.
Tillery compares self- reports with data gathered through indirect elicitation
and through observation in several studies of Texas and Oklahoma and

concludes that self-reports are "at least as valid as" the other methods (2000: 65). Direct questioning may, in fact, provide a more accurate usage picture for some variables than would less metalinguistic approaches. Included here would be items that appear infrequently in free conversation and are difficult to elicit through indirect questioning. On these grounds, Bailey, Wikle, and Tillery (1997: 57) argue that their self-reported data on the use of the double modal construction, *might could*, in Texas are a better measure of the extent of this feature that the data from the Linguistic Atlas of the Gulf States, which were collected using indirect elicitation. Indirect approaches may also bring problems of interpretation. Tillery and Bailey (1998) encountered such difficulties in their research on the use of the second person pronoun *yall* with singular reference. When a speaker asks "How are yall doing?" of a single addressee, it is possible that he or she has in mind just the addressee, but it is also possible that *yall* is meant as an "associative plural" covering the addressee's family or colleagues, etc. Tillery and Bailey conclude "The only way to resolve such disagreements, of course, is to ask users what they mean when they use *yall*" (1998: 263). Nevertheless, such direct questioning can be more problematic when it requires subjects to consider less common linguistic phenomena such as is often required in making grammaticality judgments about syntactically unusual sentences (see further section 7.2).

Fieldworker-administered surveys are traditionally very time-consuming. For example, the data collection for the Linguistic Atlas of the United States and Canada began in the 1930s, continued intermittently for decades, and is still incomplete in its coverage. As noted above, this inefficiency is one of the motivations that Chambers (1994) cites for his use of postal questionnaires. Other researchers have used the telephone as an efficient means of gathering data. Contacting subjects on the phone obviously eliminates the time and money costs involved in fieldwork travel. The time savings is demonstrated by Labov's Telsur project which has surveyed all of the US and Canada within a period of about eight years (Labov, Ash, and Boberg forthcoming). This project focuses on pronunciation features, especially on sound changes like the Northern Cities Shift and the *cot/caught* merger. The project utilizes a range of strategies to collect data on the speech production, combining elements of a questionnaire format with those of a traditional sociolinguistic interview. The researchers ask questions to elicit particular forms (e.g., "What's the name for the type of foldable bed often used in the army?") as well as more open-ended questions to capture examples of extended discourse (e.g., "How has your community changed over the years?"). Labov and his colleagues are also interested in speech perception, particularly in whether sounds are judged to be merged. This information is gathered by directly asking respondents whether certain pairs of words (e.g., *cot* and *caught*) sound the same.

Guy Bailey together with Jan Tillery and others have utilized telephone surveys in their work in Texas and Oklahoma (see, e.g., Bailey, Wikle, and Tillery 1997; Tillery and Bailey 1998; Bailey and Dyer 1992). In some cases, this research has been coordinated with general (i.e., non-linguistic) survey projects. In Texas, for example, Bailey and his colleagues received permission to add questions about the usage of certain lexical and grammatical variables to the protocol for the Texas Poll, which is "a quarterly survey of approximately 1,000 randomly selected telephone households" in the state (Bailey and Dyer 1992: 4). They also tape-recorded the interviews to collect phonological data. The fact that such surveys, unlike most strictly linguistic surveys, employ a properly constituted random sample increases the power of the statistical inferences that can be drawn from the results (see section 2.2.1 and Bailey and Dyer 1992). Another advantage of "piggybacking" onto non-linguistic surveys is the reduced potential for interviewer bias. Since the interviewers conducting the survey have no training in linguistics and no knowledge of the issues being studied, the risk of their influencing the results is minimal (Tillery and Bailey 1998: 264). On the other hand, this ignorance of linguistics imposes certain limits on the data to be collected since untrained interviewers could not be expected to record, for example, variable pronunciations reliably.

3.2.3 Rapid and anonymous surveys

A special type of fieldworker-administered survey is done without the awareness of the subjects. In this approach, known as the rapid and anonymous survey, the investigator seeks to elicit a set word or phrase in entirely naturalistic conditions. The prototype for this kind of research is Labov's famous "fourth floor" study in New York City department stores (1972b). In this project, Labov examined the pronunciation of /r/ among employees of three stores seen as catering to different socioeconomic strata. His procedure was to ask various employees in each store for the location of an item already known in advance to be on the fourth floor. He then obtained a repetition by pretending to mishear the response. In this way he elicited four instances of the target feature in two separate phonetic environments (pre-consonantal in *fourth* and word final in *floor*). Pronunciations of the target feature were covertly marked down in a notebook on the spot, using a simple preset schema.

The same principle was used in Philadelphia to investigate the alternation between [str] and [ʃtr] in word initial clusters. In this case, the data were collected in the following way:

We obtained data on (str) in a wide variety of Philadelphia neighborhoods by asking for directions in the neighborhood of a given street which had a name of a form *X Street*. However, we asked

"Can you tell me how to get to X Avenue?"

In the great majority of cases, the informants would respond "X Street?" with considerable emphasis on street. (Labov 1984: 50)

Another example of this type of survey is described by Rimmer (1982) whose research was carried out in Birmingham, England. Penelope Gardner-Chloros' (1997) study of language choice and code-switching in Strasbourg department stores represents a slight variation on this style of survey. Rather than eliciting responses, she surreptitiously observed interactions between customers and salespeople, recording on notecards the language used.

Plainly, considerable ingenuity is needed to design rapid and anonymous survey questions that will reliably elicit the target feature, and the main advantage of the method is that a clear view of the distribution of a single variant, geographically and sometimes socially, can be obtained quickly. In fact, the [ʃtr] variant appears to represent an innovation in Philadelphia, and Labov was able to track its distribution through various types of residential areas in the city. Nor is the observer's paradox an issue, since speakers are not tape-recorded and are not even aware that they are being observed.

The method is, however, applicable only if the investigator has in mind extremely clear goals that have been well formulated in advance. A major disadvantage is the very limited nature of the data that this method is capable of yielding. Not only is the investigator restricted to a single linguistic feature, but social information on the speakers is likely to be only approximate.

3.3 Sociolinguistic Interviews

3.3.1 The structure and design of the interview

Interviews have traditionally been the most common approach to data collection among sociolinguists. Typically these are one-on-one exchanges conducted in person, though occasionally they are conducted over the phone (e.g., Labov's Telsur project discussed in section 3.2.2 above) and occasionally they involve either multiple fieldworkers or multiple subjects (see section 3.3.3 below). The sociolinguistic interview typically differs from a survey in being relatively less structured. Whereas survey questions are usually asked in a predetermined order and a prescribed form, interview protocols are more flexible. Surveys seek brief responses to fairly direct questions;

interviewers attempt to elicit more extended stretches of unscripted, conversational speech. The basic objective has often been to observe the subject's relaxed, "natural" usage. As we noted earlier, however, the idea of the "vernacular," as this usage is sometimes termed, is problematic. In this section we introduce the interview as a data collection strategy and discuss some examples of its use.

Considering the open-endedness of the interview format (relative to a questionnaire), one question that emerges is: How long should an interview last? Labov has suggested that interviewers should obtain "from one to two hours of speech from each speaker" (1984: 32); but, in fact, it is difficult to be categorical about the appropriate length of an interview. Useful phonological data can often be obtained in a relatively short time – perhaps as short as 20 to 30 minutes, but a very different picture of a speaker's pattern of language use is liable to emerge over a longer period, and it is this pattern that will be of interest to an analyst who wants to get an idea of fluctuations in a speaker's use of key phonological variables. Thus, Douglas-Cowie (1978) suggests that, even when interviewed by a stranger, speakers will settle down to a pattern approximating to their everyday interactional style after about the first hour, and speech produced before this period has elapsed may show radically different patterns. On the other hand, recent research on style-shifting, especially that of Schilling-Estes (1998), suggests that interviewees may move in and out of styles throughout the course of an interview for a variety of reasons (see further section 8.3). Thus, researchers should be careful in assuming that speakers will adopt or maintain a particular style simply based on the fact that some period of time has elapsed in an interview. Furthermore, on the question of interview length, Cheshire (1982) noted in her study of Reading that, for the purposes of *syntactic* analysis much greater quantities of data were required since the relevant structures were not likely to emerge as predictably or as frequently as phonological elements (see further section 7.2). It is for this reason, in fact, that some researchers have adopted more direct approaches to data collection (see section 3.2.2). The question of interview length can therefore, like so many methodological questions, be answered primarily in terms of the goal of the research.

Successful interviewing requires careful planning. While the goal may be to engage the subject in free conversation, the interview situation is very different from the spontaneous discussion that might arise among friends. Most importantly here, the responsibility for keeping the conversation going rests with the interviewer who manages the discussion by asking questions. For this reason, it is essential to have a prepared list of topics that will generate talk in each interview.

Labov's interview techniques for his neighborhood studies in Philadelphia illustrate the preparation involved in successful data collection. These

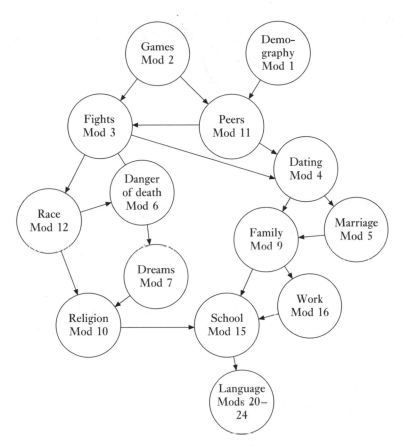

Figure 3.1 Characteristic network of modules for adolescent or young adult speaker (adapted from Labov 1984: 35)

interviews are structured in terms of *modules* or sets of questions organized around specific topics. These modules may then be organized into what Labov (1984) describes as *conversational networks*. The topics of the modules are selected using two criteria. First, previous experience had shown some topics to be successful in engaging speakers in interaction (the danger of death question discussed in section 3.3.3 is of this type). Second, and equally important, is the information that a given topic can yield on neighborhood norms and on general social and background information of value to the researchers. The fieldworker on any given occasion selects modules from a larger set in order to construct a conversational network appropriate to a given speaker; a typical network selected for an adolescent or young adult in Philadelphia can be seen in figure 3.1.

The general idea of this interview schedule is to use interlocking modules to simulate the seamless topic-shift structure of normal conversation. There is no fixed order for working through the modules and the fieldworker is expected to allow the subject's interest in any particular set of topics to guide transition through the network from module to module.

Question design is always given very careful attention in terms of phrasing and ordering within modules: the initial and final questions from each module are designed to facilitate topic shifts to other modules in the system. Module 3, "Fights," ends with the questions:

(1)   Do girls fight around here? Did you ever get into a fight with a girl?

This can lead, for example, directly into the module dealing with dating patterns:

(2)   What are girls *really* like around here?

All questions, as illustrated by those quoted here, are designed to be brief; Labov notes that questions formulated without preparation can often be lengthy and unclear, containing spontaneous conversation phenomena such as hesitations and false starts. Module questions are also formulated to be as colloquial as possible, avoiding any "bookishness" in syntax and lexicon. While experienced interviewers may adapt the wording of some questions to fit their own style, other questions are to be asked exactly in the prescribed form.

In a large-scale project like Labov's Philadelphia research, the use of a detailed conversational network plan helps to establish consistency across the many interviews conducted by various fieldworkers. In many cases, however, interview preparation need not involve such an elaborate structure as that suggested by figure 3.1, and certainly every question need not be formulated beforehand. For example, Gordon's (2001b) study mentioned earlier (section 2.4) involved interviews with adolescents and adults in two different small towns. Before beginning the fieldwork, he prepared a list of topics to be raised in the interviews. Some items were discussed by all participants while others were relevant only to one or the other age group. All the questions pertained to the general topic of life in the subject's town; they did not cover anything like the range of areas in figure 3.1. Nevertheless, the fairly restricted list of topics generated 60 to 90 minutes of conversation with each interviewee. The key, in addition to locating cooperative speakers, is preparing topics that the participants will eagerly discuss at length. In the small towns investigated by Gordon, the adults spoke fondly of their childhoods and had much to say about how the town had changed since they were young. With the adolescents, the conversation focused on school, their social lives, and their plans for the future.

Clearly, not all topics will work for all speakers. Interviewers must be flexible and willing to adjust their approach to their subjects. For example, in his Michigan research, Gordon interviewed one man who refused to answer any direct questions about his personal history including his educational and employment background. This refusal came at the beginning of the interview and suggested that the interview would not be fruitful. However, the man was happy to talk about more general matters ranging from local history and culture to national politics. The interview thus kept to topics with which he was comfortable. The discussion was as lively as any, and over the course of the interview the man revealed many of the personal details that he had initially refused to discuss. The interview was a success, though it was unlike any other that Gordon conducted.

While interviewers need to be concerned with preparing questions that will generate extended conversational responses, they can use their questions to learn about who their subjects are as well as how they talk. Basic demographic information about the speakers, such as age, sex, and possibly ethnicity and socioeconomic class, must be recorded for later analysis of covariation between social and linguistic variables, and any such personal information that might have some relevance in explaining speech behavior can be pursued. Interviews often produce valuable qualitative data that can complement quantitative analyses. For example, Gordon (2001b) discovered patterned speech differences between pairs of adolescent girls in one of the Michigan communities he examined. These quantitative differences in usage were explained by referring to social differences including the types of friends the girls had and the way they spent their free time. This kind of information was specifically targeted in the interviews because previous research, especially that of Penelope Eckert (e.g., 2000), had demonstrated its relevance in adolescent social structure (see further section 3.4).

3.3.2 Interviews as speech events

The preceding discussion of interviews has sketched some of the basic characteristics of this technique. It was noted that the interview has been the most common method of data collection among variationist sociolinguists. In this section, we examine this method further and argue that, despite its popularity, the interview offers a rather problematic solution to the needs of data collection. This is particularly true when the research seeks to elicit natural conversational speech.

Much of the difficulty involved in interviewing stems from the fact that an interview in western society is a clearly defined and quite common speech event to which a formal speech style is appropriate. It generally involves dyadic interaction between strangers, with the roles of the two participants being quite clearly defined. *Turn-taking rights* are not equally distributed as they are in conversational interaction between peers. Rather, one participant (the interviewer) controls the discourse in the sense of both selecting topics and choosing the form of questions. The interviewee, on the other hand, by agreeing to be interviewed, has contracted to answer these questions cooperatively. Once the interviewer has obtained a response, the obligation rests upon him or her to follow it up with a further question. People are generally quite well aware of the behavior appropriate to these roles, and of their implications in terms of unequal distribution of rights to talk.

The first point that might be made is that individuals who are being questioned will seldom produce large volumes of speech in their replies. This may in part be a consequence of the "cooperative principle", in the sense that they are attempting to comply by responding relevantly and briefly (Levinson 1983: 100). Interviewers may work to 'fudge' the nature of the event in an attempt to encourage the interviewee to relax and produce larger volumes of speech, but the well-defined nature of the interview as a speech event, along with the associated social and discourse roles of the participants can make such efforts very difficult. Interviewers may risk confusing or even angering research subjects if they stray from the expected interview format. For example, during fieldwork in Michigan, Gordon interviewed the owner of a café, asking a series of questions about the operations of the business. This line of questioning was pursued not only because it seemed likely to produce extended replies but also because it provided information about the interviewee's experience and the business environment in that community. The owner, however, became very suspicious, and objected, "You don't care about this stuff; you just want to get me talking." After assurances that the information was important, the interview continued and, in the end, was quite successful. This example indicates, however, the need for interviewers to make clear the relevance of their questions since it is one of the expectations speakers bring to the interview.

Labov has suggested that the basic counter-strategy of the sociolinguistic interview is to acknowledge the "position of the interviewer as a learner, in a position of lower authority than the person he is talking to" (Labov 1984: 40). An experience described by Briggs (1984) illustrates the fruitfulness of this strategy in dealing with some subjects. After a series of disastrously uninformative interviews with the Lopezes, a wood carver and his wife in Cordóva, northern New Mexico, Briggs reports a successful set of interviews with another community elder: "He agreed to both the interviews and their tape-recording. When I returned from my car, Mr Cordóva asked me 'Now what is it that you wanted to know?' I provided him with one of the questions that had fared so badly with the Lopezes. He then proceeded to produce a long, flowing narrative of the local carving industry" (Briggs 1984: 23). Although Briggs attributes his success with Mr Cordóva and his failure with the Lopezes to different factors (cross-cultural differences in conversational structure), it may be significant that by addressing to Briggs the question "Now what is it that you wanted to know?," Mr Cordóva has, to some extent, reversed the roles of interviewer and interviewee in such a way as to be congruent with the deference due to him as a knowledgable older man. Attempts to downplay the asymmetrical roles characteristic of interviews are, however, not always so fruitful (see Wolfson 1982 for a critique of Labov's recommendation).

A rather different type of challenge posed by interviews relates to the nature of the data they are likely to produce. The basic format of the interview may impose limitations on the structural characteristics of the data. Certain speech phenomena may be difficult or even impossible to study using interviews. One concern relates to the frequency of occurrence of the phenomena under investigation. Many interesting syntactic variables, for example, appear infrequently in the course of everyday conversation (e.g., relative clauses), and their rarity may present challenges to quantitative analysis – an issue that is addressed in more detail in chapter 7. As we mentioned earlier (section 3.2.2), this problem has led some researchers to trust more direct methods of investigation such as surveys to measure usage of certain syntactic features (see, e.g., Bailey, Wikle, and Tillery 1997).

In some cases, the problem relates to the pragmatic constraints of the interview. An obvious example is interrogative constructions, which are plentiful in spontaneous speech in a range of discourse functions, but are likely to be inhibited in the speech of interviewees. One of the variables studied by Cheshire (using a participant observation method (see section 3.4)) in the speech of Reading adolescents was the *tag question*. Tag questions do not usually function in discourse as requests for information, but rather are conducive forms seeking confirmation of a previously stated proposition:

(3)   She's here already, isn't she?

(4)   This is your book, right?

Since their main function is to compel a (normally minimal) response from the addressee it is unlikely that they will often be used spontaneously by a speaker whose perceived social role is to respond to questions put by another.

The question-and-answer format of the typical interview may, in fact, inhibit the use of a number of potentially interesting variables. For example, the so-called *hot-news perfect* (McCawley 1971), a feature of Irish English, is unlikely to occur in interview sessions since it indicates an event in the immediate past:

(5)   A young man's only after getting shot out there.
      [St. E. "A young man has just got shot out there."]

Commenting on these discourse and pragmatic constraints on higher-level syntactic variation, Harris (1984: 316) makes the additional point that tokens of the hot-news perfect are absent from Irish rural data collected by formal interview methods in the Tape-Recorded Survey of Hiberno-English. Conversely, examples such as this turned up in some quantity in the Belfast urban sociolinguistic projects (see section 3.5), which utilized participant-observation techniques.

The formality of the interview may also limit efforts to examine certain variables. The use of overtly stigmatized features (e.g., multiple negation in English) is likely to be affected by the act of answering questions from an interviewer. This is true of syntactic as well as phonological features. For example, in the Belfast project, the researchers encountered severe difficulties in collecting examples of the vernacular pronunciation of words such as *meat, beat, heat, leave* (the MEAT class, as it is commonly known to historians of the language). Among vernacular speakers, the vowel in this class of words approximates to, but is not identical with, the vowel in items like *mate* and *bait* (the MATE class). This feature is of considerable theoretical interest, as it sheds light on a notorious historical problem of an apparent merger in early Modern English and subsequent reseparation between words of MEAT and MATE classes (see Milroy and Harris 1980; Milroy 1992 for details and historical references).[2] The Belfast investigators had heard this pronunciation in casual exchanges but were frustrated in their efforts to capture examples on tape. The vernacular alternates that were recorded nearly all occurred in peer conversations and only very rarely in speech addressed directly to the fieldworker.

A related problem particularly associated with data collected by means of interviews is that the effects of *speaker correction* of socially stigmatized items are often indirect, and can also give a misleading impression of phonological structure. In working-class West Belfast, tokens of /k/ are frequently heavily palatalized, with a palatal glide appearing between the initial consonant and a following front vowel. Pronunciations like [kjap, kjat, kjɪd] ("cap," "cat," "kid") are stigmatized and apparently recessive, being used mainly (but not entirely) by middle-aged and older men. During an interview, a middle-aged, West Belfast woman described a visit to a shop where she stood in a queue [kuː]. One possible explanation of this realization was that the Belfast urban dialect, like many others (such as Norwich, for example), deleted in some contexts the palatal approximant /j/. But only after vernacular pronunciations like [kjap] "cap" had occurred in informal conversations did a clearer picture of the structure of the dialect emerge; the speaker had *hypercorrected* standard [kjuː], classifying it along with non-standard /kj-/ items. Interestingly, this process revealed a misanalysis of phonological structure since the vernacular palatalization rule affects only items with a following front or low back unrounded vowel; a word like *cool*, for example, does not show [k]/[kj] alternation.

These examples demonstrate the limitations of the interview – even the informal interview – as a means of collecting linguistic data. Briggs (1986) offers a more general critique of interviewing as a social-scientific method and discusses alternative approaches of particular relevance to research outside the context of western, industrialized cultures. Sociolinguistic interviewers need at the very least to be alert to possible problems, since, particularly at the level of pragmatic and discourse constraints on syntactic structure, they are not always immediately obvious. Various techniques that have been developed for dealing with such constraints by investigators into *syntactic* variation are discussed in chapter 7. Techniques for dealing with the problem of investigating vernacular forms are discussed in the next section.

3.3.3 Interview strategies for eliciting casual speech

As noted in the opening to this chapter, the speech in which sociolinguists have traditionally taken the greatest interest has been the spontaneous, everyday style that is often called the vernacular. For reasons outlined in the previous section, the interview is far from an ideal instrument for gathering data on this speech style. Nevertheless, there are steps that can be taken by interviewers to encourage subjects toward more casual speech. Such strategies are basically of two types: (1) attempts to influence the content of the interview; and (2) modifications to the dynamics of one-on-one interviewing.

When people are emotionally involved (excited, angry, fearful, etc.) in a discussion, they are more concerned with what they say than with how they say it. Following this logic, interviewers can obtain less self-conscious speech by asking questions that bring about such emotional reactions. The best known of these is Labov's "danger of death" question which asks subjects about situations in which they feared for their lives (see Labov 1972b: 93 for details and rationale of the technique). Despite his success with this technique, attempts by others to use it have frequently backfired. For example, Trudgill comments on its lack of success in Norwich, suggesting that perhaps Norwich people have led somewhat less eventful lives than New York City people. But in Belfast it was inappropriate for quite different reasons. During a conversation with a working-class family about the general hardships of life, it emerged that one 19-year-old man had already had a number of narrow escapes from death. First, as a merchant seaman he had almost drowned in the Baltic, his ship having been run down by a Russian vessel; then he had been held up by gunmen in a Belfast alley-way; arrested and beaten by troops as a Republican sympathizer; and two months before the period of the research he had been shot in the legs during an intergroup Republican feud. His response to these alarming events was not at all the

Data Collection

one predicted by Labov, but nevertheless accorded closely with Ulster norms of behavior. It may be described as a rather world-weary cynicism at the duplicity of the authorities combined with a tendency to low-key black humor. On this occasion the danger of death question was not put explicitly; but on the two or three occasions when it was, the characteristic response of Belfast people was a matter-of-fact account of what were often quite unpleasant and dangerous experiences. The question proved equally ineffective for Butters (2000) who used it in a series of interviews with North Carolinians. In contrast to the stoic Belfast reactions, the Americans who had experienced brushes with death were often hesitant to discuss them because they considered them "too terrible or frightening to speak of" (2000: 73). Those who did discuss such experiences tended to use very careful and often philosophical or theological language – hardly their most casual style.

As these difficulties show, the danger of death question does not translate well into every speech community. Nevertheless, many researchers have found other questions that fulfill the function of engaging the speaker's attention in the way Labov describes. Wolfram and his colleagues working in North Carolina have had good success with the strategy of asking interviewees to tell ghost stories (Herman 1999). Even less-structured approaches can be productive; the key is hitting upon a topic that will engage the interviewee. Gordon (2001b) found that questions about childhood experiences had the desired effect for adult speakers, while adolescents often responded well to inquiries about the social structure of their high schools (e.g., Are there cliques in your school?).

Changing the dynamics of the interview away from the one-on-one format can also facilitate the production of casual speech. This may be accomplished by having either two or more interviewers or two or more interviewees. The North Carolina research team headed by Wolfram has taken the former approach (see Wolfram and Schilling-Estes 1996; Wolfram, Hazen, and Schilling-Estes 1999). They use pairs of interviewers to create a three-way conversation which eliminates some of the awkwardness of two strangers having to speak one-on-one. The questioning seems to proceed more smoothly since the fieldworkers can work together to keep the discussion going; and there are fewer lulls in the conversation when one fieldworker needs to look at notes for the new questions. Also, one fieldworker can monitor the recording equipment which is often a distraction in one-on-one interviews.

In their approach to breaking down the interview structure, Labov et al. (1968) studied groups rather than individuals for their Harlem research. As demonstrated in Labov's famous account of an interview with Leon, an African American 8-year-old, and his friend Gregory (Labov 1972a: 210) this has the effect of "outnumbering" the interviewer and decreasing the likelihood that speakers will simply wait for questions to which they articulate responses. In fact Leon and Gregory tended to talk to each other rather than to the interviewer. Often, fieldworkers can attach themselves to the fringes of the group. Although Labov and his colleagues used both individual recording sessions and group sessions, it was during the group sessions that the richest data were recorded. The speech of each member was recorded on a lavaliere microphone (worn round the neck) on a separate track, and the atmosphere of the sessions was more like that of a party than an interview.

One critical point is that if a speech event can be defined as something other than an interview, it is very likely that group members will talk to each other rather than adopt the role of respondents. The effect of group dynamics seems also to be important, as Nordberg (1980: 7) explains:

> . . . the stylistic level is controlled in quite a different way than in an interview, i.e. the members of the group themselves exercise social constraint on one another's language. It would be quite unacceptable for someone in the group to put on an act during the recording and use a form of language which was not normally used in that speech community or among the individual speakers. The more closed the social network of the discussion group is, the stronger the social pressure will be to speak in accordance with the group norm. But even in the case of discussion groups which must be described as open social networks we are on safer ground when it comes to the authenticity of the language used than we are in the case of an interview.

In support of these remarks, Nordberg cites experimental evidence from Thelander's work in Burtrask, northern Sweden, where the linguistic effects of manipulating group composition in various ways were systematically examined. Other researchers have described episodes which illustrate the kind of control that a close-knit group in particular exercises on the language behavior of its members (Labov 1972a; Milroy 1987).

The point at issue then is not whether or not the presence of the group in some way allows participants to "forget" that they are being observed. This is unlikely since, for example, the groups studied by Labov et al. had been convened specifically for the purpose of recording, and the microphones worn by speakers must have constrained their physical movements considerably. But it does appear that the tendency of outside observation to encourage careful, standardized styles and inhibit the emergence of vernacular structures is to a considerable extent *counteracted* by the operation of the group dynamics described by Nordberg.

For these reasons, a number of researchers have adopted the strategy of collecting data from groups rather than individuals (Reid 1978; Edwards 1986). Hewitt's study of the use made of patois by London adolescents focused on groups (Hewitt 1982), while Edwards finds very great differences in the language of British black adolescents, depending upon whether it is collected in a group session or in response to the questions of a single interviewer. Cheshire, like Hewitt and Edwards, combined the strategies of studying groups and focusing on adolescent language; she was plainly very successful in obtaining large amounts of quality data. In some cases, researchers have taken the study of groups even further by removing the investigator from the scene. For example, Stuart-Smith (1999) collected samples of Glasgow speech by placing pairs of speakers in a room with a recorder and leaving them to discuss whatever suited them.

In conclusion, it is important to note that although interviews are not ideal instruments for sampling informal speech styles, they can with some "fudging" be fruitful in this regard. The various strategies that we have discussed here need to be used carefully and appropriately in conjunction with each other, and with local conditions very much in mind. In the end, however, investigators who, for whatever reason, need to examine speech styles that are unavailable even in the most relaxed interviews, would do well to consider more ethnographic approaches. In the following section, we consider such an approach as we examine issues related to participant observation.

3.4   Participant Observation

In most cases researchers investigate communities of which they are not members. Their outsider status poses a challenge to their ability to overcome the observer's paradox. In an attempt to change this status, investigators may adopt the role of participant observer. This ethnographic approach entails long-term involvement in a community and is fundamentally a pursuit of local cultural knowledge (Johnstone 2000b: 82). The principal benefits of participant observation are (a) the amount and quality of the data collected, and (b) the familiarity with community practices gained by the investigator.

These benefits can be illustrated by the work of Penelope Eckert (1989a, 2000), whose research in Detroit-area schools was mentioned briefly above (section 2.3). Eckert spent two years studying a suburban high school, and although her research was authorized by school authorities, she intentionally avoided an official role in the school. Any association with the institution might have limited students' willingness to speak frankly with her. Eckert spent her time in the school outside of classrooms, in public areas such as the library and the cafeteria or just wandering the halls. She observed students' behavior and interacted casually with them. She also conducted and tape-recorded interviews with 200 students alone and in groups (2000: 82). Throughout her fieldwork, Eckert took care to circulate among the entire student body and not to limit her investigation to particular social networks.

The linguistic data produced by Eckert's research are difficult to match in terms of quality and quantity. Her interviews resulted in hundreds of hours of informal speech from a variety of students. The comfort the students felt with Eckert is evident in the content of the interviews. They discuss fairly taboo subjects including sex, drugs, and crime, and they share very personal thoughts and stories. Clearly, Eckert's long-term involvement at the school made her a familiar presence, and she gained the trust of students. As she explains, "Students introduced me to their friends, and as my reputation spread, some came and introduced themselves to me on their own" (1989a: 32). Her extended contact with the school also meant that she spoke with students on multiple occasions. In fact, none of the individual interviews represented her first interaction with the student (2000: 79). Knowing the interviewees beforehand helped to eliminate any discomfort in participating in a tape-recorded interview.

Eckert's familiarity with this community gave her not only access to the students' speech but also the insight to make sense of the linguistic (and other) behavior she observed. The depth of this insight is seen most clearly in her treatment of the distinction between two categories of students: the jocks and the burnouts. This division plays a central role in the social structure of the school. It is the "means by which socioeconomic class is constructed in and for the adolescent population" with jocks and burnouts constituting "middle class and working class cultures respectively" (Eckert 2000: 2). While these social categories could be explored in a less ethnographically oriented study, Eckert argues for the broadened perspective that long-term participant observation provides:

> [T]he significance of the jock and burnout categories lies not simply in their existence and membership, but in their day-to-day motion. The two categories are based in practices that unfold in daily and mundane activity, interaction, and movement. And membership is not an either-or matter, but composed of many forms of alliance, participation, comings and goings. Viewing jocks and burnouts as members or representatives of categories would not only gloss over the histories, uncertainties, and multiplicities that constitute social affiliation, but would also freeze the categories and mask the fact that they exist only in practice. (Eckert 2000: 74)

Simply put, the practices associated with being a jock or a burnout can be better understood by a researcher directly observing them than by just hearing about them in interviews.

In order to develop her understanding of the social world she investigated, Eckert spent two years at the school, attending "regularly" for the first year and "occasionally" for the second (1989a: 28). While the rewards of a project such as Eckert's are considerable, few researchers can afford to spend so much time in the field. Fortunately, many of the benefits of participant observation can be achieved without such a tremendous commitment of time. Patricia Cukor-Avila, for example, utilized participant observation in her study of the small town of Springville, Texas (Cukor-Avila 1997; Cukor-Avila and Bailey 1995). She made daily trips to the town for nearly two months. Rather than circulate through the town conducting individual interviews, Cukor-Avila spent her time in the general store, a focal point for the community and a place frequented by nearly every resident on a daily basis (in part because it also served as the post office). Initially she conducted some interviews with residents visiting the store, but soon these "became closely intertwined with the day-to-day business of the store and began to include a wide range of unsolicited interactions, including teasing, arguments, jokes, business transactions, and the routine conversations that make up much of the community's linguistic activity" (Cukor-Avila and Bailey 1995: 167).

Cukor-Avila's approach proved fruitful in gaining access to everyday speech in fairly natural situations. The fact that her subjects shared town gossip with her and got into heated arguments in her presence suggests the comfort they must have felt with her (and her tape-recorder). The methods represent an innovative approach to overcoming the observer's paradox by allowing the fieldworker to move into different conversational roles. As Cukor-Avila and Bailey (1995) discuss, in most sociolinguistic interviews, the fieldworker remains the addressee. In the Springville corpus, however, she often becomes an overhearer or even an eavesdropper, in the sense of Bell (1984), as conversations among community members go on around her.

There are practical difficulties involved with an approach such as this. The fieldworker sacrifices control over the recording situation which can become somewhat chaotic as several participants interact. Cukor-Avila and Bailey (1995) note the challenges that parallel conversations can pose for intelligibility and recommend that fieldworkers keep notes on who is present, where they are situated, etc. Another potential problem for researchers pursuing quantitative analysis may be ensuring that enough speech is recorded from each speaker. This difficulty can be remedied by seeking follow-up interviews. Cukor-Avila, for example, has returned regularly to Springville.

Participant observation works well in small, well-delineated communities where suspicions about outsiders might inhibit other approaches to data collection. Such is the case with the research directed by Walt Wolfram on Ocracoke Island off the coast of North Carolina (Wolfram, Hazen, and Schilling-Estes 1999; Wolfram and Schilling-Estes 1996; Schilling-Estes 1999). This project differs from those discussed above in that it involved multiple fieldworkers. Wolfram and his team made repeated visits to Ocracoke over the course of several years, staying for periods of up to two weeks (Wolfram and Schilling-Estes 1996: 106). During their visits, the investigators conducted interviews with islanders and engaged in participant observation of local activities. The interviews were designed to fit with local norms in order to reduce their formality. For this same reason, many were conducted by pairs of fieldworkers. As Wolfram and Schilling-Estes (1996: 107) explain, "[f]or example, the husband and wife team of Walt and Marge Wolfram, or another natural pair of fieldworkers, might make an after-dinner visit to a home for an interview, thus fitting into a fairly natural and recognized type of social occasion."

In the Ocracoke case, as with others, participant observation was crucial to developing a deeper understanding of the community than might other-wise be accessible to outsiders. The objective is "to understand the sociolin-guistic dynamics of the community from the perspective of the community itself" (Wolfram and Schilling-Estes 1996: 106). Local knowledge expands researchers' explanatory possibilities; it allows them to move beyond the standard macro-social categories like age, sex, and socioeconomic class. For example, Wolfram and his colleagues encountered the "poker game network," a group of men who meet regularly to play poker. These men come from different educational backgrounds and have varying degrees of contact with non-islanders. Still, they share a "strong belief in the positive value of being true islanders" (Wolfram and Schilling-Estes 1996: 106). These men are also united linguistically in their embrace of traditional vernacular features, especially the backed and rounded pronunciation of the /aj/ diphthong which has become a stereotype of Outer Banks speech (see further section 4.4.3).

Participant observation is particularly valuable as an approach to studying variation in a bilingual context. The observer's paradox can be especially problematic for bilingualism researchers because of the influence of audience in determining language choice. The presence of a community outsider, the researcher, will likely bias the results. For this reason, Sarah Shin chose participant observation in her study of Korean/English bilingual children in New York City, adopting the role of a teacher's assistant in their first grade classroom (Shin 1998; Shin and Milroy 1999, 2000). In this capacity, she was able to casually observe what was apparently characteristic linguistic behavior in the classroom (including language choice and mixing). Her own bilingual abilities permitted Shin to engage the children in either code. More-over, she recorded peer interactions by having the children wear a small wireless microphone while they engaged in various school activities.

As the examples mentioned here illustrate, participant observation can be an enormously fruitful method for sociolinguistic analysis. It produces a tremendous supply of high-quality data and crucial insight into community dynamics. Nevertheless, there are some important disadvantages associated with this approach. We have already hinted at one disadvantage in noting the amount of time investigators like Eckert spent in the field. Such studies are extremely demanding for the fieldworker not only in time but also in energy, tact, and emotional involvement with community members. Related to this is the fact that participant observation is rather inefficient as a data collection procedure. It can be quite wasteful since many more speakers and many more hours of speech are recorded than can ultimately be analyzed. A useful rule of thumb is that a minimum of ten hours will be needed to analyze every hour of recorded speech. A more substantive analytical problem relates to the challenge of locating the results of a focused, ethnographic study of a particular community in a wider sociolinguistic context. Examining one high school or one small town alone cannot tell us how that situation at that site fits into the system of sociolinguistic variation in the city or region as a whole. For this reason, investigators engaged in participant observation often supplement their study with forays into similar communities in order to broaden their perspective (e.g., Eckert 2000; Wolfram, Hazen, and Schilling-Estes 1999). Alternatively, researchers might combine participant observation with other approaches, as illustrated by the case study in the following section.

3.5   Balancing Fieldwork Strategies: The Belfast Project

In an ideal world, a researcher interested in sociolinguistic variation in a given community would collect speech samples from every member of the community in every situation of use. Furthermore, the researcher would examine every linguistic variable as they relate to every social variable and present an analysis that accurately describes the local norms and practices shaping sociolinguistic variation. An endeavor of such scope is clearly beyond the reach of even the most-talented, best-funded researchers. Instead every investigator makes choices about the breadth and depth of coverage to be pursued based on limited time and resources.

Breadth and depth generally operate in inverse proportion to each other, and they influence sampling as well as data collection. A comparison of two studies discussed earlier in this chapter – Labov's Telsur project and Eckert's high school study – illustrates this relationship. In surveying all of the US and Canada, Telsur certainly offers geographical breadth. This project can, for example, indicate the range of areas affected by sound changes like the Northern Cities Shift (NCS) (see chapter 6). However, it does not offer depth of coverage for any one location since it surveys only two speakers for most cities and at most six speakers for even the largest urban areas. Thus, Telsur cannot tell us the extent to which a feature like the NCS has penetrated a given community. Eckert also investigated the NCS, but from a very different perspective. Her study examined only a single location but provided in-depth coverage of that location by interviewing some 200 students. Clearly, Eckert can make no claims about the geographical status of the NCS, but she can offer information about the social distribution of such features.

Decisions about data collection are also influenced by the need to locate investigations on the breadth/depth continuum. Techniques that efficiently gather data from a large number of people are generally limited in terms of the kinds of information they can investigate. For example, written questionnaires can provide broad coverage of a population but cannot tell us much about intraspeaker variation such as how frequently individual speakers use a given feature. On the other hand, approaches that provide a more holistic view of a variety of linguistic variables typically examine fewer speakers. In fact, some studies concentrate on one or two speakers whose usage is examined in detail (e.g., Coupland 1980).

Decisions about how broadly and how deeply one's project will cover a target population and the language of that population are faced by every researcher, and every researcher makes greater or lesser sacrifices in both dimensions. What is critical is that the limitations of the chosen approach be recognized. In many cases, these difficulties can be addressed in follow-up research employing alternative approaches with complementary benefits and limitations. The following discussion considers an example of a project that utilized multiple strategies for data collection. It is presented here as a case study illustrating how various approaches can be integrated. Labov's descriptions (1984, 2001b) of his Project on Linguistic Change and Variation – a series of studies examining sound changes in Philadelphia – serve the same purpose, and readers may wish to consult Labov's account for a comparative perspective on ways of balancing research strategies.

The research discussed here was carried out in 1975–81 in and around the city of Belfast, Northern Ireland, under the direction of James and Lesley Milroy, and many of the key findings have been presented elsewhere (Milroy and Milroy 1978; Milroy 1987, Milroy 1981; Pitts 1985). Our discussion here focuses on the design of the project which included three distinctly different approaches to the study of language variation and change in the city. These are a series of community studies involving participant observation, a doorstep survey based on a random sample of area households, and a study of a rural community in the hinterland of Belfast.

3.5.1 The community studies

A total of five communities within the city were selected for in-depth neighborhood studies. In choosing communities, the investigators attempted to give broad coverage of major geographical, status, and ethnic divisions in the city (see figure 3.2). The first three, Ballymacarrett, the Clonard, and the Hammer, are very low-status inner-city areas. Ballymacarrett is located

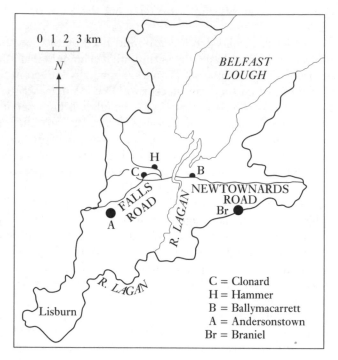

Figure 3.2   Location of five speech communities in Belfast

east and the Clonard and the Hammer west of the River Lagan, which bisects Belfast and constitutes an important socio-geographical boundary. The other two, Braniel and Andersonstown, are both located on the outer edges of the city and might be described approximately as upper-working to lower-middle class. Braniel is east of the river and is exclusively Protestant, while Andersonstown is west of the river and is exclusively Catholic.

Ballymacarrett and the Clonard can be viewed as somewhat lower-status "feeder" areas of Braniel and Andersonstown respectively. Many Andersonstown people originated from or had family ties with the Falls Road, the area where the Clonard is located; the Braniel population on the other hand are in East Belfast, and many have ties with the Newtownards Road where Ballymacarrett is located. The identification of these interrelationships between the areas is well motivated; when Belfast people change their place of residence, for whatever reason, there is a strong likelihood that the new location will be selected in accordance with a highly predictable set of urban sectoral preferences. To some extent, these sectoral preferences are related to ethno-religious lines of demarcation (Boal and Poole 1976); certainly it is reasonable to view inner-city communities east and west of the river as each having a higher-status ethnic counterpart.

The general idea of selecting communities that were interrelated in this way on the dimensions of status and ethnicity was to "match-up" linguistic data from the four areas in order to obtain some fairly detailed information on the linguistic strategies that Belfast people employed as they moved from urban vernacular to slightly higher-status speech patterns. The investigators were also curious as to whether east/west differences in the structure of the vernacular (see Milroy 1987) would be maintained by higher-status speakers. Thus, the choice of communities was constrained quite sharply by the analytical goals of the research.

The fieldworkers were eager to reach central community networks in each area in order to gain access to vernacular speech. Since contacts made through individuals with a clear institutional status – such as teachers, priests and community leaders – can often lead to rather standardized speakers, these contacts were avoided. Instead, communities were always approached initially through persons encountered directly or indirectly in the course of everyday living who had no institutional status in the communities, but were members of them. The Andersonstown fieldworker however, an anthropology graduate, was a local resident and was also one of the subjects. It was in this community that the closest approximation to a traditional participant-observation study was achieved, since the observer had for her entire life been part of the social setting which she was observing.

This guiding principle of participant observation – that the observer should be part of the setting which he or she is studying – was followed as closely as possible in the other communities. It was for this reason that the fieldworkers in the other areas, who were not local residents, adopted the role of "a friend of a friend" which gave them a clear position in the community as noted earlier (section 2.3). Following this strategy, the fieldworker introduced herself initially in each community not in her formal capacity as a researcher but as a "friend of a friend" (see Boissevain 1974 for a discussion of the significance of this relationship) mentioning the name of a person categorized as an insider with whom she had previously made contact and who had given her the names of people who might initially be approached. As a consequence of the reciprocal rights and obligation that members of close-knit groups contract with each other, the mention of the insider's name had the effect of guaranteeing the fieldworker's good faith; moreover, members of the group appeared to feel some obligation to help her in her capacity as a friend of their friend, so that she acquired some of the rights as well as some of the obligations of an insider. In all communities, but most particularly in the poorer inner-city areas (largely as a consequence of the denser, more multiplex structure of local networks), the fieldworkers were passed from one family to another, being received with warmth, friendliness, and trust. The research was presented as an investigation of the way life and language in the community had changed, and general permission was sought to record interactions at which the fieldworker was present. Once people had agreed to participate, this permission was never refused. As a consequence of the local norm of extended visiting (which was commonest in the low-status inner-city areas and least common in Braniel) many of the recordings were of two, three, or four people talking among themselves, often with minimal fieldworker participation.

The investigators used snowball sampling (section 2.3), recording subjects as described above until a quota sample of 16 people in each community had been filled. The target quota consisted of eight young adults (18–25 years) and eight middle-aged adults (40–55 years), equally divided between males and females. In practice, of course, many speakers fell outside the target quota. The quality and quantity of data collected during these community studies was excellent, including many group sessions with little or no linguistic participation by the fieldworker.

In the Belfast research, no attempt was made to provide an interview schedule such as that developed by Labov (section 3.3.1); fieldworkers were simply briefed on the kind of social information (such as occupation, educational background, family connections, and previous residence of speaker) that they would need to have acquired by the end of the observation period. The topics associated with this information – such as local attitudes and local networks of relationships – generally provided a more than adequate conversational resource.

The Belfast methods in these neighborhood studies were developed primarily for the study of *close-knit* communities – and indeed they are particularly suitable for urban or rural communities of this type. Bortoni-Ricardo's (1985) work in Brasilia provides an example of a sociolinguistic "network" study of a close-knit migrant community from a very different kind of society, using methods similar to those described here.

3.5.2   The Belfast doorstep survey

The doorstep survey was designed to complement, by means of a rather wider but shallower study, the detailed information collected in the five communities. This study was developed after intensive work on three inner-city areas had already been completed. Consequently, the basic facts about sociolinguistic patterns in the city were more or less known to the researchers, and the doorstep survey was employed to obtain quite specific and limited linguistic information.

The speakers surveyed were drawn from a random sample of households provided by the Northern Ireland Housing Executive. The sample population used by the project was actually drawn from a larger sample of 500 households which the Executive had used for their own survey of housing patterns in the city (cf. Labov's subsampling procedure in New York City). In the end, a total of 73 speakers were interviewed, and an analysis was made of data from 60 speakers, 32 males and 28 females. In order to ensure comparability, the main effort in the interviews was focused on recording carefully designed word lists, which sampled realizations of several phonological variables in a range of phonetic environments. Some spontaneous speech was also recorded.

The interviews could be completed on the doorstep in as little as 10 minutes, but most lasted between 15 and 45 minutes and more often than not the fieldworker was invited into the house, offered tea and biscuits – and on one occasion two meat pies!

In view of the brevity of the basic interview, subjects were not contacted in advance; fieldworkers simply knocked on the door and requested interviews. It was hoped in this way to reduce the high refusal rate which is a hazard in sociolinguistic surveys, and indeed the method seemed in general to be successful in this respect; altogether, out of 40 addresses visited, only eight refusals were recorded. As these refusals were mainly from relatively high-status households, interviewers had to be careful to substitute comparable households in order to maintain the social balance of the sample.

The purpose of the research was presented as an investigation of change in Belfast life and language. The rather vague account satisfied and stimulated the interest of most people; fieldworkers began asking interviewees how long they had lived in the area and moved on to discuss their general attitudes and background. The minimum social information required for each speaker was (approximate) age, sex, housing type and (where possible) occupation. Since the word list was considered to be particularly important, it was usually produced early in the proceedings. Where possible, fieldworkers attempted to record a male and a female at each address, but since both were seldom at home at the first visit, a second and even a third visit was often necessary.

The general principle of the Belfast doorstep survey is quite similar to that of other surveys (see section 3.2) as they are not designed to attain any depth of insight into, for example, stylistic variation, or the general structure of a speaker's phonology. Rather, information is sought on broad patterns of variation across a wide social range in the urban community. The major effort of the Belfast research was focused on the community studies; and the main function of the doorstep survey was to provide a context within which to place the findings of those studies. Although the data collected were quite adequate for this purpose, no attempt was made to claim representativeness for the doorstep survey.

It should be emphasized that brief, shallow surveys like that described here are most rewarding when they are designed to solve specifiable and well-understood problems. They are not suitable instruments for exploratory research, which is best carried out by in-depth investigation of a small number of speakers. For example, in order to prepare instruments like word lists which allow for efficient data collection in such surveys, the researchers must already have a fairly solid understanding of local speech patterns, including information about the linguistic conditioning of the variables to be studied (see further section 6.4).

3.5.3   The rural hinterland study

This part of the Belfast project was motivated by a question of considerable sociolinguistic interest – the relationship between dialects of cities and those of surrounding areas (for other explorations of this relationship see Callary 1975 and Gordon 2001b). Since linguistic change and rapid dialect mixing appear to be a general characteristic of urban dialects (see section 5.3; Labov 1972b: 300; Kerswill and Williams 1999, 2000), it seems reasonable to assume that insight can be gained into the processes of their formation if a set of data from a city is compared with a set from a surrounding area. Belfast, being a relatively young industrial city, is an excellent site for such an investigation (see Milroy and Milroy 1978 for details).

The hinterland area selected for study (see Pitts 1983, 1985 for details) was Lurgan, a small rural town in the Lagan Valley, 17 miles southwest of Belfast and outside the urban overspill area. It had been noted previously that certain phonological features characteristic of west Belfast where both Clonard and Andersonstown were located were also characteristic of the mid–Ulster dialect spoken in Lurgan (as opposed to the Ulster-Scots dialect of Belfast's northern and eastern hinterland). Hence, it seemed likely that information on similarities and differences between the five Belfast communities on the one hand and Lurgan on the other could be used for a variety of theoretical purposes.

The participant–observation techniques in this study were similar to those used in the urban community studies. The "network" method was adopted as a general principle, and several Belfast University students who were Lurgan residents were located as initial contacts. On a number of occasions, the fieldworker arranged for subjects to record themselves and their friends, with excellent results. Altogether, 28 speakers were recorded, 16 men and 12 women. As in the community studies, they fell into two generational cohorts.

Altogether, the six studies that comprised the Belfast project – five from Belfast and one from Lurgan – allowed language variation to be analyzed on the following dimensions: rural versus urban; high-status versus low-status (relatively speaking); east of the city versus west of the city. In addition, the social network approach adopted in the fieldwork proved to be a powerful analytical construct (see further chapter 5).

3.6 Research Ethics

We conclude our discussion of data collection by outlining a range of problems that may be characterized as *ethical*. Some consideration of ethical issues is an important part of any discussion of sociolinguistic fieldwork methods. Our treatment here is necessarily brief, though fuller discussions of many of the issues we outline here can be found elsewhere (e.g., Johnstone 2000b; Neuman 1997; Hammersley and Atkinson 1995).

3.6.1 Informed consent

Most universities and other research institutions have established guidelines for investigators working in any field that utilizes human subjects for research. In our experience, these guidelines are taken very seriously by the institutions since violations can damage much more than reputations. In the US, for example, a violation of federal policies by a single researcher can result in a suspension of funding for all research across the institution. To protect against such problems, institutions typically require investigators to submit research proposals for internal review by an Institutional Review Board (IRB). The human subjects concerns that sociolinguistic research raises are generally much milder than those stemming from, for example, medical research. There are, however, significant issues to be addressed, and we recommend that researchers go through the proper channels since the stakes are so high. The need to gain IRB approval before any data collection can begin necessitates careful planning on the part of the researcher. Fortunately, the procedures, at least in the US, allow for expedited review of studies involving minimal risk to subjects, as is typically the case with linguistic research.

One of the fundamental elements of ethical research using human subjects is the principle of informed consent. Subjects must voluntarily agree to participate in the research and must know what their participation entails. Informed consent is often obtained by having subjects sign written statements, and research involving minor children may require the consent of parents or guardians. The written statements typically contain the following: (a) a short description of the project including its objectives; (b) a description of the procedures used, detailing what the subject can expect and any risks that might be involved; (c) an assurance that the subject will remain anonymous and that all information will be confidential; (d) a confirmation that the subject's participation is voluntary and that he or she can withdraw from the study at any time; and (e) information for contacting the investigators and the sponsoring institution's review board (Neuman

1997: 450). Sample consent forms used for sociolinguistic research are reprinted in Johnstone (2000b: 44–7).

Investigators attempting to record casual speech may be concerned about the potential impact of presenting a formal written document to their subjects. The informed consent statement is an explicit reminder that the investigator's purpose is linguistic research, and thus it may counteract efforts to overcome the observer's paradox. Fortunately, written consent may not be required in every case; it may be acceptable to obtain consent verbally as long as subjects are properly informed in accordance with those elements described in the previous paragraph. Of course, there are some projects for which no informed consent is required. This is likely to be the case for analyses of public language such as published written works or mass-media broadcasts. Also, research that gathers data anonymously through written surveys is typically exempted from the need to obtain informed consent, but investigators usually need to complete the IRB review process to verify that their project is exempt.

The obligation to inform subjects about the nature of the research may also concern sociolinguists. If subjects know that the investigator is studying the use of, for example, multiple negation, /h/-dropping, or some other socially marked feature, this knowledge could easily affect their usage of that feature. Fortunately, statements of informed consent need not be so detailed, and it usually suffices to describe the research as a study of language – though even this general label may put speakers on guard about their usage. For this reason, the investigator may frame the research in even more general terms as examining social changes or life in the community (see Belfast example section 3.5.1). In this context, language can be mentioned as one of many aspects of the study – an accurate description in view of the role that social information plays in sociolinguistic analysis.

3.6.2   *Preservation of anonymity and access to recordings*

Informed consent is typically given with the understanding that the information provided by participants will remain confidential and that their identities will remain known only to the researcher. Reporting only group data is one means of meeting this obligation. At times, however, it is necessary to refer to individuals. In such instances, sociolinguists may identify people by pseudonyms, initials, or numbers. Some researchers also identify neighborhoods and even towns by pseudonyms. The decision of whether to use pseudonyms for place names is based on the potential for identifying individual research subjects. Gordon (2001b) uses the real names of the two towns he studied, whereas Cukor-Avila (1997) refers to the small-town site of her research by a pseudonym. Population numbers figured into these choices; the communities on which Gordon reports are towns of over 3,000 residents while Cukor-Avila's site has a population of less than 200. In addition, Cukor-Avila provides transcripts of extended conversations that include personal information and narratives that might facilitate identification of individuals if the location were known. As a general rule, pseudonyms should be used for locations if the researcher has any doubts about preserving the anonymity of subjects. However, sometimes the precise identification of the research site is critical to the study, or difficult to avoid in reporting on the research. In Gordon's case, for example, the research sites were chosen because of their locations relative to a major highway and certain urban areas, and these elements were crucial to the analysis. The need to describe such characteristics of the sites meant that the towns under investigation would have been readily identifiable even if pseudonyms had been adopted, and anyway individual subjects in the study were referred to only by their initials. Nevertheless, if the communities had been much smaller, Gordon would have had to take steps, including using pseudonyms for names of the towns, to avoid jeopardizing the anonymity of subjects.

Concerns about anonymity also necessitate that sociolinguists adopt a firm policy with regard to access to tape-recordings. It is common to restrict access to members of the research group or scholars who are temporarily affiliated for the purpose of carrying out a specified piece of work, and tape-recordings should by no means be freely available as a resource to all. Occasionally material from one investigation may be requested for bona fide research by another scholar or, more commonly, the original investigators may present their material, including excerpts from tapes, in public lectures. Policies regarding these matters should be specified in the informed consent procedures so that the subjects are aware of such possible uses of the material they provide. Some institutions may require researchers to obtain a separate permission for public presentation of recorded material, even in the classroom setting. In all instances where recordings are shared, the tapes involved should be carefully vetted for sensitivity of content or for material that can lead to the identification of speakers.

3.6.3 Surreptitious recording

It may appear that the easiest way of overcoming the observer's paradox is to record speakers covertly. Such deception, however, raises serious legal and ethical concerns. The legal issues are detailed by Murray and Murray (1992, 1996) who review the relevant statutes and case law for the US and Canada. As their discussion makes clear, the question of the legality of surreptitious recording is quite complex with standards varying by jurisdiction. It appears, however, that there are several circumstances in which this technique is legal. For example, in some states the law allows for conversations to be recorded when only one party is aware of the recording. Thus, a professor could covertly record conversations held in his or her office with students. Other jurisdictions are more restrictive and would not allow for surreptitious recording even in public venues such as parks and street corners (Murray and Murray 1992: 34–45).

For many researchers the fact that surreptitious recording may be legal does not suffice to license its use; they view this deceptive technique as a violation of ethical principles. Labov has been a particularly strong opponent. During his term as president of the Linguistic Society of America, he established an ethics committee that condemned the practice (see Shuy 1993). Nevertheless, linguists not working within Labov's general framework seem less troubled than variationists are by covert recording. For example, Dixon (1984: 80) quite openly states that some interesting material was obtained from Aboriginal speakers by candid recording. Similarly, Harvey (1992) was interested in certain features of "drunken speech" in the Peruvian community she studied. She decided that the only way to gather the data she needed was by surreptitiously recording drinking sessions. Such techniques appear to be less common among researchers working in Western, industrialized societies though Murray (1986) stands as an exception. For a study of St. Louis, Murray used a concealed tape-recorder to gather data from speakers in a variety of public venues, including singles bars, supermarkets, laundromats, churches, and funeral parlors. In some cases, the deception of these speakers was taken further when Murray inquired about their age and whether they were native to the city. Understandably, the informants became suspicious, but Murray pacified them by claiming to be either a government employee who was gathering demographic statistics or a marketing consultant for the business they were patronizing or "a dear friend of someone who bore [the subject] an amazing resemblance, but who lived in another state and was a few years younger or older and on the brink of death" (1986: 8). Fortunately for the reputation of the field, such outright deception of research subjects marks Murray's study as exceptional.

The ethical dilemma associated with covert recording may be lessened if speakers are informed after the fact. It is acceptable in other social scientific fields, especially psychology, for investigators to deceive subjects initially about the nature of the research provided that they are debriefed afterward and given the opportunity to withdraw themselves from the study. Such an approach was taken by Crystal and Davy (1969) who tape-recorded colleagues, friends, and family surreptitiously and subsequently requested permission to use the material. It is important to note, however, that Crystal and Davy are focusing on the language of a few speakers well known to them whereas variationist methods are designed to have more general application to communities not known to the investigator. In the former case the nature of the personal ties between investigator and subject seems to make candid recording a less pressing ethical issue.

Some *practical* disadvantages of candid recording have been noted by Labov (1984). First of all, it can jeopardize the researcher's relationship to the community, and access to subjects is likely to be hindered if people think they are being spied on. Secondly, the quality of recordings is likely to be poor. Imagine, for example, the sound quality of Harvey's tapes that were made by "hiding a Walkman-sized recorder in a pocket or bag" (1992: 78). Shuy (1993) describes a much more elaborate set up used by researchers at the Center for Applied Linguistics in the 1960s. They converted a house into a recreation center and installed microphones in the chandeliers in order to record the speech of the children who came to play there. The technique failed because "[t]he naturalistic conditions produced a great deal of inaudible shouts along with the sounds of ping-pong balls hitting various surfaces, toilets interminably flushing, doors slamming, and unidentifiable fragments of human speech" (1993: 105).

Although we personally endorse Labov's views on the matter of candid recording, it has to be admitted that the issues are not always as clear-cut as they seem. Particularly during successful long-term participant observation, the borderline between overt and covert recording can become blurred and quite difficult problems emerge.

During the community studies carried out in Belfast, for example – and no doubt this experience is quite general – conversations were often interrupted by several people entering the room. Indeed, sometimes the original participants would leave in the course of a long recording session. Although the recording equipment was not concealed, and was monitored quite openly by the fieldworker, it was not always clear whether all participants were aware that they were being tape-recorded. In such situations it was not the researchers' practice to interrupt proceedings in order to renegotiate permission to record; in Belfast such permission was sought at the first contact with each household. There was, moreover, a standing agreement that the equipment would never be concealed and that before leaving the house the fieldworker would erase from the tape any material that subjects or fieldworkers considered sensitive. In fact, more often than not the fieldworker took the initiative in this matter; investigators who build up long-term relationships with communities frequently hear and record material about which they would prefer to remain ignorant.

As the Belfast example indicates, even researchers who reject the intentional use of surreptitious recording such as practiced by Harvey or Murray may face ethical dilemmas related to this issue. While there remains some disagreement on the ethics of candid recording, Labov's general principle seems to offer a good guideline: the researcher should "avoid any act that would be embarrassing to explain if it became a public issue" (Labov 1984: 52).

3.6.4   The researcher's responsibilities to the community

Treating research subjects with respect by obtaining informed consent, protecting their anonymity, and so forth, is one dimension of the investigator's responsibility to the community being studied. Still, many linguists have argued that it is not enough simply to do no harm and that we should work to give something back to the communities we investigate. Cameron and colleagues distinguish "ethical research" in which the concern is "to minimise damage and offset inconvenience to the researched" (1992: 14) from "advocacy research" which is conducted not only *on* but also *for* the subjects (1992: 15). The basic idea is that research should benefit the community as well as the investigator.

Labov has been a strong proponent of this advocacy position. In his view, linguists are motivated to take social action by their commitment to certain basic principles:

The Principle of Error Correction
A scientist who becomes aware of a widespread idea or social practice with important consequences that is invalidated by his own data is obligated to bring this error to the attention of the widest possible audience. (Labov 1982b: 172)

The Principle of the Debt Incurred
An investigator who has obtained linguistic data from members of a speech community has an obligation to use the knowledge based on that data for benefit of the community, when it has need of it. (Labov 1982b: 173)

The principle of error correction motivated linguists in the 1960s to speak out against widespread belief among educators and language pathologists that vernacular speech features were evidence of language deficit. Labov's influential paper "The logic of nonstandard English" (reprinted in Labov 1972a) illustrates these efforts which succeeded in "pushing the definition of linguistic normalcy toward a dialectally-sensitive one" (Wolfram 1993a: 226).

The call for linguists to respond to community needs raises the question of what we have to offer. How can linguists' specialized knowledge be applied to benefit the community? The areas most relevant to sociolinguistic research might include language testing especially as it relates to speakers of non-standard dialects, language policy in multilingual societies, and efforts to preserve moribund languages and dialects (e.g., Nagy 2000; Wolfram and Schilling-Estes 1995). However, by far the greatest attention from sociolinguists seeking to repay some of their incurred debt has been given to issues in education.

Labov (1982b) discusses the "Ann Arbor trial" as an example of the contributions that sociolinguists can make to educational issues. This case involves a 1977 lawsuit that was brought against school officials in Ann Arbor, Michigan, by the parents of several African American children. The parents alleged that the school system had failed "to take into account the cultural, social, and economic factors that would prevent [the students] from making normal progress in the school" (1982: 168). Language took on a central role in the case as the plaintiffs argued that the children's dialect, a variety of African American Vernacular English (AAVE), posed a barrier to their educational success that the schools had not taken adequate action to overcome. These arguments gained support from the evidence of Geneva Smitherman and other linguists who testified about the structure and history of AAVE. In the end the plaintiffs prevailed, and the judge's ruling led the school district to conduct workshops to raise the teachers' awareness of the nature of sociolinguistic variation (Wolfram and Schilling-Estes 1998: 264).

Many of the issues involved in the Ann Arbor trial were revisited nearly two decades later when the school district in Oakland, California, presented a resolution on Ebonics, the term they chose to refer to the dialect of their urban African American students. A storm of controversy arose surrounding this action due in part to misrepresentations of the district's intent by the media as well as to some problematic phrasing in the resolution itself (see Wolfram 1998a). As they had in Ann Arbor, linguists spoke out about the nature of AAVE and generally offered support for the Oakland proposal. The members of the Linguistic Society of America made clear their support in a resolution that was passed at the annual meeting in 1997. Several linguists stated their case in letters and articles in newspapers and other mass media forums (see especially Rickford, e.g., 1997a). Eventually, the US Senate convened a hearing on the issue during which Labov and other linguists gave testimony. Unlike the Ann Arbor case, there was no definitive resolution of the "Ebonics controversy." Over time the media, and apparently the politicians, simply lost interest in the issue.

The examples discussed so far are cases in which linguists stepped forward to offer their assistance in reaction to situations of perceived need as required by the principle of debt incurred. However, Wolfram has argued that our responsibilities extend beyond such "reactive advocacy" and that researchers should take the initiative in serving the communities they investigate (1993a, 1998b). Following Labov's model, he formulates a principle of linguistic gratuity:

> Investigators who have obtained linguistic data from members of a speech community should actively pursue positive ways in which they can return linguistic favors to the community. (Wolfram 1993a: 227)

Guided by this principle, Wolfram and his research team have developed a series of language awareness programs that are designed to communicate basic facts about regional and social dialects and, ultimately, to promote greater tolerance and even appreciation of linguistic diversity. Schools offer a useful venue for such programs. Wolfram (1993a) discusses a language awareness program piloted in the schools in Baltimore, Maryland. The curriculum for this program includes a series of exercises that systematically guide students through the discovery of phonological and grammatical patterns in varieties such as AAVE. In this way, the program exposes children to "a type of scientific inquiry into language that is generally untapped in the students' present instruction about language" (1993a: 230). In addition to this intellectual benefit, such programs may offer some measure of emotional benefit. They may promote respect for non-standard varieties by demonstrating that they are as regular as the standard language. Moreover, by exploring the sociohistorical context that gave rise to current varieties, they can encourage students to be proud of their linguistic heritage.

Wolfram's work on Ocracoke, an island community off the coast of North Carolina, provides several models for language awareness programs outside the context of the schools. Because many of the features of the local dialect appear to be fading from use, much of the work on Ocracoke has had a preservationist flavor. For example, Wolfram and his colleagues established a permanent exhibit on the dialect at the local historical museum. They also produced a video documentary describing the dialect and published a book for the general readers (see Wolfram 1998b: 272 for citations). Profits from the sale of these items, as well as from the sale of the dialect-themed T-shirts they designed, are shared with the Ocracoke Preservation Society. As such examples indicate, linguists can be creative in pursuing avenues for returning "linguistic favors" to the community.

The discussion thus far has focused on the positive value of initiatives undertaken in accordance with the principle of linguistic gratuity. In most cases, these efforts seem fairly uncontroversial, at least among linguists. However, it is important to bear in mind some of the problems that might arise from such efforts despite the good intentions of the researcher. Wolfram (1993a, 1998b) details several ethical considerations related to initiatives like his language awareness programs. There is, for example, an element of paternalism involved in linguists performing what they consider to be favors in areas where they perceive a need rather than "responding to the explicitly stated needs of a community" (1993a: 233). In this regard, Wolfram cautions linguists to be aware of their own sociopolitical agendas and how they might influence their work, a concern that may be particularly acute when promoting language awareness programs in the schools. He also raises issues related to the representation of non-standard varieties. The need to describe a dialect in terms that a non-specialist audience can understand may lead to oversimplification of the sociolinguistic facts. Our descriptions tend to include a list of characteristic features that distinguish the dialect from other varieties, including the standard. Most audiences are not used to thinking about language as variable and thus might assume the use of dialect features to be categorical. The picture that emerges, then, is of a variety more vernacular, more basilectal than any dialect actually is.[3] Nevertheless, while the potential for entering such ethically problematic territory is real, this discussion is not intended to discourage researchers from seeking ways of benefiting the communities they study. The bottom line is that linguists need to be sensitive to community needs and tread lightly as they work to meet those needs.

3.7   Concluding Remarks

These first chapters have attempted to provide a critical overview of variationist approaches to research design and data collection. One conclusion emerging from this discussion is that a wider variety of approaches is being practiced today than ever before in the field's nearly four-decade history. As the field expands, so too do the choices faced by investigators. Thus, while our focus has largely been methodological, we have stressed the need for decisions to be grounded in a defensible framework. In the following chapters theoretical issues become even more central, as our emphasis shifts from largely practical concerns to matters of interpretation.

4

Language Variation and the Social World: Issues in Analysis and Interpretation

4.1 Introductory

Researchers look for two very different kinds of regularity in a corpus of recorded or transcribed language data: language internal patterns which reflect, for example, phonological, morphological, or syntactic constraints on the distribution of variants, and those which reflect preferences for particular variants by different kinds of speaker. This chapter and chapter 5 explore analytic and interpretative issues arising from this second type of pattern.

We noted in chapter 1 that the methods of dialect geography were not primarily designed to investigate variation within a specified geographical area between (for example) status groups, male and female speakers, generation cohorts, distinct ethnic groups, or socially patterned variability in the language of a single speaker. In providing explicitly for a range of speaker types and speech styles to be sampled, the data collection methods pioneered by Labov allow data to be analyzed on all of these dimensions. The key to direct systematic comparison of large amounts of socially and stylistically differentiated data is the concept of the *linguistic variable*.

Crucially, variant realizations of a linguistic variable do not encode different referential meanings (an issue discussed further in chapter 7) but covary with other units in the system and/or with social categories such as those mentioned above. Quantitative statements can be made about language use, so that a speaker of type A might be said to use *more* or *less* of a particular variant than type B speakers, rather than categorically to use it or not to use it. Equally, type A speakers may be said to use more of variant X in situation Y than in situation Z, rather than categorically to use X in either situation. In principle, a statement of this kind can be made with reference to any kind of social category or situational context that the analyst can justify. Comparisons between the language of individual speakers or between the language of the same speaker on different occasions can be made in the same way (see Coupland 1980).

We look first at a small amount of straightforwardly presented material from investigations in two English cities, Bradford and Norwich, which shows relationships between phonological variation and the social class of speakers of a kind commonly reported in the literature. The figures in table 4.1 refer to the variable (h), and list the percentages of zero realizations of word initial /h/ in stressed syllables (e.g., *hammer, heart*) recorded for five social class groups in these cities, ranging from lower-working to middle-middle class. The zero variant has been heavily ideologized in England since around the middle of the nineteenth century as an index of low social status (see further Mugglestone 1995), and as Milroy (1992: 135) points out, a pattern of alternation between zero and [h] is of considerable antiquity. It is still found in most of England except for an area in the extreme north of the country. Although Bradford and Norwich are located several hundred miles apart in distinctively different dialect areas, it is clear that in both places the higher the status of the speaker, the greater the tendency to approximate to a spoken norm which retains [h]. However, levels of use of the two variants are quite different in the two locations, with each social group in Bradford using the zero variant more than the corresponding group in Norwich.

This difference between the two communities in the pervasiveness of *h-dropping* raises an issue developed further in this chapter and in chapter 5, namely that specific social meanings indexed by linguistic variables are local, despite the robust supralocal character of the relationship between language and social class. In this case, Bradford middle-middle-class speakers and Norwich lower-middle-class speakers use comparable proportions of the stigmatized zero variant, so that a level of use by a given speaker of around 14 percent will index high social status in Bradford, but a somewhat lower status in Norwich. Social meanings of even heavily ideologized variants such

Table 4.1 (h) in Bradford and Norwich: percentage of zero realization (after Chambers and Trudgill 1998: 59)

Social class	Bradford	Norwich
Middle-middle	12	6
Lower-middle	28	14
Upper-working	67	40
Middle-working	89	60
Lower-working	93	60

as this are therefore not constant across communities, nor do social categories such as class operate in the same way across communities (cf. section 2.6 above). The need to interpret social categories locally rather than globally is a recurrent theme of our discussion.

Table 4.1 relates language variation to a single social category, but in practice social categories usually do not affect linguistic variables independently of each other. Tables 4.2 and 4.3 show variant realizations of the vowel variable (o) (in words such as *home* and *boat*)[1] by 16 men and 16 women in the northern English city of Newcastle upon Tyne. Effects of social class (working class versus middle class) and age (45–65 versus 16–24) on linguistic variation are also shown. Four variants of (o) are identified, as follows: (i) [œ]: a centralized rounded, usually monophthongal mid vowel localized to limited areas around the city of Newcastle upon Tyne; (ii) [oː]: a much more widely distributed but characteristically northern English variant, widely distributed also in Scotland and Ireland; (iii) [oə]: a variant localized to the far north of England, the distribution of which is less localized than [œ] but more so than [oː]; (iv) [ou]: one of several diphthongized variants with a closing glide associated with the Midlands and the South (see Kerswill 1996) which has been gaining territory northwards for about 200 years.

Table 4.2   (o) as realized by Newcastle women, by age and social class

Variants:	1 [œ]	2 [oː]	3 [oə]	4 [ou]	Total
WC (45–65)	0	144	0	0	144
WC (16–24)	0	144	0	2	146
MC (45–65)	0	179	0	0	179
MC (16–24)	0	95	0	9	104
Total	**0**	**562**	**0**	**11**	**573**

Table 4.3   (o) as realized by Newcastle men, by age and social class

Variants:	1 [œ]	2 [oː]	3 [oə]	4 [ou]	Total
WC (45–65)	55	80	4	0	139
WC (16–24)	30	96	1	6	133
MC (45–65)	10	129	0	0	139
MC (16–24)	55	76	0	15	164
Total	**150**	**381**	**5**	**21**	**557**

Several patterns are evident in tables 4.2 and 4.3, most obviously a dramatic gender difference which arises chiefly from the women's overwhelming preference for the widely distributed northern variant [oː]. The variant [ou] represents a southern English norm external to the far northern city of Newcastle approximating also to a high-status RP variant. It seems to be quite marginal to the speech community as it appears only occasionally and is used only by young speakers (chiefly men) in both social class groups. Neither of the more localized variants [œ] and [oə] are used at all by women.

The male pattern is dramatically different. While [oː] is the preferred variant for men also, table 4.3 shows that three out of the four male subgroups use [œ] extensively. The older middle-class group are relatively infrequent users – in fact, one man in this group does not use [œ] at all. The other localized variant [oə], also entirely absent from women's speech, is mostly restricted to occasional use by older working-class men. This distribution suggests that it is recessive. The distribution of the heavily used variants [oː] and [œ], gives rise to an overwhelming and dominant gender effect, although, as we have noted, age and class are also implicated (for details see Milroy 1999; Watt and Milroy 1999).

Recent work by Dubois and Horvath (1998) provides a further example of the complex, multidimensional relationship between social categories and linguistic variation, highlighting the interacting effect of gender, age and social network on realizations of the variables (th) and (dh) – respectively the voiceless and voiced consonants occurring initially in words such as *think* and *that*. Table 4.4 reports the incidence of stop versus fricative realizations in a sample of 28 speakers from the Cajun community of St. Landry parish, Louisiana, the stop variants being heavily ideologized as stereotypical of Cajun speech. This bilingual English/French-speaking community is now

Table 4.4 Percentage of dental stop realizations of (th) and (dh) according to age and sex split by type of network (after Dubois and Horvath 1998: 254)

	Old		Middle-aged		Young	
	(th)	(dh)	(th)	(dh)	(th)	(dh)
Women						
Closed network	51	65	15	12	35	49
Open network	0	0	11	6	5	8
Men						
Closed network	44	69	19	39	47	55
Open network	46	40	5	64	56	87

undergoing language shift, but is acutely aware of its distinctive Cajun ethnicity. Community members draw on a range of symbolic resources, including those provided by phonological variability, to display and enhance their distinctiveness. The network variable is relevant to the maintenance and display of distinctiveness as it distinguishes different orientations to the Cajun community; speakers with closed networks have always lived and worked in the local town, while those with open networks contract less localized ties.

Table 4.4 shows that while men use both [t] and [d] variants much more than women overall, this difference relates to age and personal network type of the speakers; the sharpest distinction emerges between men and women with open networks. Women with closed networks use very much more of the ethnically marked variants [t] and [d] than those with open networks, while the effect of network type on male patterns of use is much less evident. This sex-related network effect holds across all three age groups. Age effects are also clear, in that the middle-aged group as a whole uses a much lower proportion of stopped variants than the older and younger groups, with the young male group particularly favoring these variants.

Dubois and Horvath (1998: 255) point out that while female patterns of use are comparable for both (th) and (dh) variants, all male groups use [d] more than [t], with different patterns emerging in each age group. While the middle-aged closed network group uses [d] less than younger and older speakers with closed networks, younger men with open networks use this variant dramatically more than their elders.

Such complex data invite the analyst to consider the roles of gender, age, ethnicity, social class, and social network in yielding these systematic patterns, raising the question also of what such patterns mean to speakers, as opposed to analysts. Dubois and Horvath make it clear that answers to such questions require an understanding of the local social world specific to this Louisiana community whose language choices are part of a larger set of local social practices defining them as distinctively Cajun. In the remainder of this chapter we consider not only such interpretative issues, but the question of how global social categories such as class, gender, and ethnicity might themselves best be conceptualized and related to local social practices.

4.2   Social Categories and Theories of Change

The general tenor of Labov's work throughout his career makes clear that he does not interpret patterns yielded by his quantitative methods primarily as an elucidation of the relationship between social and linguistic structure (e.g., Labov 1972b, 1994, 2001b). His goal, shared by many variationists, is to obtain insights into processes of linguistic change and to challenge linguistic theories that model language as a static entity, identifying homogeneity with structure. Systematic differences in apparent time of the kind shown in table 4.2, 4.3, and 4.4 are, under certain conditions, interpreted as evidence of change in progress, differences between generation cohorts being assumed to mirror changes over real time (see section 2.5 above). But a less obvious kind of evidence is provided by irregularity in the expected pattern of differentiation according to the speech style or sex or social class of the speaker. An example is Labov's well-known analysis of the variable (r) in New York City, which shows a robust pattern of stratification by social class except that one social group, the lower-middle class, use in their more careful styles *more* rather than *less* of the prestige variant [r] than the status group immediately above them. Labov interprets this irregularity as indicative of the important role of the lower-middle class in diffusing a change throughout the speech community following their adoption and emulation of an innovatory pattern introduced by a higher status group (Labov 1972b: 122). Similar structural irregularities might involve a social group unexpectedly using variants associated with *lower-status* values (see, for example, Trudgill 1974: 111; Trudgill 1988), and might also be associated with social categories other than class – particularly gender (Labov 1990; Milroy and Milroy 1985).

The central role of gender in the social trajectory of language change as exemplified in tables 4.2–4.4 has received a good deal of attention in the literature and is discussed at various points in Labov's recent account (2001b) of social dimensions of language change. With the benefit of information on the language behavior of older speakers in Newcastle and the dialect at an earlier period (see Watt and Milroy 1999) we can infer that the monophthongized variant [oː] is advancing at the expense of more localized variants, with women leading this change. A more complicated picture emerges in the data from the Cajun community shown in table 4.4, where the open network men appear to be taking the lead in consolidating the use of a variant strongly associated with Cajun ethnicity.

Labov (1990) proposes two general principles governing the role of gender in language change, as follows:

Principle I: For stable sociolinguistic variables [i.e., those not involved in change] men show a higher frequency of non-standard forms than women.

Principle Ia: In change from above [i.e., change which takes place above the level of consciousness] women favor the incoming prestige form more than men.

Principle II: In change from below women are most often the innovators.

Debate on the social dynamics of language change remains prominent in variationist research, much of it critical of these principles. Note that Principle Ia assumes the importance of prestige in explaining which variants are preferred by women. However, the data presented in tables 4.2 and 4.3 suggest that it is the supralocal variant [oː] rather than the high-prestige norm [ou] which is preferred by women, while men continue to use the localized variant [œ] at quite high levels. Further evidence of women's preference for supralocal variants, which may or may not coincide with a variant evaluated globally as prestigious, is discussed in section 4.4.2 below. Eckert's study of Detroit adolescents shows how the interaction between gender and the local social categories "jock" and "burnout" shapes the direction of change (1989b, 1998, 2000). She reports that, in general, girls signal social category membership by linguistic means more dramatically than boys. However, she emphasizes that gender should be considered in conjunction with the ideologies and social practices associated with the jock and burnout categories and (contrary to Labov's principles) as a local rather than a global category (Eckert and McConnell-Ginet 1994).

Dubois and Horvath (1999) have recently contributed to the linguistic change debate, and their discussion of several changes in the Cajun community of Louisiana also shows that generalizations about the role of gender in language change cannot be made independently of interactions between gender and other variables. They further suggest that the debate would benefit from some distinctions that have not generally been made – such as whether the change originates from inside or outside the speech community, and whether the phenomenon under consideration is the spread of an existing variant or an innovation. They also note difficulties with Labov's distinction between changes from above and below conscious awareness, as used in Principle Ia and Principle II.

The work reported in this section shows that behind the apparent robustness of relationships such as those shown in tables 4.1 through 4.4 lie pervasive difficulties of both definition and interpretation in relation to social categories and their role in language change. Much recent sociolinguistic research, including that of Eckert and of Dubois and Horvath, has criticized a tendency to treat categories such as class, gender, and ethnicity as predetermined and unproblematic factors against which linguistic variation can be measured. An alternative conceptualization of social categories as constructed by members' everyday practices challenges researchers to show their specifically local relevance, and to consider how an individual's category affiliations are related to everyday linguistic practices. In the following sections we explore such questions with reference to three social categories that are particularly salient in the literature: social class, gender, and ethnicity.

4.3 Social Class and Sociolinguistic Research

4.3.1 Models of social class

The nature of the social class model that underlies variationist thinking is seldom specified, and the linguistic anthropologist Kathryn Woolard is one of several critics who suggests that it is in need of explicit formulation and critique: "... sociolinguists have often borrowed social concepts in an ad hoc and unreflecting fashion, not usually considering critically the implicit theoretical frameworks that are imported wholesale along with such convenient constructs as three-, four-, or nine-sector scalings of socioeconomic status" (Woolard 1985: 738). Thus, a particular social class model is adopted not primarily for its theoretical properties but for the purely pragmatic reason that it has been widely used in sociological surveys and so is readily operationalizable. As a consequence, a satisfactory theoretical framework within which to interpret recurrent and robust correlations between language and class has not been clearly articulated. Furthermore, several principles based on undertheorized assumptions about stratificational social class have become almost axiomatic.

As discussed by Rickford (1986) and Milroy and Milroy (1992), the functionalist sociology which generally underlies variationist analysis treats social stratification as a product of shared values and broad social consensus, contrasting with perspectives derived from the work of both Marx and Weber where conflict is treated as the basis of class divisions. Functionalists characteristically see classes as forming a continuum rather than as sharply divided, and for them the basis of social hierarchy is not different relations to the market (as both Marx and Weber proposed), but different status values assigned to different occupations. The close agreement found between persons who are asked to rank-order a list of occupations by relative prestige is cited as evidence in support of this analysis (cf. Chambers 1995: 41ff and section 2.6 above). Divisions between classes are most commonly drawn on the basis of occupation and are seen as arbitrary; functionalist thinking does not expect agreement on the number and composition of classes, nor on the location of the boundaries between them which are, in any event, readily crossed by the socially mobile. Hence, a class is rather vaguely said to consist of a group of persons sharing similar occupations and incomes, life-styles and beliefs. Differences in market orientation are downplayed, the emphasis being overwhelmingly on the values shared within and between classes. While the fact of class conflict is not denied, it is seen as only one of several sources of conflict within society rather than as the basis of class structure.

Most sociolinguistic research within the paradigm established by Labov's *Social Stratification of English in New York City* implicitly adopts such a consensus view of social class, and there is no doubt that the results achieved within this framework have been remarkably consistent (see, for example, Chambers 1995: 34–101). Particularly impressive is Macaulay's (1978) detailed demonstration of the consistency of language variation as a fine-grained index of social class. Composite indices for four Glasgow vowel variables reveal only one of 48 speakers out of the rank which might be predicted by individual social class indices. Moreover, the indexicality revealed in these rankings supported an analysis of social class in Glasgow as tripartite, consisting of a unitary working-class group, a white-collar group, and a professional and managerial group (Macaulay 1978: 138). But however well this model works at an operational level, we would agree with Woolard that its controversial nature and implications should be acknowledged; otherwise, it is difficult to address the question of what constitutes an appropriate social model for variationists.

Consensus models of class inform not only analytic procedures, but also variationist theory. Labov's key concept of speech community, with its emphasis on shared norms and common evaluation of the very linguistic variables that differentiate speakers, embodies a view of the community as fundamentally cohesive and self-regulating (Labov 1972b: 120–1). Yet, the vitality and persistence of non-standard vernacular communities is more readily interpretable as evidence of conflict and division in society than as evidence of consensus. It is clear that sociolinguists need to assume cross-community consensus to account for data such as the cross-class agreement on the phonolexical rules for raising and tensing of (æ) in Philadelphia (Payne 1980) – an agreement which extends even to the socially insular upper class of the city (Kroch 1996). However, Rickford's (1986) work in the village of Cane Walk, Guyana where a bipolar pattern of variability co-occurs with a sharp social division into two distinct classes, defined largely in terms of their relationship to the market, has led him to conclude that conflict models of social class have been unduly neglected (Rickford 1986; see also Eckert 2000: 18). He comments on the relevance of conflict models to other sharply opposed groups such as black and white speakers in American cities where progressive segregation and linguistic differentiation are reported (Labov and Harris 1986; Anderson and Milroy 1999). In tending to view class as the ultimate source of all divisions in society, conflict models emphasize the relationships between class and ethnicity, whereas consensus models appear to force an analysis of black and white speakers as belonging to separate speech communities.

Similar comments could be made about the model appropriate to an analysis of the social and linguistic behavior of the adolescents studied by Eckert, who define themselves and their associates in relation to the polarized categories of "jock" and "burnout." Eckert suggests that the communities of practice engaged in by mutually hostile adolescent networks (see section 5.2 below) provide both the conditions for the emergence of opposing linguistic norms and the dynamics of linguistic change (2000: 213–28). In general, linguistic change appears always to be associated with social division or conflict, and indeed Labov has acknowledged that "a thorough-going structural–functional approach to language could be applied only if linguistic systems did not undergo internal change and development" (1986: 283).

4.3.2   Linguistic markets

Weber's model of classes as groups of people with different orientations to the market is identified by Rickford (1986: 217) as being particularly relevant to both social structure and linguistic variation in Cane Walk. That is the rationale for Bourdieu's concept of the *linguistic market* where linguistic differences between speakers are analyzed in terms of "the importance of the legitimized language in the socioeconomic life of the speaker" (Sankoff and Laberge 1978: 241; see also Sankoff et al. 1989). The thinking underlying this analysis is that language constitutes symbolic capital which is potentially convertible into economic capital, and some types of job (such as a business executive's personal assistant) require more than others (such as a chemical engineer) the employee's control of a widely marketable standard language variety. Dittmar, Schlobinski, and Wachs (1988) provide an interesting exposition of the linguistic market concept in relation to their analysis of Berlin vernacular. However, Woolard (1985) has suggested that the standard/vernacular opposition which emerges from much sociolinguistic research is better understood in terms of alternative linguistic markets, contrary to Bourdieu's (1984) view of a single dominant linguistic market where the rule of the legitimate language is merely suspended, and its domination is temporarily absent, when the vernacular is used. Eckert (2000: 16–25) adopts a perspective similar to Woolard in an extended discussion of different conceptions of linguistic and other relevant markets.

Bourdieu's and Woolard's different proposals complement, respectively, consensus and conflict perspectives on class, and while it is clear that the issue for sociolinguists is the relative weight given to these perspectives rather than an absolute opposition between the two (cf. Giddens 1989: 705), we have suggested that a social class model based on conflict, division, and inequality accounts well for many recurrent patterns of language variation, particularly those reported for small-scale studies of communities (cf. Eckert 2000: 18). The overall impression emerging from such studies is not of cohesion but of social division and distinctiveness. For example, the phonological structure of Belfast vernacular (reported in Milroy 1987; Milroy 1992; etc.) can be coherently described only if it is analyzed as internally consistent and systematically variable, rather than an unsuccessful approximation to a standard; yet, evidence of a clear orientation to the latter is what a consensus model seems to require. Similarly, the new contact varieties emerging as a result of mass migrations to contemporary cities such as Stockholm, Sweden (Kotsinas 1988) and Christchurch, New Zealand (Gordon 1991) need to be analysed in their own terms rather than as poor approximations to Standard Swedish or "cultivated" New Zealand English. Similar comments might be made about the emergence of the distinctive Cajun variety of English documented by Dubois and Horvath.

4.3.3   Interpreting correlations between language and social class

A wide range of personal characteristics and behaviors have been found to covary with social class, which also affects the most fundamental events in people's lives, ranging from their chances of surviving the first year of life through likely age of marriage and number of children, to the kind of diseases they are most likely to die of (Reid 1977). Social class influences are particularly pervasive in education, showing an effect even at the nursery stage (Tizard and Hughes 1984). As a global category, social class thus encompasses distinctions in life-style, attitude, and belief, as well as differential access to wealth, power, and prestige. Without some kind of more detailed analysis of social practice, it is not at all clear why a person's life-style, behavior (both linguistic and non-linguistic), and opportunities should be so radically affected by his or her father's occupation.

Eckert's work with Detroit adolescents has important implications for an understanding of the social practices underlying social class differences, and their relationship to language variation. She shows that there is no direct correlation between the categories *working-class: burnout* on the one hand and *middle-class: jock* on the other; on the contrary, contrasting patterns of language variability in Belten high school reflect parents' socioeconomic characteristics only to a very limited extent (Eckert 2000: 108). Suggesting a more subtle relationship between adolescent category and class, she argues that the orientation of jocks to institutions such as school and college rather than to informal local networks, to suburban rather than urban, and to supralocal rather than local places is characteristically middle class. These contrasting orientations are displayed in everyday social practices such as dress, adornment, demeanor, use of leisure time and preferred hangout places, and the adolescents make use of the rich symbolic resource offered by language variability to construct styles which situate them socially in relation to others in the high school between the polar values of jocks and burnouts.

Eckert argues that these choices set up a series of contrasting sociolinguistic patterns which constitute the foundations of a future adult sociolinguistic class stratification system.

Work such as this links the regular correlations between language and class of variationist research to concrete social practices. Recall also that (in Britain and North America at least) occupation is the class-related measure that is thought to correlate particularly closely with language variation (cf. Macaulay 1977; Labov 1990). Eckert suggests that these correlations emerge because occupation is "an indication of the adult's actual forms of participation in the standard language market, while education is primarily a preparation for this participation" (2000: 164). Haeri (1997) similarly offers an account of variation oriented both to the market and to social practice, with specific reference to the *qaf* index among men in Cairo (*qaf* is the name given to a uvular stop variant associated with Classical Arabic). Haeri reports that men whose occupations require control of Classical Arabic use *qaf* significantly more than men whose jobs do not require Classical Arabic (Haeri 1997: 180).

Most researchers in Arabic-speaking countries (Haeri is an exception) handle social class somewhat differently from their colleagues in Britain and North America in treating education as the chief indicator of class (e.g., Al-Wer 1997; Abd-El-Jawad 1987; Abu-Haidar 1989). Al-Wer's (1997) comments on the social significance of education in the Arab world suggest a clear relationship between changes in a speaker's social networks as he or she becomes educated, and patterns of linguistic variation. She notes first that a high level of education does not imply proficiency in Classical Arabic and, in agreement with Haeri and others, emphasizes the marginality of Classical Arabic to overall community patterns of language variation and change. The important point about education, according to Al-Wer, is that it accurately indicates a speaker's degree of contact with speakers of other varieties because "in most cases, college and university education involves leaving one's home town and interacting with speakers from different linguistic backgrounds. Educated speakers appear to be leading linguistic changes, most often in the direction of urban and koineized regional standards" (Al-Wer 1997: 259). This analysis constitutes a practice-related explanation of why education in the Arabic-speaking world is likely to be a good indicator of class, and of how class is related to linguistic variation. Educational institutions in Arabic sociolinguistic contexts may thus be seen as the domains where the standard language is constructed, in contrast to their less central sociolinguistic role in the United States as places where young adults are prepared for participation in the standard language market.

Al-Wer's comments further suggest a need to consider precisely what is meant by a "standard," a term generally used by variationists to denote a variety used by high-status speakers. In the Arab world, however, it is a supralocal variety rather than the prescriptive norm of Classical Arabic that shows this distribution. Although we have seen that Classical Arabic variants are available as a marketable resource to the Cairene male speakers studied by Haeri, she agrees with Al-Wer in stressing the marginality of Classical Arabic to overall patterns of sociolinguistic variation in Cairo. This marginality is essentially a consequence of the diglossic relationship between Classical Arabic and local koineized or urbanized varieties such as Cairene. Haeri comments on the special position of Cairo as a major intellectual, cultural, and commercial center, pointing out that Cairo's distinctive and longstanding urban variety (described as a "non-classical standard") commands its own local and national prestige. It corresponds much more closely than Classical Arabic to entities like "standard English" or "standard French" (Haeri 1997: 168–9).

4.4   Sex and Gender

4.4.1   Introduction

Although "gender" is often used as little more than a synonym for "sex," sex is generally understood to be a biological attribute of individuals, and gender a social construct which does not map directly on to (apparent) biological sex. Strictly speaking, therefore, it makes sense at the data collection stage to talk of sampling speakers according to sex, but to think of gender as the relevant social category when interpreting the social meaning of sex-related variation. Reviewing recent developments in research on language and gender, Eckert (1998) argues that gender should not be treated as a binary variable, but rather as a continuum where speakers situate themselves socially between two reference points. She also demonstrates that generalizations about the role of gender in language change (of the kind discussed in section 4.2 above) make sense only with reference to the meaning of gender in specific communities and in relation to other local social categories. Nor does gender have a constant effect on language, since linguistic variables relate to gendered behavior in very different ways.

   In this section we review early work on the relationship between gender and language variation and highlight issues emerging from the more careful conceptualization of gender described by Eckert. Coates (1998) provides extensive coverage of the large literature on language and gender, which includes not only some classic articles within the variationist paradigm but others dealing with style, ideology and discourse.

4.4.2   Social class and gender

Recall that early variationist research tended to privilege social class, so that gender-related variation was often explained with reference to, and as dependent on, social class (see section 4.3 above). Thus, women were said to approximate to the prestige norm more closely than men of corresponding social status, and Labov's (1990) statement of the general principles governing the role of gender differentiation in linguistic change assumes a relationship between social class and gender of this general type (see section 4.2). Since recent work suggests that theories of change are better articulated somewhat differently, we begin by noting some recurrent problems associated with the traditional account.

In a recent review of the issues surrounding gender and sound change, Holmes (1997) points out that no satisfactory explanation has emerged of why women should orient more readily than men to a prestige norm. Furthermore, specifying the prestige norm to which they are said to orient is not always straightforward. The question of how such a norm should be characterized emerged in section 4.3.3 in our review of Haeri's work in Cairo, and is also discussed elsewhere. Milroy (1987: 105) and Romaine (1978) noted the difficulty of specifying a single prestige norm to which Belfast (Northern Irish) and Edinburgh (Scottish) speakers respectively orient. More recently, Holmes (1997) has observed that images of linguistic prestige are currently changing in New Zealand. Similarly, change in the hegemonic role of RP in England has been the subject of comment for some time and the norms to which speakers there orient are not always clear (Holmes 1997; Newbrook 1999). Dubois and Horvath (1999: 308) discuss this kind of change in some detail, reporting that the older speakers in St. Landry, Louisiana, generally orient to an externally mandated English language norm. The values and linguistic practice of younger speakers are, however, quite different, following a revival of Cajun language and culture (see further section 4.4.3 below). In general, prestige norms, like other kinds of norm, appear to be something of a moving target.

A further difficulty with traditional variationist assumptions about the nature of the interaction between social class and gender is that class is not necessarily the variable that accounts for the greater part of the variability. For example, the effect of gender on patterns of language variation emerges clearly in the distribution of variants of the vowel (o) summarized in tables 4.2 and 4.3, although age and social class are also implicated (see section 4.1 above). Statistical analysis confirms an overwhelming gender effect, but neither age nor class has an effect anywhere near statistical significance, nor do they approach the effect of gender when considered in isolation (Milroy 1999; Watt and Milroy 1999). Similarly, Horvath's (1985) reorganization of

Labov's New York City data in accordance with the linguistic groupings where speakers seem to cluster, rather than initially in terms of social class, suggests quite strongly that variants of (dh) (the alternation between a fricative [ð] and a stop [d] in *there, the,* etc.) are more clearly stratified by gender than by class. Coates's (1986) reanalysis of a substantial amount of data from several sources also shows that sex of speaker quite commonly accounts for variability at least as well as, and in some cases better than, social class.

Schatz's (1986) study of the dialect of Amsterdam provides an example of the problems that can be created by conceptualizing gendered language patterns in terms of social class. Since gendered patterns in the distribution of variants of the vowel variable (a) emerge in low-status speakers only, women cannot be viewed as orienting to the norms of a higher social group (1986: 102). Mees (1987: 185) also reports that current sociolinguistic thinking could not account for gender- and class-related variation with respect to several phonological variables in Cardiff English which are affected in different ways by the sex and social class of speakers. One of these, (t), is realized by a range of variants in many varieties of British English, and represents a particular challenge to standard accounts of the interacting effect on variation of gender and social class.

The glottal stop variant of /t/ in British English (in intervocalic and word-final position) has a male, working-class image and has been tradition-ally heavily stigmatized (see, for example, Romaine and Reid 1976; Macaulay 1977; Trudgill 1974). However, it has recently been observed to be spread-ing rapidly in several British cities, and has for some time been a salient characteristic of the speech of young RP speakers (Wells 1982: 106). Trudgill (1988) confirms a change in the social evaluation of the glottal stop in Norwich, reporting that 18 years after his original fieldwork it has spread into careful styles. Gender differences appear to be involved in the spread of the glottal stop in a complex way which is difficult to interpret within a framework which assumes the orientation of women to prestige norms. Mees (1987) and Mees and Collins (1999) report that in Cardiff the glottal stop is most advanced in middle-class speech and that despite the male, working-class image of the variant, the change is being led by young women. Kingsmore (1995) reports that in Coleraine, Northern Ireland, it is again females who favor the glottal stop, and Holmes (1997) shows that in New Zealand as in Britain the social value assigned to this once stigmatized variant is changing, with women strongly leading the change. A series of studies in Newcastle upon Tyne (Milroy 1992; Milroy et al. 1994; Docherty et al. 1997) reveals the same pattern, but complicates the picture somewhat. In general, boys and men use many more glottalized variants than girls and women. However, when glottal replacement (the glottal stop) is distinguished from glottal reinforcement (a traditional feature of Tyneside English affecting not only /t/, but also /p/ and /k/), it is apparent that females are leading in the spread of the glottal stop, whereas males favor glottal reinforcement.

Taken together, these developments suggest quite strongly that the establishment of the glottal stop as a middle-class form in both Britain and New Zealand is dependent on and secondary to its gender-related pattern – in other words, the association of the glottal stop with women's language may be instrumental in bringing about a social re-evaluation. The generalization that best accounts for the interacting effects of social class and gender so widely reported in the literature may then not be that women favor prestige variants; rather, they create them, as the variants that females prefer become ideologized as prestige variants. This generalization not only accounts for some otherwise difficult data, but avoids the problem that emerges in some speech communities of identifying the relevant prestige variant. Women seem very generally to prefer supralocal variants, which may or may not be identifiable as prestigious; examples discussed so far are the monophthongal variant of (o), the glottal stop variant of (t), or the standard fricative variants of (th) and (dh). In all these cases and many others, men appear to favor localized variants, which are often stigmatized.

The association of men with localized forms and women with forms more widely distributed both socially and regionally is treated by Chambers (1995) as quite central to gendered language patterns, and noted (but not pursued) by Labov (1990: 219). Armstrong and Unsworth note a similar pattern with respect to schwa-deletion, a vigorous change in southern France spreading from northern French urban dialects. Females lead in the adoption of the deleted variant, but males favor schwa-retention, a localized pattern stereotypically associated with southern French dialects. Armstrong and Unsworth argue that the incoming variant is better described as supraregional than as standard (1999: 152). Al-Wer (1997) characterizes class- and gender-related patterns in Arabic-speaking countries in exactly the same way (cf. Haeri's account, reported in section 4.3.3 above):

> The data from various parts of the Arab world show overwhelmingly that Arab men opt for the localized and older features (which in most cases happen to be stigmatized at some level) while Arab women favor features which have a wider regional acceptance and usage regardless of the status of these features *vis-à-vis* C[lassical] A[rabic]. (Al-Wer 1997: 261)

4.4.3   Gender and language variation: Some further issues

We conclude this discussion of the effect of gender-related language variation by looking at two broad issues which overlap somewhat: patterns arising from the interaction of gender with other social categories, and difficulties with the traditional view of gender as a binary variable. In the course of this discussion we show that a satisfactory interpretation of patterns of variation greatly benefits from a historical perspective as well as an understanding of contemporary local norms and values.

Walters (1991) and Jabeur (1987) present information on gender- and age-related patterns of variation in two different Tunisian towns which, at first sight, seem rather similar but in fact index quite different social meanings. Jabeur reports that in the township of Rades, a suburb of Tunis, the capital, the effects of gender and age interact. One of the Tunisian Arabic variables that he examined involved alternation between monophthongal and diphthongal variants of the items /aj/ and /aw/. The diphthongized variants (as opposed to the monophthongs [iː] and [uː]) are described as "markers of old urban female speech". Examples cited are [bajt]: [biːt] "a room"; [nawm]: [nuːm]; "sleep" (Jabeur 1987: 110). This pattern of variation is heavily ideologized; older women are reported to take some pride in their use of the diphthongized variants, while young women avoid them. However, Walters has recently supplemented Jabeur's account (pers. com.), noting that the diphthongal variants constitute a relic feature historically associated with the highest status families who lived within the "medina" of Tunis, the old walled city which still stands. Further, the diphthongal variants are the ones required by Modern Standard Arabic (MSA), the prescriptive High variety described by Haeri and other sociolinguists as less relevant than local standards (such as Cairene Arabic) to the trajectory of contemporary language change. An example of a variety in the United States, characterized by features which in much the same way are evaluated simultaneously as indexing low status and (historic) high prestige, is perhaps provided by Boston's relic non-rhotic Brahmin dialect. Walters draws a further comparison with the American Southern white dialects spoken by people who claim descent from old plantation families.

Gender- and age-related patterns of variation in the small Tunisian town of Korba, which at first sight seem similar to those described above, are reported by Walters (1991: 211). He examines the phenomenon of raising with respect to a vowel variable (ɛː) (as in [mustəwɛː] "level") where speakers agree in stigmatizing raised variants. In Korba, as well as in Rades, older women differ from younger women (and also from men) in using stigmatized variants at relatively high frequencies, and in Korba this particular raised variant also represents a relic feature. However, the social meaning of the relic features in each town differs in important ways, despite the superficial similarity of their social distribution. In the case of Korba, Walters notes (pers. com.) that raising is associated with the isolation of the community and is stigmatized except in in-group settings. Furthermore, unlike the relic diphthongs in Rades raising in Korba involves a movement away from the requirements of the High MSA variety. Walters also points out that at the time of his research in Korba (1985) no one could name a woman over the age of 45 who could read or write, while some younger women were already receiving a university education.

It is certainly true that in both Korba and Rades older women form a distinguishable social group (Abu-Lughod 1986) which in both places is involved in the retention of relic features. But to present an account of both sets of gender- and age-related patterns which stops short at this observation misses essential differences in social meaning. While the variants used by the Rades women are associated with the high variety of Arabic and index an association with the highest social group of a former era, the raised variants in Korba are associated with geographic isolation and membership of a non-elite group, and are stigmatized both in Tunisian Arabic and in the High variety. The educated older women of the next generation are likely to display quite different patterns of language variation. For this reason, a focus on the interacting effects of the variables of age and gender which implicitly treats both sets of women as similar is less relevant than an understanding of the local historical and social factors, different in each case, which make it likely that women of a particular age at a particular point in Tunisia's history will retain particular relic forms which themselves have particular social meanings.

We turn now to a different speech community. Recall that gender differences in the use of the Cajun variables (th) and (dh) were heavily dependent on the age and network characteristics of speakers (section 4.1 above). Dubois and Horvath (1999) discuss more generally the interaction of gender with other social categories and the effect of specific historical events in shaping the trajectory of language change. They show that gender indexing affects language quite differently in each generation and that each generation orients to different norms. The oldest group studied was bilingual in French and English, and so was able to use both languages as a resource for indexing gender, as well as other social meanings. However, their way of speaking English provided the pool of features involved in future language change, which are later interpreted as indexing Cajun ethnicity and recycled by younger speakers. Members of the middle-aged group were subject to strong pressures to learn English, and both men and women appear to orient to a community-external norm in the course of the language shift process. This group shows less evidence of gender differentiation, at least in English, the focus of Dubois and Horvath's analysis. The youngest speakers, however, are influenced by the so-called Cajun Renaissance, which resulted in the commodification of the distinctive "Frenchness" of Louisiana. Since these young speakers use French only with the oldest members of the community, Cajun ethnicity is indexed by variation in English. Crucially however, the Cajun Renaissance, with its market implications, has largely affected traditional male activities. The authors therefore attribute the male preference for Cajun features such as stopped variants of (dh) and (th) not only to their desire to display Cajunness, but to a shift in local gender roles associated with the loss of French as a community language:

> The shift from French to English, which largely took place within the middle-aged generation, means that young women no longer have any responsibility for passing on French to the children. Their roles as Cajun torchbearers have been taken over by young men. Young women have not moved to recycle the Cajun English features because they have fewer reasons than do young men to associate themselves linguistically with the current understanding of Cajun identity, which is largely masculine. (Dubois and Horvath 1999: 307)

This example highlights some difficulties with decontextualized generalizations about the role of gender in linguistic variation and change, partly because gender interacts with other social factors and partly because gendered language behavior and gendered roles – such as that of cultural and linguistic torchbearer – are influenced by historical events.

Eckert (1998) argues particularly strongly for a view of gender as a construct that derives from the details of actual social practice, and as interdependent with other social categories. Gendered linguistic practices "differ considerably from culture to culture, from place to place, from group to group, living at the intersection of all the other aspects of social identity" (1998: 66). For example, Eckert suggests that males and females in the United States stand in very different relationships to both adult and adolescent markets. Just as men's actions and values define the adult world of work, so do boys' actions (as athletes or bikers, for example) define opposing jock/burnout adolescent categories. Typically, females are excluded from a central role in these marketplaces, and may deal with this marginalization by using symbolic means to establish identities. Hence, Eckert finds that, in their respective social categories, girls are more likely than boys to identify themselves clearly and extremely with the polarized jock or burnout categories by language use as well as by other social behaviors such as demeanor, dress, adornment, or social activities. Localness being a burnout value, burnout girls make more use of variants that indicate local accent than any other group. Jock girls, on the other hand, make the greatest use of variants that identify them as suburban, with boys in each category occupying less extreme positions than the girls (Eckert 1998: 73). In their patterns of language use, speakers thus demonstrate a complex relationship between gender, social category, and urban versus suburban orientation. Eckert's account suggests that women, more than their male peers, may have clear social motivations to exploit the symbolic resources offered by language variation that locate them unambiguously in a given social category.

Schilling-Estes' (1999) account of variation in the island of Okracoke off the southeastern coast of the United States demonstrates particularly clearly the advantages of caution in treating men and women as members of undifferentiated binary categories. She explores patterns in the use of local variants of the diphthongs /aj/ and /aw/ – respectively raised variants of /aj/ as in *high tide* and fronted variants of /aw/ as in *house, sound*. Patterns of variation are examined both with reference to three generations of males and females and "among members of same sex groups whose gendered identity is not a mere by-product of sex" (Schilling-Estes 1999: 509). The male groups considered in this way are all in the middle generation. The group described as the Poker Game Network characteristically espouse values associated with the highly masculine fishermen of the island and explicitly exclude women from their weekly poker games. Since they project a stereotypically masculine image, these men might be expected to index extreme masculinity in language as well as other behaviors. The other male groups considered by Schilling-Estes are a group of gay men and a group of straight men who are not Poker Game Networkers.

Schilling-Estes reports that the traditional raised variant of /aj/ is receding, with women using it somewhat less than men in the oldest and youngest generations. However, the patterning of raised /aj/ in the middle generation is much more complex, to the extent that a general statement that associates the vernacular with men and the standard with women is extremely misleading. In this age group the predicted male/female distinction emerges only between the women and the Poker Game Network men, but women use raised /aj/ more than other male subgroups, with gay men showing the lowest levels of use. Schilling-Estes (1999: 513) comments: "Issues of gendered identity play a crucial role in the delimitation of all three men's groups, not merely the division into gay and straight. Men in the poker group project a highly 'macho' image, and there are no avowedly gay men in this group."

The gender-related pattern for the localized variant of the variable /aw/ is different, but varies with generation. The canonical pattern of women using lower levels of the vernacular variant than men holds only for young speakers, and in the middle-aged group, women show particularly high levels of the localized glide-fronted variant, followed in turn by the gay men and the straight men. The Poker Game Network shows the lowest level of use of all speaker groups. Schilling-Estes suggests that these asymmetrical patterns of use with respect to /aw/ and /aj/ reflect the availability of two different phonological elements as resources on which speakers can draw in indexing "islander" identity. Recall that the vernacular variant of /aj/ carries strong connotations of masculinity, and is also associated particularly with the island fishermen. While this indexicality makes it unavailable for all women and for some middle-aged men, the vernacular variant of /aw/ is available as a symbolic resource for these speakers. The poker players for their part avoid using high levels of the variant associated with women and with men outside the Poker Game Network. When both variables are considered, localized variants are not uniquely associated with men nor standard variants with women, nor are preferences split in a straightforward way according to biological sex. More generally, this interpretation, like that of Eckert and of Dubois and Horvath, requires a good deal of knowledge of local history, ideology, and social practices. Gender affects language differently in different generations because of various life experiences, and gendered language differences index salient intra-community social categories which need to be uncovered by researchers rather than treated as previously given.

4.5   Ethnicity and Race

4.5.1   Introduction

Giddens (1989) discusses ethnicity and race as systems which, along with class, underlie the distribution of power and inequality in society. Ethnic groups are formed by persons who share, or believe they share, common cultural characteristics. These are wholly learned, typically very early in life, and usually involve a sense of place and of a common history and destiny, a shared religion and social ideology, and a shared language or set of communicative conventions. Ethnic distinctions are rarely neutral, usually being associated with marked inequalities of wealth and power so that, in practice, most discussions of ethnicity involve minority groups whose members are discriminated against by the majority population (Giddens 1989: 244). Like class boundaries, ethnic boundaries are flexible and permeable, as Rampton (1996) points out. Just as ethnic differences are best understood as socially constructed rather than reliably corresponding to any verifiable differences in history, culture or place of origin, so ethnolinguistic distinctions may not correspond to any major structural difference between languages. For example, the spoken forms of Urdu and Hindi are almost identical but are commonly treated as distinctive because of their strong association with Muslim and Hindu ethnicity where these ethnic distinctions are socially salient (Linguistic Minorities Project 1985: 45; Blom and Gumperz 1972). However, such perceptions are subject to review as social configurations change. For example, women interviewed in the South East Asian migrant community in Newcastle, England, insisted to the (European) fieldworker that Hindi and Punjabi/Urdu were the same language. This change in language ideology appears to follow a social change whereby the Muslim/Hindu contrast receded as the relevant opposition that developed was between British and South Asian communities as a whole (Milroy and Raschka 1996). Dyer (2000, 2002) discusses the same kind of change in a different community.

Race has in the past notoriously been subject to a good deal of pseudo-scientific theorizing, and it is still often believed that humans can be separated by biological criteria into different races. However, the genetic diversity within populations that share, for example, the same skin color is as great as differences between visibly different groups. Giddens suggests that racial differences are therefore best understood socially as being closely associated with ethnicity, in referring to "*physical variations singled out by members of a community and treated as ethnically significant*. Differences in skin colour are often treated as significant in this way, while differences in hair colour are not" (Giddens 1989: 246; original italics).[2]

Giddens suggests that the persistently problematic character of race relations in the United States is best understood within a historical context, since from the earliest colonial days the racist views of European colonists were more extreme toward the blacks who had been brought to the Americas as slaves than toward other non-Europeans, including native Americans. He notes that "ever since then racial conflicts and divisions have tended to have pride of place in ethnic conflicts as a whole. In particular, racist views separating 'whites' from 'blacks' became central in European attitudes" (Giddens 1989: 254). The effect of this outcome in subordinating other kinds of social divisions in the United States to a division based on race appears to be relevant to sociolinguistic treatments of language and ethnicity.

Given its place in structures of inequality, ethnicity often needs to be understood in relation to social class. Because migrant populations are frequently recruited as low-paid workers, they tend in many countries to cluster in the poor areas of inner cities close to workplaces and to be concentrated in low-status occupations. Even members of ethnic minorities who were relatively prosperous in their country of origin tend to become occupationally declassed, taking a step down in status relative to their former positions, particularly if they migrated originally as political refugees (Linguistic Minorities Project 1985: 74). Sugrue's (1996) extended analysis of race and inequality in Detroit – and to some extent in American "rust belt" cities generally – conceptualizes class as a system which promotes inequality in capitalist societies. In the United States, the class system works along with the longstanding patterns of discrimination and segregation described by Giddens, so that inequality has a disproportionate impact on African Americans.

Documenting a steady increase in residential segregation in Philadelphia, Labov and Harris (1986) note that de facto segregation persists in much of the United States. Farley, Danziger, and Holzer (2000) single out Detroit as a particularly racially polarized city, as a result of a number of local historical factors. They describe patterns of residential and activity segregation and long-term discrimination in the workplace as well as differences in attitudes, including attitudes to language, between blacks and whites. An important distinction between the operation of class in the United States and, for example, in Britain is the extent and effect of the interaction between race and class noted by Farley et al., Sugrue and others. Like social class and gender, ethnicity means different things in different communities, and its significance for patterns of language variation needs to be understood with reference to local conditions and local social practices. The heightened sense of racial distinctiveness that results from historical events and contemporary social conditions in the Unites States is accompanied by salient linguistic distinctiveness.

4.5.2   Language, race, and ethnicity in the United States

Not unexpectedly, given the social and historical underpinning reviewed above, much public commentary on issues of language, race, and ethnicity in the United States focuses on the variety of English spoken by African Americans. Since research agendas are likely to reflect local ideologies, it is equally unsurprising that work by American scholars on ethnically distinctive varieties is overwhelmingly on this variety. Wolfram and Schilling-Estes (1998: 169) note that more than five times as many publications are devoted to African American English (AAE) than to any other ethnic or regional group of speakers.

AAE is a variety distinguished by a number of features at all linguistic levels, some of which are shared with varieties spoken in the southern United States. Furthermore, while African Americans appear in earlier times to have maintained some measure of ethnolinguistic distinctiveness, many speakers are progressively developing norms increasingly distinct from those of adjacent white groups. For example, over four generations, African Americans in Hyde County, North Carolina have moved away from a peripheral rural dialect, quite similar to the variety spoken by local white residents, toward a contemporary supralocal AAE norm (Wolfram and Beckett 2000; Wolfram, Thomas, and Green 2000). Poplack and Tagliamonte (2001) present copious historical evidence of AAE's vernacular English dialect antecedents, consistent with this general picture. Labov (1998 and elsewhere) reports that African American speakers in northern cities do not participate in the Northern Cities Shift, a salient set of coordinated vowel changes affecting ethnically unmarked varieties spoken in urban areas of the Northern dialect region. Gordon (2000) confirms the pattern among African Americans in the Chicago area, and Edwards and Diergardt (2000), Anderson (2002), and Anderson and Milroy (1999) present similar findings with respect to inner city African American Detroiters. Anderson and Milroy also report that

Detroit AAE appears to be moving toward a general southern phonological norm, a change that has the effect of distinguishing AAE sharply from adjacent ethnically unmarked varieties.

The phonological, grammatical and stylistic features characteristic of AAE are described and discussed by (among many others) Wolfram and Schilling-Estes (1998), Rickford (1999), Mufwene et al. (1998), and Poplack (2000) – some of which will be reviewed in detail in subsequent chapters. Research on AAE has tended to concentrate on a limited number of issues: relationships between AAE and comparable (mainly Southern white) varieties; the history and development of AAE; and changes currently taking place within AAE (Wolfram and Schilling-Estes 1998: 169–81). Despite the volume of work published on AAE, this selective focus has resulted in notable gaps in the research literature. Particularly, the dialect tends to be treated as if it were invariant, and much less information is available on social, generational, and regional dimensions of variability within AAE than on white dialects (Wolfram and Schilling-Estes 1998: 174–5). Wolfram (1969) constitutes the only major study of social stratification in an urban variety of AAE, and variation according to gender and age has been investigated only to a limited extent (e.g., Nichols 1998; Wolfram and Beckett 2000). In addition to understating the internal variability of AAE, researchers have tended to emphasize the distinctiveness of the dialect, but Rickford points out that since very few studies examine the effects of contact between AAE and adjacent varieties, the precise character of the ethnolinguistic boundary is unclear (1999: 90). Recently, however, Wolfram and Sellers (1999) and Dannenberg and Wolfram (1998) reported on the effects of contact between AAE and two other varieties in a tri-ethnic situation (see further below).

In addition to the large volume of research on AAE, there is a small but growing variationist literature on the ethnic dialects of other groups in the United States, of which Dubois and Horvath's work on Cajun English is an example (see further Wolfram and Schilling-Estes 1998: 181–3). Like contemporary Cajun English, these varieties are usually learned as first languages – particularly in the case of Native American varieties – and display internal variability. They therefore need to be treated as ethnically distinct contact varieties rather than as products of imperfect learning destined to vanish as a new generation successfully learns and orients to ethnically unmarked norms.

Dannenberg and Wolfram (1998) and Wolfram and Sellers (1999) describe a pattern in the English spoken by the Native American group, the Lumbee, with respect to forms of the verb BE which distinguishes this dialect from varieties used by the surrounding African American and white population. Reporting on AAE, Lumbee English, and Anglo varieties in Robeson County, North Carolina, they conclude that ethnic distinctiveness is maintained by drawing on existing dialect resources in quite subtle and localized ways. For example, the inflected third singular verb form *bes*, once characteristic of local white varieties, is now obsolescent in those varieties, but it is used by both Lumbee and AAE speakers with somewhat different grammatical constraints that serve to distinguish them from each other. Anderson (1999) documents subtle distributional differences with respect to variants of the sociolinguistically sensitive diphthongs /aj/ and /oj/ between Cherokee English and adjacent varieties in Graham County, North Carolina.

Mendoza-Denton (1999) reviews sociolinguistic work on Latino speech communities, who constitute an important cluster of distinctive ethnic groups in the United States. The situation varies a good deal in accordance with country of origin – for example, between Puerto Ricans and Chicanos, who are of Mexican descent. Since Spanish shows no sign of disappearing from the sociolinguistic landscape, accounts of Latino communities generally need to consider speakers' deployment both of a bilingual repertoire and of an ethnically distinctive variety of English as resources for expressing social meaning. Zentella (1997), whose work is discussed in chapter 8, examines the distribution of both monolingual and bilingual repertoires of Puerto Rican speakers in New York City. In a study of the language practices of Chicana girls in a north California high school, Mendoza-Denton (1997) shows that many kinds of intersecting identities are mediated both through language choice between Spanish and English, and through monolingual variation at phonological and discourse levels. Fought (1999), however, finds evidence of /u/-fronting among speakers of Chicano English, a vigorous sound change characteristic of Californian speakers generally.

Reporting on the Jewish community in Grand Rapids, Michigan, Knack (1991) describes phonological patterns with respect to length and height variation in (ɔ) and voicing of (s) different from those of local gentile speakers. Realization of these variables within the Jewish community is patterned in accordance with a complex interaction between ethnicity, status, and gender. It is likely that much ethnolinguistic distinctiveness is of this subtle kind, and may also be marked by limited participation in large-scale changes that the ethnically unmarked dialects are undergoing (see, for example, Gordon 2000). Labov (2001b: 245–56) discusses the linguistic effects of ethnicity in various communities in the United States.

4.5.3　Language and ethnicity in Northern Ireland

We discuss here a community where ethnicity is indexed linguistically in a very different way, and much less directly, than in any considered so far. The ethno-political conflict in Northern Ireland between Catholics and Protestants, whose political orientations are respectively Irish and British, has a history stretching back to the seventeenth century Plantation of Ulster by Scottish and English settlers. Protestants and Catholics believe themselves to be different peoples with different histories, and for the most part maintain different cultural traditions in prominent domains such as education, religion and leisure activities. Although Northern Ireland as a whole has traditionally suffered high levels of unemployment and other kinds of social malaise, Catholics have suffered disproportionately and the current phase of the conflict began in the late 1960s as Catholics protested against longstanding discrimination and disadvantage. Political conditions in Northern Ireland continue to maintain a powerful sense of ethnic distinctiveness which is marked in a number of culturally codified ways, as discussed by Larsen (1982: 135).

The variationist study described in chapter 3 was carried out in Belfast in the 1970s during a particularly intense period of conflict (Milroy and Milroy 1978; Milroy 1987). At this time, Catholic and Protestant communities had entrenched themselves in different urban sectors, east Belfast having become more Protestant and west Belfast more Catholic. The clearest result of a pilot study undertaken to identify the main social and linguistic dimensions of variation was a sharp linguistic division between the more Protestant east of the city and the more Catholic west. Differences between Catholic and Protestant communities in the west (Clonard and Hammer respectively) were much smaller, with Catholics revealing a generally more conservative pattern with respect to several phonological variables. However, systematic phonological differences between Protestant and Catholics communities of east Belfast (Ballymacarrett and Short Strand respectively) did not emerge from the pilot study. These communities were mutually hostile, sharply segregated, and both were located adjacent to the shipyard, which offered the main source of employment in east Belfast.

On the basis of these observations, the systematic (but variable) differences that often emerged between Catholic and Protestant groups in Belfast were treated as regional differences, a distinction which, perhaps surprisingly in view of the intensity of the ethnic conflict, corresponded to local language ideologies. Thus, for example, community members referred to east and west Belfast accents, but not Catholic and Protestant accents, as distinctive. Ethnicity was widely believed to be linguistically indexed in Belfast in the 1970s not by the kind of systematic phonological and morphosyntactic distinctions documented for Cajun, Latino, or African American communities in the United States, but by variant pronunciations for names of letters of the alphabet. These shibboleths (such as the characteristic Catholic pronunciation of the letter *h* as [hetʃ] versus Protestant [etʃ]) lie outside the phonological system, and probably arose as the product of a segregated educational system (see further Milroy 1981: 41–3). Although the chief dimensions of variation in Belfast were associated with urban location and with locally constituted networks, a clear distinction between local and ethnic differences in language use is, in practice, difficult to maintain in a city with a high level of Protestant/Catholic residential segregation. Thus, in terms of ethnicity, an east Belfast accent is, to a certain extent, associated with Protestants and a west Belfast accent with Catholics. More recently, McCafferty (1998, 1999, 2000) has shown that the ethnic boundary is linguistically indexed elsewhere in Northern Ireland in quite subtle ways, while being careful to emphasize that "there is no such thing as 'Catholic English' or 'Protestant English'" (2000: 1). In a study of phonological variation in the predominantly Catholic, northwest Ulster city of Derry, he reports that Protestants are more likely than Catholics to adopt innovations from Belfast and from the predominantly Protestant eastern part of the province. This general movement of sound change from east to west with Protestants adopting changes earlier than Catholics was observed by Pitts (1985) in the small mid-Ulster town of Lurgan and is consistent with the trajectory of change reported in Belfast (e.g., Milroy 1981; Milroy 1987; Milroy and Milroy 1992). McCafferty also reports that Catholics tend to orient toward localized norms and Protestants to more general Northern Irish norms. Gunn (1990) and Harris (1991) similarly suggest that middle-class Belfast speakers orient to different norms, depending on whether their political affiliation is nationalist (Catholic) or Unionist (Protestant); recall the discussion in section 4.4.2 of problems in identifying a single "standard" in Northern Ireland.

Ethnolinguistic boundaries in Northern Ireland and the United States thus differ in a number of ways, particularly in the interaction between ethnicity and other social variables. In the United States, where it makes sense to talk about distinctive ethnic varieties, ethnic marking is most visible in the language of the lowest status speakers, but in Northern Ireland it may manifest itself in the different norms to which educated speakers orient. Furthermore, a trajectory of linguistic change associated with an interaction between regional and ethnic boundaries, of the kind described both in Belfast and in Derry, has not been reported in the United States. The case of the Protestant/Catholic division in Northern Ireland has important methodological implications for any researcher working with ethnicity as a speaker variable. As we emphasized in section 4.5.1, ethnicity is a culturally created category and is in no sense objectively "given." Thus, it is quite possible (even commonplace) in Northern Ireland for an ethnic Catholic to be a non-believer, or conversely for an English or Scottish migrant who identifies as an adherent of the Catholic religion to be categorized as Protestant. While religion and ethnicity do not directly map on to each other, religion is a culturally accepted indicator of ethnicity, and the terms "Protestant" and "Catholic," as generally used in Northern Ireland, refer to ethnicity rather than religion.

4.6 Concluding Remarks

The social categories of class, age, gender, and ethnicity are prominent in variationist research and have often been used to elucidate the global patterning of linguistic variation across broad populations. More recently, researchers have emphasized that the way in which these variables relate to language variation is determined by local norms and local practices, so that, for example, social class does not mean the same thing in different communities. Nor can gender be assumed to have a uniform effect on language across all communities, or to be a straightforward binary category which maps directly on to biological sex. Similarly, the linguistic effects of ethnicity vary dramatically from community to community. In the following chapter we consider frameworks for studying local dimensions of language variation and change, and thus reach some understanding of the practices underlying recurrent sociolinguistic patterns of the kind that have so far dominated our discussion.

5

Social Relationships and Social Practices

5.1 Introductory

Categories such as class, gender and ethnicity are macro-level *analyst* constructs that have certainly proved useful to variationists in revealing remarkably consistent sociolinguistic patterns. But despite this consistency, they may relate somewhat indirectly to the procedures of *participants* in constructing and categorizing social worlds that reflect their analysis of locally meaningful social groupings. Thus, for example, the distribution of a set of linguistic variants according to gender (such as variants of (o) in Newcastle), class (variants of (h) in Bradford and Norwich), or ethnicity (variants of (dh) and (th) in Louisiana) suggests that these variants are important in the everyday lives of men and women, of people of different social statuses, of people who identify as Cajun – but it does not tell us what the variants mean. To understand the correlations between language and these global social categories, we need procedures which allow us to examine the specifics of local practice and local conditions, and which are sensitive to the local social categories and locally contracted ties with which speakers operate in their everyday lives.

In the following sections we focus on the closely related concepts of social network and community of practice in order to suggest ways in which local practices give rise to global sociolinguistic patterns. Both of these concepts are better understood as a means of capturing the dynamics underlying speakers' variable language behaviors than as social categories parallel to class, gender, or ethnicity. The chapter concludes this analysis with a discussion of the sociolinguistic consequences of social mobility, particularly in relation to changes in social network structure.

5.2   The Concept of Social Network

Recall that Dubois and Horvath (1998) found that speakers with closed networks – that is, those with a relatively large number of local social contacts – used the resources of linguistic variability available to the Cajun community somewhat differently from those whose social orientation was less local (section 4.1). As their analysis suggests, an individual's social network is the aggregate of relationships contracted with others, a boundless web of ties which reaches out through social and geographical space linking many individuals, sometimes remotely. First-order network ties, i.e., a person's direct contacts, are generally the focus of interest. Within the first-order zone it is important, for reasons to be discussed below, to distinguish between "strong" and "weak" ties of everyday life – roughly, ties that connect friends or kin as opposed to those that connect acquaintances. Second-order ties are those to whom the link is indirect, and are often an important local resource, enabling persons to access a range of information, goods, and services.

Social network analysis of the kind generally adopted by variationists was developed by social anthropologists mainly during the 1960s and 1970s (see further Milroy 1987; Li Wei 1996; Johnson 1994). Contrary to the assertions of Murray (1993: 162), it is clear from even a cursory reading of the literature that no canonically correct procedure for analyzing social networks can be identified; scholars from many different disciplines employ the concept for a range of theoretical and practical purposes. For example, Johnson's (1994) survey alludes to a wide range of approaches within anthropology that hardly overlap with the largely quantitative modes of analysis described by Cochran and colleagues (1990). This international and interdisciplinary team of scholars is interested in the role of networks in providing support for urban families. Accordingly, their methods are to a great extent driven by a concern with social policy and practice.

Personal social networks are always seen as contextualized within macro-level social frameworks of the kind analyzed with reference to such global categories as those discussed in chapter 4. These frameworks are "bracketed off" for purely methodological reasons, in order to focus on less abstract modes of analysis capable of accounting more immediately for observed variable behaviors. A fundamental postulate of network analysis is that individuals create personal communities to provide a meaningful framework for solving the problems of daily life (Mitchell 1986: 74). These personal communities are constituted by interpersonal ties of different types and strengths, and structural relationships between links can vary. Particularly, the persons to whom an individual is linked may also be tied to each other to varying degrees. A further postulate with particular relevance to students of language change (or its converse, language maintenance) is that structural and content differences between networks impinge critically on the way they directly affect individuals. Particularly, if a personal network consists chiefly of strong ties that are also multiplex or many-stranded, and if the network is also relatively dense (i.e., many of those ties are linked to each other), then such a network has the capacity to support its members in both practical and symbolic ways. More negatively, however, such a network type can impose unwanted and stressful constraints on its members. Thus, we come to the basic point of deploying network analysis in variationist research. Networks constituted chiefly of strong (dense and multiplex) ties appear to be supportive of localized linguistic norms, resisting pressures from competing external norms. By the same token, a weakening of these ties produces conditions that are favorable to particular types of language change. Hence, a network analysis can help to explain why a particular community successfully supports a linguistic system that stands in opposition to a legitimized, mainstream set of norms, and why another system might be less focused or more sensitive to external influences.

5.2.1   *Social network and community of practice*

Individuals engage on a daily basis in a variety of endeavors in multiple personal communities and the people who comprise an individual's personal communities change, as indeed do the everyday problems that such personal communities help to solve. Eckert employs the concept of *community of practice*, an idea related to social network, to locate the interactional sites where social meaning is most clearly indexed by language, and where language variation and social meaning are co-constructed. A community of practice can be defined as an aggregate of people coming together around a particular enterprise (Eckert 2000: 34–5), and in her analysis of the social dynamics of language variation among Detroit adolescents, Eckert focuses on intersecting clusters of individuals engaged in socially relevant enterprises (2000: 171–212). Such clusters constitute gendered subgroups showing an orientation in their social and linguistic practice to the adolescent social categories of jock and burnout which participants themselves construct.

Eckert comments that the construction of such local styles was possible only insofar as individuals were integrated into local networks and so had access to information, the importance of information being particularly clear at the level of clothing style. She points out that

> [c]ertain aspects of linguistic style are also negotiated consciously. I can recall explicit discussions in my own high school crowd of "cool" ways to say things, generally in the form of imitations of cool people. . . . But in general, linguistic influence takes place without explicit comment and all the more

requires direct access to speakers. The adoption of a way of speaking, like a way of dressing, no doubt requires both access and entitlement to adopt the style of a particular group. (Eckert 2000: 210–11)

Thus, individuals who are well integrated into local networks are socially positioned to access multiple communities of practice. Eckert is here describing very general social mechanisms by which local conventions and norms – of dress, religion, and general behavior, for example – are negotiated and created, and linguistic norms are no exception. Close-knit networks of the kind where this activity takes place are commonly contracted in adolescence. These are the linguistically influential peer groups that are of particular interest to sociolinguists attempting to understand the kinds of language change associated with different points in the life-span (see Kerswill 1996; Kerswill and Williams 2000). However, such norm-supporting (and norm-constructing) networks also flourish in low-status communities in the absence of social and geographical mobility and foster the solidarity ethos associated with the long-term survival of socially disfavored languages and dialects.

The concepts of network and community of practice are thus closely related, and the differences between them are chiefly of method and focus. Network analysis typically deals with the structural and content properties of the ties that constitute *egocentric* personal networks, and seeks to identify ties important to an individual rather than to focus on particular network clusters (such as those contracted at school) independently of a particular individual. Eckert (2000) explains in detail her procedures for identifying the clusters that form the crucial loci of linguistic and social practice in the social world of the high school. Because it does not attend to the identification of particular clusters or the enterprises undertaken by members which, combined, constitute communities of practice, network analysis cannot address the issues of how and where linguistic variants are employed, along with other network-specific behaviors, to construct local social meanings. Rather, it is concerned with how informal social groups are constituted in such a way as to support local norms or, conversely, to facilitate linguistic change. In the following section we flesh out our discussion with details of specific variationist studies that have employed the social network concept.

5.2.2 Social networks and language variation

The effect of interpersonal relationships on language choices has long been explored in sociolinguistics: Gauchat's (1905) account of variation in the vernacular of the tiny Swiss village of Charmey is cited by Chambers (1995) as an early example. Labov's much later sociometric analysis of the relationship between language use and the individual's position in the group (Labov

1972a) resembles, in important respects, Eckert's account of communities of practice as the sites where linguistic norms and social meaning are co-constructed, as does Cheshire's (1982) account of language variation in adolescent peer groups. Working in an ethnographic, non-quantitative tradition of research which strongly influenced variationist methods, Gumperz (1982a)[1] discusses the effects of changing network structures on language choice in bilingual communities.

A network approach is potentially attractive to variationists for several reasons. First, it provides a set of procedures for studying small groups where speakers are not discriminable in terms of any kind of social class index – as, for example, the southeastern United States island communities investigated by Wolfram, Hazen, and Schilling-Estes (1999). Other examples are minority ethnic groups, migrants, rural populations, or populations in non-industrialized societies. A second advantage is that since social network is intrinsically a concept which relates to local practices, it has the potential to elucidate the social dynamics driving language variation and change. Finally, network analysis offers a procedure for dealing with variation between individual speakers, rather than between groups constructed with reference to predetermined social categories. It was employed chiefly for these reasons in a number of other studies carried out in the 1980s and 1990s in many different kinds of community. Examples of such studies are Milroy (1987) in Belfast; Russell (1982) in Mombasa, Kenya; Schmidt (1985) of Australian Aboriginal adolescents; Bortoni-Ricardo (1985) of changes in the language of rural migrants to a Brazilian city; V. Edwards (1986) of the language of British black adolescents; Schooling (1990) of language differences among Melanesians in New Caledonia; Lippi-Green (1989) on dynamics of change in the rural alpine village of Grossdorf, Austria; W. Edwards (1992) of variation in an African American community in inner-city Detroit; and Maher (1996) of the persistence of language differences in the isolated island community of St. Barthélemy, French West Indies. Milroy (1987), Lippi-Green (1989), Edwards (1992), and Bortoni-Ricardo (1985) are reviewed below, to illustrate a range of applications of the network concept, always with attention to the specifics of local social structure and local social practice.

The Belfast study carried out a detailed quantitative analysis of the relationship between language variation and social network structure. It adapted many of Gumperz's ideas, particularly in its ethnographically oriented fieldwork methods (see 3.5.1 above) and in its attention to local practices in interpreting sociolinguistic patterns. As first reported by Milroy and Milroy (1978) the language patterns of 46 speakers from three low-status urban working-class communities – Ballymacarrett, Hammer, and Clonard – were examined. Eight phonological variables, all of which were clearly indexical of the Belfast urban speech community, were analyzed in relation to the network structure of individual speakers. In all three communities networks were relatively dense, multiplex, and often kin-based, corresponding to those described by many investigators as characteristic of traditional, long-established communities minimally impacted by social or geographical mobility (see, for example, Young and Wilmott 1962; Cohen 1982). The extent of individuals' use of vernacular variants was found to be strongly influenced by the level of integration into neighborhood networks. The kind of network ties that were locally relevant emerged, in the course of observation, as those of kin, work, friendship, and neighborhood. As discussed by Milroy (1987), a considerable body of anthropological research had already noted the particular importance of ties of these four types. Some of the Belfast participants worked outside the neighborhood and had no local kin and few local ties of friendship, while others were locally linked in all four capacities. Such differences in personal network structure appear to be associated with a range of social and psychological factors, and in the Belfast communities interacted with a number of other variables such as gender, generation cohort, and neighborhood settlement patterns.

A major challenge for researchers is to devise a procedure for characterizing differences in network structure which reflects local social practice, so that, not surprisingly, the studies reviewed in this section all measure social network structure in quite different ways. The Belfast study developed a Network Strength Scale (maximum score, 5) which assessed speakers' network characteristics with reference to various relationships *within the neighborhood* of kin, work, and friendship that had emerged in the course of the fieldwork as significant to participants. Speakers scored one point for each of the following conditions they satisfied:

- were members of a high-density, territorially based group (e.g., a bingo or card-playing group, a gang or a football team, or football supporters' club)
- had kinship ties with more than two households in the neighborhood
- worked in the same place as at least two others from the neighborhood
- worked in the same place as at least two others of the same sex from the neighborhood
- associated voluntarily with workmates in leisure hours.

A series of statistical analyses revealed that the strongest vernacular speakers were generally those whose neighborhood network ties were the strongest, a pattern complicated, as we might expect, by the interaction of other social variables such as age and gender.[2] Milroy (2001b) discusses patterns of this kind in Ballymacarrett, where variants of a single variable are examined in relation both to network structure and to gender. Labov's (2001b: 331) re-analysis of the Belfast data confirms the patterns reported by Milroy, and he discusses in particular detail interactions between network and gender in Belfast and Philadelphia (2001b: 329–56). In both communities network structure affects language quite differently for men and women, as shown also by Dubois and Horvath's study of the Louisiana Cajun community (see section 5.1 above).

The relative socioeconomic homogeneity of the inner-city Detroit African American neighborhood studied by Edwards (1992) made social network analysis an attractive procedure for dealing with intra-community linguistic variation, and he operationalized the network concept in accordance with the specifics of local social practice. While the principal factor associated with choice of variant was age, the most important factor distinguishing age-peers of a comparable social and educational background was participation in neighborhood culture. Edwards interpreted such participation as indicative of relative integration into local networks, and measured this integration by means of a Vernacular Culture Index. This was constructed from responses to ten statements which could range from Strongly Disagree (1 point) to Strongly Agree (4 points). Five statements were designed as indicators of the individual's physical integration into the neighborhood and, like the Network Strength Scale used in Belfast, focused on localized interactions with kin, workmates and friends. (e.g., "Most of my relatives live in this neighborhood or with me"; "Most of my friends live in this neighborhood"). Convinced of the importance of attitude in accounting for variation, Edwards designed the other five statements to indicate evaluations of the neighborhood and of black/white friendship ties (e.g., "I would like to remain living in this neighborhood"; "I do not have white friends with whom I interact frequently").

Quite a different set of indicators of integration into localized networks was relevant to Lippi-Green's (1989) study of language change in progress in Grossdorf, an isolated Austrian Alpine village with 800 inhabitants. Commenting specifically on the unhelpfulness of macro-level concepts such as social class in uncovering the relationship between language variation and social structure, Lippi-Green examined in detail the personal network structures of individuals, constructing a scale that used 16 differentially weighted indicators. Some of these were associated with the familiar domains of work, kin and friendship, while others dealt with more specifically local conditions – such as the number of grandparents familiar to the speaker who were core members of the village, or the involvement of the speaker's employment with the tourism industry. Particularly important were indicators that linked speakers to major family networks in the village. Overall, the best correlate of conservative linguistic behavior was integration into three important networks, including those which involved workplace and exposure to non-local language varieties. However, the subtlety of Lippi-Green's network measurement scale allowed her to examine correlations both with all of it and with some parts of it, revealing among other things gender-specific social trajectories of language change and variation of the kind discussed earlier in this section.

In addressing the changing language behavior of mobile individuals, Bortoni-Ricardo's account of the sociolinguistic adjustment of rural migrants to Brazlandia, a satellite city of Brasilia, operationalized the network concept very differently from any of the studies discussed so far. Again, social class was not a particularly useful category in this context, since it did not discriminate between the individuals studied, all of whom were relatively poor. Taking the group's own linguistic norms as a starting point, Bortoni-Ricardo examined the extent to which speakers had moved away from their stigmatized Caipira dialect, rather than attempting to identify a linguistic standard "target." Much as Labov in New York City, she was able to build on ongoing work by sociologists in developing her social framework.

Bortoni-Ricardo's main hypothesis was that the change in social structure associated with rural to urban migration involves a move from an "insulated" network consisting largely of kinsfolk and neighbors to an "integrated" urban network where links are less multiplex but are contracted in a wider range of social contexts. The linguistic counterpart of this change is increasing dialect diffuseness – a movement away from the relatively focused norms of the Caipira dialect (see Le Page and Tabouret-Keller 1985) for an elaboration of the notions of "focusing" and "diffusion"). Two separate network indices are constructed to measure the changing patterns of the migrants' social relationships: the *integration index* and the *urbanization index*. The integration index assesses relevant characteristics of the three persons with whom each migrant most frequently interacts – for example, whether they are kin or non-kin, and whether ties were contracted prior to migration. The final score measures progress in the transition from an insulated to an integrated type of network – effectively the gradual loosening of close-knit network ties. These changes are correlated with a linguistic movement away from the norms of the Caipira dialect. The urbanization index focuses not on the migrant, but on the characteristics of members of his or her personal network, such as educational level and mobility; indicators are selected to assess the extent to which the migrant's contacts are integrated into urban life. In developing these two quite different types of index Bortoni-Ricardo extends the application of the network concept beyond an analysis of small, close-knit groups of the kind described so far to consider the extent to which individuals have detached themselves from such groups and the linguistic consequences of that detachment. We shall return to this issue in section 5.2.4.

5.2.3   Network structure and language shift in
bilingual communities

We have concentrated thus far on the language/network relationship in monolingual communities. However, researchers investigating the social mechanisms of language maintenance and shift in bilingual communities have employed a variant of the same general principle: networks constituted chiefly of strong ties support minority languages resisting institutional pressures to language shift; but when these networks weaken, language shift is likely to take place. This section reviews some of this work, considering first the network structure characteristic of immigrant communities.

It has sometimes been suggested that close-knit networks such as those studied in Belfast and Detroit are marginal to contemporary urban life since traditional working-class communities like the Italian American "urban villagers" described by Gans (1962) or the close-knit Yorkshire mining communities described by Dennis, Henriques, and Slaughter (1957) have all but disappeared in North America and western Europe. There is a large sociological literature on "the stranger," the mobile, marginal individual often seen as typical of a modern city dweller (Harman 1988), and while this perception certainly reflects important characteristics of contemporary urban life such as social and geographical mobility and high proportions of incomers, it does not tell the whole story. Giddens (1989) points out that neighborhoods involving close kinship and personal ties still seem to be created rather than discouraged by city life, since those who form ethnically distinctive urban communities gravitate to form ties with, and often to live with, others from similar linguistic or cultural backgrounds. Hence, far from being a residue of an earlier type of social organization, the older style of close-knit working-class community has apparently been replaced in industrialized countries by similar types of community created by newer immigrants. Dabène and Moore (1995) describe the supportive function of such migrant networks during the period when immigrants are developing resources to integrate more fully into urban life.

Not only recent immigrants, but also long-term stigmatized and marginalized minorities like the New York Puerto Ricans studied by Zentella (1997), construct personal communities that serve as powerful support systems in a hostile environment. Gal (1978) and Li Wei (1994), whose work is discussed in more detail below, have correlated observed patterns of language use with specific network patterns in much the same way as researchers working in monolingual communities. Indeed, Gal explicitly compares her model of language shift to a variationist model of language change, in being both gradual and rooted in synchronic patterns of language variation. Zentella also adopts a broad variationist perspective, but, like Gumperz, uses the concept of network informally and non-quantitatively.

Gumperz's (1982b) vivid account of the Slovenian/German bilingual community in a remote part of Austria's Gail Valley demonstrates relationships between language, network structure, and large-scale social and political structures, associating the move toward monolingualism particularly with economic changes. Members of the poor and socially stigmatized farming community that he studied had traditionally been embedded in close-knit networks of mutual support which linked them in many capacities – as co-workers, neighbors and friends who socialized together within the boundaries of their community. However, such behaviors changed as the economy shifted from a dependence on subsistence farming to, primarily, a service economy. Improvements in the road system gave rise to a host of further changes which affected network structure and everyday social practices, including language behavior. Farmers sold produce to incomers and to factories rather than deal with other local farmers; farm buildings were converted to tourist accommodation for the many visitors entering the area; and work and leisure activities were no longer confined to the immediate locality. As villagers interacted increasingly with urban outsiders, reliance on the local support network diminished. Although, of course, local conditions give rise to variations, the pattern Gumperz describes here appears to be very general in much of western Europe, and perhaps elsewhere. Ó'Riagáin's (1997) description of a series of studies carried out in Ireland between 1973 and 1993 suggests a situation broadly similar to that in the Gail Valley, where change to a service economy triggered associated change in personal social network structure. Consequent changes in the categories of individual involved in face-to-face encounters shifted the balance from bilingual Irish-speaking insiders to monolingual English-speaking outsiders, inevitably resulting in the further decline of Irish. Gal's (1978) analysis of language shift in the bilingual German/Hungarian community in Oberwart, Austria, identified similar triggers. Individuals were measured in terms of the relative "peasantness" (a local category) of their networks. While operating differently for men and women (cf. section 5.2.2), this network variable correlated more closely than individual peasant status with patterns of language choice. Like the Gail Valley and the Irish Gaeltacht, Oberwart had been bilingual for several centuries and, as in those communities, changes in network structure are associated with higher level economic changes.

We now turn to the work of Zentella (1997) and Li Wei (1994) in immigrant communities, where typically pressure to assimilate to the monolingual norm of the host country is intense and, in contrast to long-term bilingual communities of the kind discussed above, a pattern of language shift within three generations is common. Grosjean (1982) and Jørgensen (1998) describe assimilatory pressures in the United States and Europe respectively.[3] In an account compiled from long-term participant observation, Zentella provides evidence of a three-generation shift pattern in a Puerto Rican community in

New York City (*el bloque*), and although the details are complex, this shift appears to be taking place despite the apparent persistence of Spanish in many Latino communities in the United States. Several distinguishable varieties of both Spanish and English give rise to multiple-code repertoires, and the choice of code is heavily network-dependent (Zentella 1997: 48; see also section 8.4.3 for details).

Zentella comments on the significance of what she describes as "the Puerto Rico language learning connection" in offering an explanation of the strength and persistence of Spanish in New York City and elsewhere in the United States. She cites the combined effect of continuing network ties of immigrants to individuals in adjacent Spanish-speaking countries of Latin America, and cyclic patterns of immigration (see also Bourhis and Marshall 1999). This Puerto Rican connection (and its counterpart in other Spanish-speaking communities in the United States) may explain why young people use a mixed Spanish–English code; in accordance with the expected pattern of language shift in immigrant communities, they have shifted substantially to English monolingualism but still need to communicate with Spanish monolingual speakers. Patterns of code-switching and language choice described by Zentella are discussed further in chapter 8.

Li Wei (1994) and Milroy and Li Wei (1995) report a quantitative analysis of social trajectories of language shift which also associates different network types with variable patterns of language use. Three migrant groups in Newcastle upon Tyne are distinguished, overlapping with (but not exactly corresponding to) a grandparent, parent, and child generation cohort. Each group contracts characteristically different types of network ties, the first associating mainly with kin, the second chiefly with other British Chinese, and the third more extensively with non-Chinese peers. Variable network patterns are in turn correlated with several different patterns of language choice, where English and Chinese were used either monolingually or in different dominance configurations. Following Milardo (1988), interactive and exchange networks were distinguished, corresponding roughly to "weak" and "strong" types of tie. Additionally, a "passive" type of tie is distinguished, which seems particularly important to migrant or mobile individuals. Passive ties – for example, to geographically distant relatives or friends – entail an absence of regular contact, but are valued as a source of influence and moral support.

Since the Chinese in Tyneside did not live within a specifiable neighborhood, assessments of network strength could not be based on the territorially restricted strong ties that were found in most of the studies reviewed in section 5.2.2. Instead, comparative analysis of individual exchange networks was based on a list of up to 20 persons who constituted significant and regular contacts for each individual, adapting a procedure described by Mitchell (1986). These sets of 20 could then be compared on relevant dimensions –

for example, different ethnic compositions. Not surprisingly, the strongest ethnic Chinese networks were associated both with the oldest generation and with the most extensive use of Chinese, and the weakest with the British-born generation and with the most extensive use of English. Most interesting were the many subtly different network patterns within each group such as those associated with one of the community's institutions, the True Jesus Church.

Religious organizations appear to be particularly important focal points for many migrant communities, as Shin (1998: 71) points out in her account of the social practices of the Korean community in New York City. Li Wei (1995) suggests that the True Jesus Church functions primarily as a support mechanism for cultural and socialization activities, noting that the original member families had contracted pre-migration network ties on the island of Ap Chau, close to Hong Kong. He further documents a markedly stronger pattern of Chinese language maintenance among the British-born members of the True Jesus Church than among the young community as a whole – a pattern attributed to the strong ties maintained by True Jesus youngsters with church members who are monolingual in Cantonese. Interestingly, Li Wei also notes a pattern of fluent Cantonese/English code-mixing as characteristic of the True Jesus teenagers, which he explains in much the same way as Zentella explains widespread Spanish/English mixing by New York City Puerto Rican youngsters. In both cases the young people have found a similar solution to the problem of their own limited linguistic proficiency, which is at odds with their desire to maintain social ties with non-English speakers. In these cases, a network analysis is invoked to explain not only the social trajectory of language shift, but specific patterns of code-switching. Labrie (1988b) also offers a network-based account of code-switching by Italians in Montreal, and Milroy (2001a) provides a fuller discussion of the role of social network analysis in an account of language maintenance and language shift.

5.2.4   Weak network ties and theories of language change

Social network analysis has most commonly been employed in communities where ties between speakers are generally strong. While studies such as those reviewed in sections 5.2.2 and 5.2.3 show that it can be operationalized relatively straightforwardly in such locations, it is much less clear how researchers might handle socially and geographically mobile speakers whose personal network ties are not predominantly dense or multiplex. In fact, network-based accounts of such speakers are rare, and the only study that has attempted this is Bortoni-Ricardo's account of the progressive urbanization patterns of Brazilian rural migrants. In this respect, the network studies over the last two decades have usually shared the orientation of both socio-linguistics and dialectology pointed out by Chambers (1992) to non-mobile speakers in isolated communities. In a recent review of sociolinguistic approaches to Latino speakers in the United States, Mendoza-Denton (1999) has criticized the tendency to treat minority groups as if they were isolated from contact with others, and we noted earlier the tendency to treat the dialects of African American speakers in this way (see section 4.5.2). Yet, geographical and social mobility and contact between communities is the rule rather than the exception in contemporary cities, and variationists are increasingly addressing the sociolinguistic consequences of mobility and con-tact (see, for example, Trudgill 1986; Trudgill and Britain 2001; Chambers 1995: 52–65; Kerswill and Williams 2000; and Milroy 2001b).

It is easy to identify the difficulties of working with loose-knit networks. Analysis of close-knit networks involves comparing speakers who differ from each other in certain quite specific respects (for example, multiplexity of ties contracted at the workplace) but are still similar enough in other relevant ways for a comparison to be meaningful. But it is difficult to see how the loose-knit network structures of individuals who differ from each other in many respects such as educational level, occupation, region of origin, and mobility might meaningfully be compared. This problem was noted in the Belfast study (see section 3.5.1), where the social networks of relatively mobile speakers in the suburbs of Andersonstown and Braniel could not be analyzed following procedures developed for the close-knit inner city neighborhoods of Ballymacarrett, Clonard and Hammer (Milroy and Milroy 1985: 363) and was also encountered in the prosperous Berlin suburb of Zehlendorf (Labrie 1988a). However, from the perspective of a person who has changed employment and place of residence several times, the networks of speakers studied in Belfast, Detroit, and Grossdorf are all close-knit, and might be compared in a general way with those of more mobile speakers, as exemplified by Kerswill and Williams (1999).

Despite these operational difficulties, loose-knit networks are of consider-able theoretical interest, for reasons to be discussed in the remainder of this chapter. We might surmise initially that if a close-knit network structure supports localized linguistic norms and resists change originating from out-side the network, then communities composed of weak ties are likely to be susceptible to such change. Following Granovetter's (1973, 1982) argument that "weak" and apparently insignificant interpersonal ties (of "acquaint-ance" as opposed to "friend," for example) are important channels through which innovation and influence flow from one close-knit group to another, Milroy and Milroy (1985) proposed that linguistic innovators are likely to be individuals who are socially positioned to contract many weak ties. Since such weak ties link close-knit groups to each other and to the larger regional or national speech community, they are likely to figure prominently in a socially accountable theory of linguistic diffusion and change. Labov (2001b: 356–65 and following) develops an account not inconsistent with the arguments set out here, which focuses on the social positioning of individuals in Philadelphia neighborhood networks.

Milroy and Milroy suggest that a "weak tie" model of change can account rather generally for the tendency of some languages to be more resistant to change than others (Icelandic versus English, or Sardinian versus Sicilian, for example). They suggest that a type of social organization based on overlapping close-knit networks will inhibit change, while one characterized by mobility (for whatever reason), with a concomitant weakening of close ties, will facilitate it. Grace (1992) explains in a similar way some puzzling developments among the Austronesian languages, which show widely differing patterns of susceptibility to change that are inexplicable in terms of traditional assumptions (see also Grace 1990). As well as explaining different large-scale linguistic outcomes by comparing different types of social organization, the weak tie model can account for specific problematic examples of change of the kind discussed below.

Innovations have been widely observed to skip from city to city, missing out intervening territory. This appears to be the pattern of the Northern Cities Shift – a vigorous change in vowel systems affecting cities of the northern United States from western New England to an unspecified point westward (Labov 1991; Wolfram and Schilling-Estes 1998: 138). Trudgill (1988) notes the relatively recent adoption by young speakers in the English city of Norwich of a merger between /f/ ~ /θ/ and /v/ ~ /ð/ (as in *fin~thin*; *lava~lather*). The use of this merger, also by young speakers, is subsequently documented in the northern cities of Sheffield and Derby by Milroy (1996); further north in Middlesbrough, a town about 50 miles south of Newcastle, by Llamas (2000); and further north still, in Glasgow, by Stuart-Smith (1999). As it saliently indexes working-class London speech, this change appears to be contact-induced rather than to originate from within the communities. However, it is hard to explain the precise mechanisms of its diffusion in terms of close contact between Londoners and other speakers. While attributing its rapid spread to Norwich to greater mobility and contact between speakers, Trudgill points out that the teenagers who use the merged variants are less mobile than their seniors and tend to contract close ties locally. Llamas, however, suggests an association between the spread of the merger and the exceptional occupational mobility of young Middlesbrough men (so-called "language missionaries") who follow a pattern of returning to their home town between periods of work on short-term contracts in the south of England in areas where the merger is already current. A weak tie model would in fact explicitly predict its diffusion from one community to another through multiple weak ties of some kind. Following the same line of reasoning, historical sociolinguists have begun, with promising results, to examine systematically the social trajectories of earlier changes with attention not only to gender and status-related patterns, but to the effects of weakened close-knit network ties (Nevalainen 1999; Nevalainen and Raumolin-Brunberg 1996; Tieken-Boon van Ostade, Nevalainen, and Caon 2000).

Milroy and Milroy (1992) propose an account of the dynamics of language change which assumes that mobile middle-class speakers are particularly likely to contract loose-knit ties and so are likely to be important agents of change – a proposal consistent with Labov's principle that innovating groups are located centrally in the social hierarchy (1980: 254). Taking Milroy and Milroy's argument as a point of departure, Kerswill and Williams (1999) have recently investigated the relationship between social class, mobility, and susceptibility to change by comparing the language behavior of low- and high-mobility speakers of different social statuses in the English towns of Reading and Milton Keynes. They conclude that network structure has the predicted effect – that is, close-knit networks maintain localized norms, while loose-knit networks facilitate change. However, following a comparison of the very different behaviors of mobile high-status and mobile low-status groups, they argue that the variables of class and network need to be considered independently.

5.3   Dialect Leveling

The weak tie model of change discussed in section 5.2 can illuminate the dynamics of dialect leveling; that is, the eradication of socially or locally marked variants (both within and between linguistic systems) in conditions of social or geographical mobility and resultant dialect contact. Leveling might reasonably be viewed as a linguistic reflex of the large-scale disruption endemic in the modern world of close-knit, localized networks that have historically maintained highly systematic and complex sets of socially structured linguistic norms. Such disruption arises from (for example) internal and transnational migration, war, industrialization, and urbanization. While these dynamics have operated earlier and more intensively in colonial contexts, as discussed by Chambers within a broad social network framework (1995: 57–66; see also Trudgill et al. 2000), they continue to affect geographically or socially mobile populations. In any event, leveling gives rise to a tendency for varieties associated with major conurbations to spread into increasingly large territories (Kerswill and Williams 2000; Britain 1997) at the expense of localized norms of the kind supported by a close-knit network structure.

Watt and Milroy (1999) discuss the female-led convergence in Newcastle on the supralocal variant of (o) and (e) and the progressive abandonment of highly localized variants (see section 4.1 above) as an example of dialect leveling. Thomas (1997) describes the operation of the same kind of process in Texas, part of the United States sunbelt, which has received a huge influx of internal migrants in recent years. He reports that rural speakers retain two stereotypical features of the Texas dialect (monophthongal variants of /aj/ and as in *dye* and lowered variants of /e/ as in *day*) while young speakers from metropolitan centers lack these locally distinctive variants. Trudgill (1999: 80) describes the effects of this process in England generally, where varieties associated with major cities have spread outwards into the surrounding territory at the expense of distinctive localized norms. Williams and Kerswill (1999) and Britain (1997, 2002) describe the effects of leveling on local distinctiveness in several locations.

An understanding of the leveling process is helpful in considering the nature of varieties traditionally described as regional standards, such as the regionally distinctive varieties associated with educated speakers in the American south (Preston 1996; Hartley and Preston 1999) or Northern Ireland, or the Tyneside area of England. Watt (2002) discusses the convergence of Tyneside speakers on socially unmarked supralocal variants (o) and (e) in these terms, arguing that regional standards originate not as modified versions of exonorms such as British Received Pronunciation, but as supralocal leveled varieties. Consider also the case of the Belfast low front vowel /a/ (as in *pat*, *pass*). As in Tyneside, higher status Belfast speakers do not usually orient to RP where low back and low front vowels are phonologically contrastive (as in *psalm*: *Sam*). Rather, they reduce the number of linguistically conditioned allophones of /a/ by eliminating the extreme back and front variants characteristic of the vernacular system, often converging on a narrow area of vowel space around the center of the vernacular range. Milroy (1982) describes this process as "normalization," a phenomenon that he carefully distinguishes from standardization, where institutional intervention is implicated.[4] At the time this research was carried out in Belfast (1975–80) no model was available to describe the dynamics of this contrast between high- and low-status speakers; following Labov (1966) most researchers operated with a single dimension such as relative vowel height or relative backness which was linearly correlated with status. However, a dialect contact framework treats speakers' treatment of /a/ in Belfast (and indeed of other vowels) as a straightforward instance of leveling, whereby socially marked or stigmatized elements are eliminated from the pool of variants. Such leveled norms indeed might function socially as standards; and this appears to have happened in the United States, where it is much easier to define the standard negatively in terms of what speakers avoid, than positively in terms of the characteristics of any putative standard variety (Wolfram and Schilling-Estes 1998: 12). However, there is an important distinction between an institutionally legitimized exonorm such as RP and a leveled norm which develops in a structurally regular fashion independently of an identifiable exonorm, since, as Watt (2002) shows, an important function of these leveled norms is to index ingroup distinctiveness.

Although leveling constitutes a pressure toward linguistic convergence, it does not follow that communities whose dialects undergo this process lose their linguistic distinctiveness. Schilling-Estes (2002) considers the tension between pressures toward supralocalism and homogenization on the one hand and the desire of speech communities to maintain a distinctive social and linguistic identity on the other. Her comparative account of two small rural American communities (Smith Island, Maryland, and the Lumbee community of Robeson County, North Carolina) shows that each responds differently to the tension introduced by these competing forces. The Smith Islanders maintain more elaborate linguistic indices of distinctiveness, while the Lumbee mark linguistic distinctiveness quite minimally, but make extensive use of material symbols drawn from their traditional Native American culture.

The structure of personal social networks and the operation of leveling processes raises both psycholinguistic and sociolinguistic issues. On the basis of evidence from language attitudes research, sociolinguists commonly assume an ideological motivation to underlie the long-term maintenance of distinctive, often stigmatized, local norms in the face of pressures from numerically or socially more powerful speech communities; speakers want to sound (for example) Welsh, Irish, northern English, New Zealandish, Canadian, African American, American Southern and be distinguished from whatever social group they perceive themselves as opposing. Yet, motivations alone appear to be insufficient to maintain non-standard patterns reliably, since spreading supralocal varieties often engulf minority dialects contrary to the desires of their speakers to maintain distinctiveness (see Wolfram, Hazen, and Schilling-Estes 1999 for a discussion of this issue in an American context). Relevant to the question of why distinctive localized norms sometimes do not survive is Payne's (1980) demonstration of the social conditions needed for children to learn the highly localized phonolexical complexities of the Philadelphia system; particularly, their parents needed to be locally born for such learning to take place (see section 2.4 above). This seems to imply that if a close-knit community network structure loosens and members become mobile, leveling and simplification processes follow naturally as the social and cognitive prerequisites for supporting highly localized norms disappear. Thus, not only does a community's sense of distinctiveness sometimes become redundant as network ties loosen, but speakers lack the extensive and regular input needed to maintain localized norms. Although close-knit networks may be viewed as the social mechanisms that support the construction, maintenance, and elaboration of local linguistic distinctiveness, from the point of view of the language learner they provide the intensive input required to master complex, localized linguistic structures in the absence of institutional support.

The age of the learner is also important in determining whether or not structural complexities will survive in a dialect contact situation, since something like the critical period hypothesized in language acquisition research also constrains the trajectory of second dialect acquisition. Chambers (1992), Kerswill and Williams (2000: 67) and Trudgill (1989: 249) present evidence that older children and post-adolescents do not acquire structurally complex features like the conditioned allophones of /a/ in Belfast or Philadelphia, and so play an important part in simplification and leveling processes. Kerswill and Williams (2000: 94) demonstrate the quite different contribution to mixed dialect formation of children who are old enough to be peer- rather than home-oriented; specifically, the child's orientation to the peer group is crucial in determining whether he or she adopts a new dialect feature rather than maintain the sometimes distinctively different norms of the family. A further point is that the peer group is the site where new dialect norms are constructed, so that "the features of the 'new dialect' are prefigured by the older children, those verging on adolescence, rather than by the home-oriented youngsters" (2000: 111).

5.4   The Sociolinguistics of Mobility: Place as a Cultural Concept

Queen (2001) provides a sociolinguistically oriented account of the effects of contact with German speakers on the language patterns of Turkish immigrant children, but variationist work that makes use, as she does, of concepts drawn from the language contact literature is rare. Dialect contact frameworks, such as those mentioned briefly in section 5.3, have been developed relatively recently in response to criticisms of a tendency to treat communities as if they were independent of outside influence, but other scholars have addressed this isolationist tendency in somewhat different ways. Labov points out that his work is restricted to intra-varietal change, and does not examine the effects of contact (2001b: 20). While his distinction between different types of change begs more questions than can be addressed here, it is clear that his basic unit of study, the speech community, is traditionally conceived as a construct that does not attend to contacts between communities or the cross-cutting influences that have been made possible through greater mobility and access to knowledge of the local practices of others.

The classical procedure in describing a speech community is for the analyst to specify a particular geographical location, and then to identify a series of putatively relevant social categories such as gender, class, or generation cohort. Analysis of variation in terms of these categories carries the implication that they influence the behavior of speakers, who are nevertheless primarily constrained by geographical location. Commenting on the speech community (or perhaps more aptly, community of practice) formed by expatriate, natively anglophone wives living with their husbands in Tunisia, Walters (1996: 526) notes that the situation of these multilingual women, whose identity derives from their contemporary practices rather than their community of origin, is by no means unique. Yet, their speech community is very different from those that variationists have imagined.

A different criticism of the traditional concept of the speech community has come from Dorian (1994) and Wolfram and Beckett (2000), who have questioned the social role of variation in small, geographically isolated communities, arguing for a larger degree of individual variation than is usually assumed.[5] In a number of publications (e.g., Johnstone 1996, 1999b; Johnstone and Bean 1997) Johnstone has discussed extensively the social dynamics underlying variation at the level of the individual. She suggests that mobility and a more general globalization has made available to speakers information about the behaviors and language varieties characteristic of many locales other than those in which they live, and that a view of place as a cultural rather than a geographical, physical entity is better suited to these conditions. Thus, for example, she examines the use made by Texan women of southern-sounding speech for reasons which relate to their everyday social and economic goals; one woman whose job involves telephone selling reports that the market value of a southern accent is considerable (Johnstone 1999b). This view of place as a cultural rather than a physical entity may help us to understand the use made by locally born African Americans in Detroit of southern norms (Anderson 2002). Similarly, Williams and Kerswill (1999), Llamas (2000), and Dyer (2002) all suggest that the rapid spread of a number of changes through English and Scottish cities, such as the *fin/ thin* merger (see section 5.3 above), constitutes part of a set of youth norms originating from the southeast of England which has become relatively independent of physical place.

5.5   Concluding Remarks

This chapter complemented the discussion in chapter 4 by moving away from large-scale social categories to focus on frameworks designed to examine local social practices and contacts between individual social actors in speech communities. We looked first at the related concepts of social network and community of practice. Applications of social network analysis to the study of variation and change in both monolingual and bilingual communities were then explored from a number of different dimensions. Our discussion of the importance of a socially oriented theory of change of loose ties between members of speech communities led to consideration of dialect-leveling processes, and a more general review of different ways to approach sociolinguistic patterns and processes in speech communities that are characterized by mobility and access to knowledge of the linguistic and social practices of others.

6

Investigating Phonological Variation

6.1   Introductory

Variationist sociolinguists seek to uncover relationships among social and linguistic variables. The previous two chapters have discussed the social dimensions of this pursuit, and we turn now to its linguistic dimensions. We treat phonological variation separately from morphological and syntactic variation though many of the issues we raise pertain to the study of any type of linguistic variable.

When examining sociolinguistic data presented in summary form, such as in the tables at the beginning of chapter 4, it is easy to forget that the numbers being reported represent the product of a long process of analysis. Fieldwork provides the raw material for analysis, but shaping that material into useful data is typically much more time-consuming. We may get a sense of the process involved by considering the example of (o) in Newcastle from tables 4.2 and 4.3. Those tables describe the usage of four variants of (o) among 32 speakers who were recorded in free conversation and reading word lists (Milroy 1999; Watt and Milroy 1999). How did the investigators proceed from having hours of tape-recorded speech to reporting the numbers in the tables?

The first step usually takes place even before the data collection is begun – that is, the identification of relevant linguistic variables. The Newcastle researchers knew from previous reports and their own experience with local speech that (o) was likely to show interesting patterns of sociolinguistic variation. Part of identifying a linguistic variable is specifying its variant forms as in the example of the four realizations of (o). Researchers will have some familiarity with the range of variation involved before beginning the analysis, though the precise definition of the variants can come only after having reviewed the collected speech samples. As was the case with Newcastle (o), the final set of variants analyzed may be the product of collapsing together a wider range of observed forms; often some degree of abstraction like this is necessary to make sense of the variation (see further section 6.2.1).

In many cases the most time-consuming step in the process is that of measuring the usage of the variable. In the case of (o), this meant counting the number of times a speaker used each of the four variants. Determining which form of (o) appeared in a given instance was done auditorily, that is by listening to the recording. In some cases, measuring usage of phonological variables may also involve the aid of acoustic instrumentation. Regardless of how the variants are measured, the counting should proceed in accordance with the *principle of accountability*, which in essence states that analysts should not select from a text those variants of a variable that tend to confirm their argument, and ignore others that do not. As Labov directs, "for the section of speech being examined all occurrences of a given variant are noted, and where it has been possible to define the variables as a closed set of variants, all non-occurrences in the relevant environments" (1982a: 30). There are, however, a number of problems underlying this concise and apparently simple statement. As we shall see, it is often difficult to specify "relevant environments" and, even more fundamentally to define the input to a given variable; Labov's suggestion that it might sometimes *not* be possible to define variables as a closed set of variants is particularly relevant to *syntactic* variation (see chapter 7).

Once usage has been measured, the search for patterns begins. Investigators must understand internal linguistic constraints in order to establish comparable data sets across their sample of speakers. With Newcastle (o), for example, the researchers noted that certain words including *old* and *know* were produced with an [aː] by some older speakers. This usage represents an archaic pronunciation which, although rare, still occurs occasionally; consequently, such items were omitted from the analysis of (o). A more common concern at this stage is the influence of phonological conditioning on the variation. If a given variant appears frequently or solely in a particular phonological context, it is important to take such facts into account in the analysis.

The final stage in the analytic process is to place the linguistic results in the context of their social distribution. The data from individual speakers may be presented or they may be tabulated to report group scores as in tables 4.2 and 4.3. Very often patterns of co-variation between linguistic and social variables are uncovered or verified through the application of statistical testing.

This chapter focuses on a range of practical and theoretical issues associated with the use of the linguistic variable as an analytic tool in the examination of phonological variation. We assume some acquaintance with the notion of the linguistic variable; much fuller accounts of this key concept are available in Labov's reports of his early work (Labov 1972b) and in many more recent surveys of the field (see particularly Hudson 1996; Wardhaugh 1986; Chambers 1995; Wolfram 1993b). Our discussion is organized in accordance with the process described above: first the initial identification of variables is discussed; second, we examine approaches to measuring variation by comparing auditory and instrumental techniques; third, the establishment of linguistic patterning is addressed; and fourth, we explore some dimensions of the problem of interpreting results. The chapter concludes with a discussion of issues associated with *quantification* of data.

6.2   Identifying and Selecting Variables

6.2.1   Types of phonological variables

Sociolinguistic methods have been fruitfully applied to the study of a wide range of phonological variables. Vocalic variation has surely received the greatest amount of attention, at least from researchers on North American English. Labov has been particularly active in this area from his early work on Martha's Vineyard to his more recent projects like Telsur (see section 3.2.2).[1] Studies of consonantal variation include work on "*h*-dropping" and glottalization in Britain (e.g., Williams and Kerswill 1999; Tollfree 1999; Docherty and Foulkes 1999) as well as work on other languages including Arabic (e.g., Haeri 1997), Dutch (e.g., Van de Velde, van Hout, and Gerritsen 1997), French (e.g., Corneau 2000), Japanese (e.g., Hibiya 1996), and Spanish (e.g., Cedergren 1973, 1987). By comparison to studies of vowels and consonants, much less attention has been given to suprasegmental features though a number of studies have examined intonation (e.g., Guy et al. 1986; Britain 1992; Yaeger-Dror 1996; Lefkowitz 1997; Grabe et al. 2000). Also noteworthy are studies – for example, Jane Stuart-Smith's examination (1999) of Glasgow speech – which explore a wide range of vocal settings through the concept of voice quality.

Some variables involve an alternation between two or more apparently discrete forms. Such is the case with (h), as shown in table 4.1, which is realized as either [h] or zero. Other variables are more continuous in nature and show variants that seem to range between two points along some phonetic dimension. The clearest cases of continuous variables are vowels that vary in terms of height and/or backness. Consider, for example, the case of (æ) which undergoes raising (and fronting) as part of a series of sound changes known as the Northern Cities Shift (see Labov 1994; Gordon 2001b). The vowel is realized sometimes as [æ], sometimes as [ɛ], and often as something in between the two.

As detailed below (section 6.3), continuous variables may be treated as having discrete variants for measurement purposes. For example, Gordon (2001b) employed the four-point scale in (1) to examine (æ) raising:

(1)   [æ] = 0; [æ̞] = 1; [ɛ̯] = 2; [ɛ] = 3

Continuous variables may alternatively be approached using acoustic measurements such as formant frequencies (section 6.3.2). In either case, it is important to recognize the theoretical implications of treating a variable as continuous. Employing a scale from A to B carries with it the implication that the two variants function as part of a single system and that the social evaluation of the variation patterns in the same way. While this interpretation may be appropriate in cases of sound changes in progress, such as the Northern Cities Shift, it may not apply in other instances (see section 6.5).

6.2.2   Choosing and specifying variables

Initial identification of variables has not generally been discussed as a problem (but see Wolfram 1993b). Researchers investigating well-studied languages and varieties or regions and speech communities may draw on previous work by sociolinguists or dialectologists. Features showing socially patterned variation are often very salient and sometimes rather general across an area. An extreme case in this sense is the alternation between [ɪn] and [ɪŋ] on the -*ing* form of verbs, which has been found to be sociolinguistically relevant in a number of places throughout the English-speaking world. But more commonly variables are relatively localized. For example, although (h) is a socially salient variable in Britain south of the River Tees (see table 4.1), it is not a variable north of this point, or in Ireland or Australia or the United States. Similarly, monophthongization of /aj/, which results in such pronunciations as [raːd] "ride," is heard throughout a large section of the American South from the Atlantic Coast through Texas, but is not as common outside this area (but see Docherty and Foulkes 1999 for a British case). Some features are even more localized, and are heard only in particular communities and often only among certain types of speakers. The fronted variant of (o) discussed in section 4.1, for example, is restricted to the small corner of northeastern England that includes Newcastle and seems to be used almost exclusively by men.[2]

Researchers investigating varieties that have not received prior linguistic study may rely on casual observations they have made about potentially interesting variables. Intuitions can be further refined through pilot studies (see section 6.2.3). In fact, any researcher should approach the choice of variables with an open mind and open ears. When working with conversational

speech samples, it is not uncommon to find features that have not previously been described or associated with the community under investigation.
For example, in a study that sought to assess the status of the Northern
Cities Shift among speakers of various ethnicities, Gordon (2000) identified two features unrelated to the shift that seemed to be characteristic
of a particular group of speakers. Similarly, in a study of Bradford, West
Yorkshire, Watt and Tillotson (2002) investigate (o), a vowel described in
the dialect literature as varying in terms of height and diphthongization,
but these investigators found an apparently new development involving
fronting of the vowel.

In a similar vein, investigators need to consider the variables they study
in terms of their local significance. The case of a much-studied variable, (r),
serves to illustrate this point. In New York City, as described by Labov,
absence of post-vocalic [r] is associated with low-status speech, is subject to
stylistic variation, and appears to be undergoing change. In England, by
contrast, r-lessness is characteristic of high-status speech and is moreover
categorical except in some (mainly) western areas. In Ireland and Scotland,
on the other hand, the traditional picture suggests that most speakers categorically pronounce post-vocalic [r]. Interestingly, Romaine (1978) describes
a change in this pattern that has been detected in Scotland whereby male
speakers appear to be adopting r-lessness (see also Stuart-Smith 1999). This
move seems to be a reaction against the prestige norm of Scottish speech;
however, "in accepting r-lessness their usage happens to coincide with a
much larger national norm [e.g., RP]" (Romaine 1978: 156). Nevertheless, the
evidence suggests that the r-lessness of the Scottish men is a local development and not one modeled on the prestige norms of southern England.

It seems then that (r) is not the "same" variable in Scotland as it is in
England or the United States. Since variables pattern differently in different places, the initial identification of even well-known variables is by no
means automatic. This point is particularly important in the specification of
linguistic contexts relevant to a given variable. Knowing the contexts within
which a variable may potentially operate is critical to an analysis of its
variation (see further section 6.4.1). Glottalization in Britain is one example
of a feature involving quite complex phonological conditioning (see Wells
1982 for an overview). Moreover, the effects vary from dialect to dialect.
Thus in most varieties glottalization does not affect word-initial stops, but
such contexts have been found to be subject to glottalization under certain
conditions in some dialects, including Cockney (Tollfree 1999).[3] For this
reason researchers examining glottalization, or indeed any feature, need to
specify the envelope of variation in local terms and cannot assume that the
variable operates in a similar manner everywhere.

Identifying phonological variables also involves specifying the formal variation associated with them. When discrete variants are involved, particularly

when the choice seems to be binary as with (h) in southern Britain, this may be a fairly straightforward matter. But, many apparently binary variables involve some intermediate forms. In the case of (aj) monophthongization, for example, the glide may be reduced rather than completely eliminated (Anderson 2002). Such cases may represent transitional forms, implying that a change is in progress. Alternatively, they may stem from "fudging" between competing varieties (Chambers and Trudgill 1998).

Previous research can certainly be helpful in specifying the variation associated with a given variable, but investigators should not be limited by prior descriptions. Widely distributed variables may show distinct developments at the local level. Such is the case with the Northern Cities Shift, which is heard across the northern US from New York State into the Dakotas. According to Labov's description (e.g., 1994), the shift involves lowering of (ɪ) and backing of (ʌ). Still, Gordon (2001b) found a much greater range of variation for these vowels in the Michigan communities he studied. Both (ɪ) and (ʌ) were sometimes lowered, and sometimes backed, and at other times both lowered and backed. This multidirectional shifting proved to be of considerable theoretical importance since it challenges the interpretation of the changes as operating in a chain shift (see further section 6.5).

6.2.3 Pilot studies

Although they need not be ambitious in scope or very systematically organized, pilot studies are in general a useful preliminary to large research projects as they help to identify unexpected difficulties of many kinds and offer guidelines to overall design. In the Belfast project described earlier (section 3.5), a small pilot study proved to be helpful in identifying relevant linguistic and speaker variables (see section 4.5.3 for a discussion of *ethnicity* in Belfast). The experiences of the investigators in that project are discussed here to illustrate some commonly encountered problems, and some solutions.

Interviews, word lists and reading passages were recorded with 20 speakers of both sexes and various ages from communities associated with both major ethnic groups in the city. The investigators had already developed some quite strong linguistic hunches, and while these often turned out to be fairly accurate, pilot work sometimes revealed that they were a little wide of the mark. It also helped to identify important variables that, previously, had not been thought to be particularly interesting. A number of hazards were revealed that had not been specifically predicted but needed to be taken into account in designing the main research project. For example there were evident differences in lexical incidence between items that had been thought to belong to the same phonological set; *get* and *never* in contemporary Belfast vernacular did not pattern in the same way as items such as *wet* and *wedding*, and so could not be considered as tokens of the variable (ε). We return to this general point in section 6.4.1 below.

The general value of a pilot study in helping to assess the importance of information gathered by relatively unsystematic observation and analysis may be demonstrated with reference to the variable (a) in Belfast. It had already been noted informally that vernacular speakers realized certain items of the /a/ class with a front-raised, lengthened, slightly diphthongized variant; [bɛ'g] is a stereotypical Belfast pronunciation of the item "bag". However, the initial hunch that Belfast, like New York City, might show innovatory patterns of front-raising of this vowel turned out to be wrong. It became quite clear that the less immediately obvious tendency to back /a/, which had also been observed, was a much more regular process and was associated with young (chiefly male) speakers. On the other hand, the more immediately obvious stereotypical raising of /a/ to [ε] emerged as a recessive feature, confined in contemporary Belfast vernacular to syllables closed by a velar consonant. Real-time evidence from more than a century ago (Patterson 1860) confirmed that the pattern had once affected the /a/ system in many more linguistic environments, and apparent-time evidence obtained during the pilot study reflected this change; for example, one 18-year-old man normally produced the form [kap] "cap," in contrast with his mother's habitual pronunciation [kεp]. Backing was apparently spreading to items that had once been fronted, but had not yet affected syllables closed by a velar consonant, like *bag*, *back*, and *bang*.

The methodological implications of this combination of historical and contemporary evidence were quite direct; syllables closed by a velar con-sonant, which were categorically non-back, could not be counted as tokens of a variable that varied on the dimension of backness. In fact, it was shown that adequate analysis of (a) in the main research projects required some adaptation of Labov's quantitative methods as they were originally formulated.

There is one particular reason to be cautious of unsystematic observa-tions (even by native speakers) as a basis for adequate identification of variables. Because most people's range of social experience has become quite limited by the time they have attained adulthood, such observations are nearly always selective and may be difficult to interpret or be simply misleading. For example, one local graduate student involved in the Belfast research was firmly convinced that front-raised pronunciations by working-class speakers of such items as *cap* and *rat* reflected attempts at correction in the direction of RP; but the more systematically collected pilot-study data confirmed that this variant was in fact a low-status and recessive feature.

One methodological point of considerable importance in pilot work concerns transcription. Transcription of any kind is invariably a selective process, reflecting underlying theoretical goals and assumptions (Ochs 1979: 44). It is therefore unwise at the pilot stage, when these goals and assumptions are still being formulated, to idealize too far from the data. Moreover, an over-abstract representation can conceal important information. When the objectives of the analysis are clearer, a selective transcription will be more useful than a detailed one, which at that later stage of the research is likely to contain much unwanted information

This principle is valid at all levels of analysis, but the implication for phonological work is that phonemic transcriptions are often unsuitable for pilot studies. The experience of the Belfast researchers was that a narrow transcription was needed to identify in the first place the range of vowel variation associated with different phonetic environments. The variable (a) illustrates this point; the speech of a number of persons was transcribed in some phonetic detail before it became clear that tokens of the vowel in a certain range of environments were *never* front-raised, and seemed moreover to be implicationally ordered with respect to their tolerance of back-raising (see Milroy 1981 for details). This information was used to construct highly selective word lists, capable of yielding a great deal of specific information about phonological structure; it was also helpful in determining the lexical input to variables (see section 6.4.1).

As the discussion in this section has implied, a general analysis of the phonological system is a prerequisite to quantitative analysis. While pilot work is an important means of obtaining the information required for such an analysis, traditional 'guess and check' methods (Longacre 1964), which draw on the skill and intuition of the analyst are also important. James Milroy's (1976) phonological analysis in the Belfast study, which provided an essential basis for subsequent quantitative phonological work, drew on the analyst's intuition and on the pilot-study data.

6.3 Measuring Variation

The greatest challenge in analyzing natural language data lies in the conversion of spoken or written samples of language into useful data. How does a researcher arrive at a quantitative measure of a person's usage from, for example, taped conversational speech? This process of conversion requires careful identification and definition of linguistic variables. In addition to these questions of what to measure, one must consider how to measure the variation.

6.3.1   Auditory techniques

Until fairly recently, the most common approach to measuring phonological variation was to rely primarily on the auditory judgments of the investigators. Through repeated listening, the investigators identify and train themselves to recognize the variants of a given linguistic variable. They then review the larger speech corpus and code the relevant forms of the variable according to the variant heard. Because the process involves the researcher's perception or impressions of the variants produced, this technique is sometimes referred to as impressionistic coding.

The categories used for coding the data will, of course, depend on the nature of the variables as well as the goals of the research. As noted earlier (section 6.2.1), some variables display relatively discrete variants that can be coded in binary terms as a choice between two possibilities. In some of these cases, the variables involve the presence versus the absence of a sound, as was seen with the (h) variable examined in table 4.1. In other cases, the choice of variants may involve alternations between two sounds (e.g., [ɪŋ]~[ɪn] in verbal *-ing* forms) or even alternations between the ordering of sounds (e.g. [æsk]~[æks] "ask"). Discrete variables may involve more than a binary choice as indicated by the example of Tyneside (o) which displayed four distinct forms (see section 4.1).

Discrete variants, as the label implies, tend to be easily distinguished and their coding is typically a relatively straightforward process. The situation is more complicated, however, with variables displaying several variants that range along a continuum. Consider, for example, the case of (æ) in the Northern Cities Shift introduced above (section 6.2.1). The raising and fronting of this vowel establishes [æ] and [ɛ]$^+$ as ends of a continuum. In treating the variable as continuous, the researcher suggests that rather than a binary choice between [æ] and [ɛ] the speaker has access to a more open-ended selection and may locate his or her production at any one of various points along the continuum. To make sense of such continuous variation, the investigator must impose some classificatory system that establishes boundaries between groups of observed forms. Thus, a coding system is developed that distinguishes points along the continuum of variation. The number of variants distinguished in this way will depend in part on the phonetic distance between the end points. A relatively great difference may allow for coding of five or more variants (i.e., the end points plus three or more forms in between), while a smaller difference may only allow for a three-way distinction. Obviously the coding system used cannot impose any more classifications than can be reliably distinguished by the researcher.

Data that have been coded auditorily can be readily quantified by simply counting the usage of each of the variants. In the case of binary variants, the results are typically presented in terms of percentage use of each form as in table 4.1. With continuous variables, it is common to use a mean score to represent a speaker's usage. Relative values are assigned to each variant according to its place on the continuum, and an index is calculated by averaging across all the coded data. In the Northern Cities Shift example, the [ɛ] variant is scored as 3, [æ] is scored as zero, and intermediate forms are scored as 1 and 2 (see section 6.2.1). An index (mean score) near zero indicates a speaker who tends to use the more conservative [æ] variant, while an index near 3 denotes someone who consistently prefers the innovative [ɛ]. The resulting measures, whether percentages or means, provide for easy comparison across speakers.

6.3.2   Instrumental techniques

A rather different approach to measuring phonological variation involves the examination of the acoustic signal using techniques and instruments adopted from laboratory phonetics. The general approach is not new even within sociolinguistics. Nevertheless, since the days of pioneering work like that of Labov, Yaeger, and Steiner (1972), this approach has become increasingly popular, due in part to technological advancements that allow spectrographic analysis to be done on a personal computer (see Thomas 2001 for a review of sociolinguistic and dialectological research using instrumental acoustic analysis).

A thorough discussion of the theoretical underpinnings of acoustic analysis lies well outside the scope of this book. Accessible introductions to this material are provided by Kent and Read (1992), Ladefoged (1993), and Johnson (1997). For the present discussion, we can note that the fundamental difference between acoustic measurement and auditory measurement is that the former involves the translation of the speech signal into a visual representation. The most common representation used is the sound spectrogram (see figure 6.1). A spectrogram shows variations of acoustic energy contained in a speech signal. The visible patterns of dark and light correspond to greater or lesser intensity of energy, respectively, and are seen to vary across time (the horizontal axis) as well as across a range of frequencies (the vertical axis).

Visual representations such as spectrograms allow the investigator to examine particular components of the speech signal in more detail than is possible with auditory techniques. Many of the variable features that are of interest to sociolinguists have acoustic correlates that can be identified in spectrograms or other representations. For example, acoustic analysis can be used to investigate consonantal features like manner of articulation

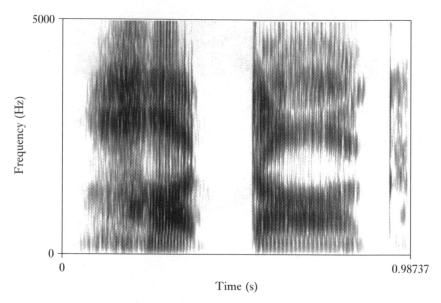

Figure 6.1   A spectrogram showing "hotdog" as produced by a male speaker

(e.g., Docherty and Foulkes 1999) as well as suprasegmental features like intonation (e.g., Yaeger-Dror 1996; Lefkowitz 1997). Working with an acoustic "picture" allows the researcher to focus attention on whichever features are of interest. More importantly, the instruments used to generate these pictures make possible precise measurement.

By far the most common use of acoustic analysis by sociolinguists has been in the study of vowels. In a spectrogram, the acoustic profile of a vowel is characterized by relatively thick, horizontal bands, called formants. These formants reflect resonances in the mouth and the pharynx and vary in frequency according to the size and shape of the vocal tract. The lowest frequency formant, called the first formant or F1, is determined in large part by the degree of openness of the mouth; the more open, the higher the frequency of F1. The second formant (F2) varies according to the size of the front oral cavity; the smaller that cavity, the higher the F2 frequency. F1 and F2 frequencies are commonly interpreted in terms of the traditional articulatory dimensions of vowel description and taken to be acoustic cor-relates of height and backness, respectively. Higher F1 frequencies are judged to indicate lower vowels while higher F2 frequencies are judged to indicate fronter vowels. Accordingly, measuring the frequencies of F1 and F2 provides the researcher with a sense of a vowel's position in vowel space. We address some of the difficulties of this interpretation in the next section.

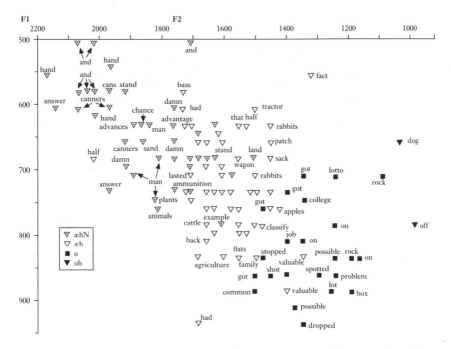

Figure 6.2   F1 and F2 frequency values of vowels as produced by a male speaker from upstate New York (from Labov 1994: 180)

Measurements from several vowel tokens can be plotted together to provide a picture of a speaker's vowel space. Often these data are presented in the form of a grid designed to parallel the traditional vowel quadrangle with F1 values along the Y axis and F2 along the X axis. Some researchers prefer to plot the difference of F2 minus F1 for the values of the X axis, arguing that this more accurately reflects perceived spacing among the vowels (Ladefoged 1993). Figure 6.2 provides an example of acoustic data presented to illustrate the relative positions of vowels. The diagram shows several tokens of /æ/, /ɑ/, and /ɔ/ plotted in an F1 by F2 grid. The data in figure 6.2 come from a male speaker from Upstate New York. One of the characteristic features of the dialect of this region is the Northern Cities Shift which involves the raising and fronting of /æ/, and these items are therefore of particular interest. While many of the /æ/ words are plotted in the middle of the graph with formant values in roughly the same range as those of the /ɑ/ items, other /æ/ words appear spread out toward the upper-left corner of the figure. The vowels in these words (e.g., *hand, and, cans, answer*) were found to have higher F2 frequencies and lower F1 frequencies, which is the expected acoustic consequence of the fronting and raising of this vowel.

6.3.3   *An evaluation of measurement techniques*

For sociolinguists interested in phonological variation, borrowing the techniques of instrumental phonetics has certainly opened new avenues for analysis. The potential benefits of this newer approach have been demonstrated by several studies (e.g., Docherty and Foulkes 1999; DiPaolo and Faber 1990), and its popularity continues to grow. In North American sociolinguistics, at least, instrumental techniques seem to have overtaken auditory methods as the dominant approach. For this reason, we offer some perspective on the relative merits of these different approaches.

Among the advantages of using instrumental techniques is the objectivity they bring to the measurement process. Judgments about a speech signal are verified by instruments rather than by human ears alone. While two listeners may hear a particular token differently, they should arrive at the same instrumental measurement assuming they follow identical procedures. Still, researchers using instrumentation are not immune to subjectivity. Consider, for example, cases of measuring formant frequencies of vowels. The values plotted in a graph like figure 6.2 come from measurements of the vowels at a particular point in the signal. The frequencies of F1 and F2 can vary greatly over the duration of a vowel, so the resulting measurements will also vary depending on where in the signal they are taken. It is crucial, therefore, that systematic procedures for instrumental measurement be established and applied consistently in order to produce meaningful results, and furthermore that these procedures be described in any reporting of the research.

Another benefit of incorporating instrumental techniques is the level of detail they make available for analysis. In some cases, acoustic methods may uncover important features that are undetectable through auditory means. A fine example is reported by Docherty and Foulkes (1999) who examined the glottalization of /t/ in Newcastle English. Auditory analysis indicated two distinct glottal forms with different linguistic and social distributions. One form was a plain glottal stop, and the other involved a combination of an oral stop with a glottal. However, close examination of the spectrographic evidence revealed a more complicated picture. First, certain acoustic elements characteristic of voiceless stops (viz., a stop gap and a period of voicelessness) were often found to be absent from the signal of tokens that appeared auditorily to be plain glottal stops. Furthermore, the other variant, which combined oral and glottal stops, was found to involve two different realizations based on the coordination of the oral and laryngeal gestures. Importantly, these two forms also showed different sociolinguistic patterning, a finding that suggests that this alternation was not a random fluctuation. It is significant that in this case the acoustic analysis did not simply reveal something that the researchers had missed in their auditory analysis. Even when returning to their data after having discovered the differences in these glottalized forms, they "did not find it at all easy to make consistent auditory discriminations of the two types, which reflects the phonetic subtlety involved in their production" (Docherty and Foulkes 1999: 57). Instrumental techniques have proven similarly useful in uncovering subtle differences in the study of reported vowel mergers (see DiPaolo and Faber 1990; Labov 1994).

On the other hand, the degree of detail made possible through instrumental analysis is not always an advantage as the precision of the measurements can make the analyst's task more difficult. We might consider, for example, the use of acoustic measurements in the study of vocalic variables. The formant frequency values associated with a particular vowel vary tremendously according to the vocal tract producing the vowel. Sex-based differences are one well-known contributor to this variation; for example, the average F2 frequency for /i/ with female speakers of English is approximately 500 Hz higher than with male speakers (Peterson and Barney 1952). The relative nature of frequency values makes cross-speaker comparison difficult. One may determine with great precision that Speaker A has an average F2 frequency of 1700 Hz for /æ/ while Speaker B's average is 2100 Hz, but these absolute values tell us nothing about the relationship between these speakers' usages. One approach to remedying this problem is through the application of some kind of normalization routine (see, e.g., Labov 2001b: 157ff). This process involves the conversion of the raw frequency values using a mathematical formula to factor out interspeaker variability resulting from physiological factors such as vocal tract size. Several techniques for normalization have been proposed (see Hindle 1978; Disner 1980; Adank, Van Heuven, and van Hout 1999 for comparative evaluations). For sociolinguists, the challenge remains that of adopting a procedure capable of normalizing away the "uninteresting" variation (i.e., that due to physiological differences) while preserving the sociolinguistically relevant variation.

In the absence of normalization, the analyst is forced to consider each speaker's vowel system on its own, noting, for example, the relative positions of the vowels. One can then make cross-speaker comparisons of these relations. Fridland (1999), for example, compares speakers based on the relative positions of several vowels involved in series of changes in American English called the "Southern Shift." One aspect of this shift is a positional flip-flop of the tense and lax front vowels, causing /e/ to be lowered and centralized while /ɛ/ is raised and peripheralized. To establish the extent of these changes, Fridland compared the frequencies of F1 and F2 for these vowels to those of a stable vowel, /ʌ/. She then used the relative distances between vowels to distinguish seven degrees of shifting across her sample of speakers.

The precise measurements that are the product of incorporating instrumental techniques can give the impression that they offer a more accurate representation of the phonological variation being studied than might be available through auditory coding. In a case such as the glottal(ized) stops discussed above (Docherty and Foulkes 1999), the acoustic picture did allow for a more precise description of the forms in use, bringing to light details that were not apparent auditorily. Whether this also results from the use of formant frequency data to represent vowels is more of an open question. One difficulty stems from the fact that, as noted above, F1 and F2 values like those plotted in figure 6.2 represent the formant structure of a vowel at a particular point in time. It is possible to take multiple measurements of a vowel at different points in its duration and to plot these together to show the trajectory of a vowel, though in practice such steps are usually only taken when analyzing diphthongal vowels (e.g., Beckford 1999; Thomas 2001). As a result, the representation of a vowel when it appears in a graph like figure 6.2 is based on a momentary "snapshot" of its structure at a specific time.

This problem is part of a much more fundamental question about the relationship between F1 and F2 measurements and perceived vowel quality. As Watt (1998) notes in his critique of dominant "sociophonetic" practices, vowel perception is a complex process that appears to rely on a wide range of elements in the speech signal. The frequencies of F1 and F2 can play a role in determining how a vowel will be heard, but they represent only part of the acoustic information carried in the signal. Many phoneticians argue that dynamic cues, such as the transitions into and out of adjacent consonants, are much more important to vowel perception (Harrington and Cassidy 1994; Ohala 1992 as cited by Watt 1998: 36–7).

A related difficulty stems from the common interpretation of F1 and F2 frequencies as correlates of vowel height and backness. Formant frequencies are certainly determined in part by the position of the tongue, but it is important to recall that other articulatory factors can influence F1 and F2. Thus, while it is true that, all things being equal, backing of the tongue body will result in lower F2 frequencies, the same acoustic effect can be caused by increased lip protrusion (as with rounding). In fact, increased lip rounding tends to lower all formants, as does lowering of the larynx. Researchers should bear in mind the uncertainties inherent in the formant model when they interpret acoustic observations in articulatory terms.

Using auditory analysis, the coder makes judgments about vowel quality based on the entire speech signal – that is, using the same input available to the listeners in the community being investigated. It is certainly true that coders would not be able to make such fine-grained distinctions between sounds as is possible with instrumentation. Nevertheless, the fact that such distinctions are available in the signal does not mean that they play a role in hearers' perception. By the same token, the fact that a trained coder can consistently distinguish variants audiorily does not necessarily mean that naïve hearers perceive those distinctions. The challenge for all researchers lies in establishing that the differences identified by the analysis are in fact the same ones that are relied upon by members of the speech community.

Auditory analysis has certain practical advantages over instrumental techniques. While spectrographic analysis can now be performed on personal computers using a variety of software products,[5] this equipment is more costly than the tape-player, which is all that is needed for auditory coding. Instrumental methods may also require a greater investment in technical training depending on the nature of the analysis. Even with training and experience, the measurement process is generally more time-consuming when instrumentation is used. Perhaps as a consequence of this, researchers employing instrumental techniques typically analyze fewer tokens than those relying on auditory techniques. For example, using auditory coding, Gordon (2001b: 47) analyzed an average of approximately 50 to 90 tokens of each of six vocalic variables for each speaker in his study of the Northern Cities Shift. Thus, a total of roughly 400 items was coded for each subject. By contrast, Fridland (1999) took instrumental measurements of around 100 items per speaker for her investigation of the Southern Shift. Since she examines 13 variables, Fridland's description of each vowel in a speaker's system is based on an average of fewer than 10 tokens. Even in large-scale projects using instrumental analysis, such as Labov's study of Philadelphia, 10 to 20 tokens of a given variable per speaker are often felt to suffice (Labov 2001b: 133).

The major concerns with auditory analysis involve questions of reliability. In contrast to the objectivity that is a principal benefit of instrumental measurement, auditory judgments are open to greater subjectivity. The potential for such problems is greater with continuous variables than with discrete variables whose variants are generally easier to distinguish. One way of reducing these risks is to analyze a greater number of tokens. The statistical impact of two or three mislabeled tokens is much less when these few occur in a pool of 70 than in a pool of 20. Another important remedy is to utilize multiple coders for the same data. If a second coder analyzes even a sample of the data, this can serve as an important check on the reliability of the coding. Choosing coders who have some training in phonetics, but are not familiar with the particular sociolinguistic variables under investigation, can help to reduce the risk of researcher bias influencing the results.

Although the preceding discussion has framed auditory and instrumental techniques in opposition to each other, it is important to note that these approaches are by no means mutually exclusive. Several studies have shown the fruitfulness of a methodology that incorporates elements of both. The acoustic work on glottalization reported by Docherty and Foulkes (1999) was part of a larger survey of Tyneside speech, much of which involved data that were coded auditorily (see Watt and Milroy 1999; Milroy et al. 1994; Docherty et al. 1997). Similarly, Gordon (2001b) used instrumental measures (F1 and F2 frequencies) to verify the multidirectionality of certain vowel movements in the Northern Cities Shift though the quantitative evidence examining the sociolinguistic distributions of these variables came from auditory coding. Ultimately, the choice of how to measure the variation in the data depends on the nature of the linguistic variables and the aims of the research. By understanding the strengths and weaknesses of the different techniques available, investigators can explore ways of combining them in order to gain the benefits of both approaches.

6.4   The Linguistic Analysis of Phonological Variables

The search for patterning in the distribution of a given variable must begin with a thorough linguistic analysis. The investigator cannot make cross-speaker comparisons without first understanding the linguistic dimensions of the variation. This entails establishing the boundaries of a variable's influence on the linguistic system and ascertaining the factors that influence the variation.

6.4.1   Defining the range of variation

Establishing the range of variation associated with a given variable is an essential first step in the linguistic analysis. The researcher needs to know what is and what is not involved with the variable under study. For phonological variables, this means knowing which words or contexts are subject to variation and which are not. Quantitative analysis cannot proceed until the investigator knows what to count.

Phonological variables differ greatly in the extent of their influence on the language system. At one extreme, they may involve the pronunciation of a single word (e.g., [ænt~ant] "aunt;" [æsk~æks] "ask" (Gordon 2000)). At the other extreme, thousands of words may be affected if the variable involves a general phonological process. Such is the case with (æ) in the Northern Cities Shift, as this variable involves the unconditioned raising and fronting of /æ/, meaning that all words containing this very common phoneme may undergo the process. The influence on the phonological system is seen as even greater if we accept the interrelatedness of the (æ) variation with the variation of other elements in the Northern Cities Shift such as (ɑ) and (ɔ) (see Labov 1994; Gordon 2001a, 2001b).

Intermediate between these extremes are cases involving more restricted phonological processes. For example, in New York City (Labov 1966) and Cincinnati (Boberg and Strassel 2000) /æ/ undergoes raising like that heard in the Northern Cities Shift though this variation only applies when /æ/ appears in certain phonological contexts. Similarly, throughout the American South, the distinction between /ɛ/ and /ɪ/ is lost before a nasal consonant (the "*pin/pen* merger").

In all these examples the task of defining the range of variation is fairly straightforward. The input for each variable, the set of items participating in the variation, is readily specifiable as a particular word, as a phonemic word class, or as a clearly delineated subset of a phonemic class. In some cases, however, the range of a variable is not an easily defined lexical set; it is not equivalent to that of any phoneme and may not even be phonologically predictable. A very clear example is the Belfast variable (u) which alternates between [ʌ] and [ʉ]. In the urban dialect of Belfast, as in most varieties of English, there is a word class of /ʌ/ consisting of items such as *cut, mud, fun*. There is also an /ʉ/ class consisting of items such as *good, food, cook, would*. There is no word class corresponding to RP /ʊ/, so that, for example, the two lexical items in the phrase *good food* are assigned in Belfast to the same rather than to different classes as in RP /gʊd fuːd/.

There is, however, a small set of lexical items which alternates between the phonetically quite distinct classes /ʉ/ and /ʌ/. The total membership of this third class cannot be predicted on phonological grounds, nor reliably specified by appealing to the intuitions of native speakers. For example, *foot, took, shook, look* have all been attested as alternating between [ʌ] and [ʉ], while *soot, cook, book, hook* seem always to be pronounced with [ʉ], at least in Belfast; the situation differs in some rural areas. The alternating set is sociolinguistically very salient, varying according to class, sex and speech style; all the items in it occur frequently and the [ʌ] variant is a stereotypical vernacular pronunciation carrying strong symbolic value.

Precisely because the composition of such "phonolexical" sets cannot be specified on phonological grounds, it is difficult to find a principled way of specifying the lexical input to such a variable as Belfast (u); in this case, the researchers eventually assigned 18 words to the set simply on the basis of observation (see further Milroy 1992: 159). Since speakers' intuitions cannot easily be accessed to define the membership of sets such as these, it is difficult to see what alternative procedure might have been adopted.

Problems of this kind are likely to be particularly common in "divergent dialect" areas (Johnston 1983) where two identifiable and radically different phonologies have in the past influenced each other, later to become an integrated part of the linguistic resources available to the speech community (see Macaulay 1978 for similar Scottish examples). But, difficulties of the same general type which spring from the apparently idiosyncratic behavior of lexical items are also reported in the United States. Perhaps the best known of such examples is the behavior of (æ) in Mid-Atlantic cities such as New York and Philadelphia (see Labov 1972b: 73–4, 1994: 430–4). This vowel is variably tensed and raised under conditions that are partly predictable phonologically. For example, tensing regularly occurs when the vowel precedes the nasal consonants /m/ and /n/ (e.g., *ham, hand*) but never when it precedes voiceless stops (e.g., *map, mat*). There are, however, a number of lexical exceptions to the phonological rules. In New York, tensing before voiced fricatives is not usual but does occur in the word *avenue*. Similarly, in Philadelphia, (æ) is normally lax before voiced stops as in *dad* and *sad* though tensing is found in the items *mad, bad*, and *glad*. This fact is crucial to the thrust of Payne's analysis of dialect acquisition patterns by out-of-state children (Payne 1980: 165; see also section 2.4). Trudgill (1983: 88) reports similar cases in relation to an ongoing vocalic merger in East Anglia.

Although difficulties in reliably specifying the appropriate lexical input to phonological variables are reasonably well documented, they may be more widespread and pose a greater methodological problem than these rather scattered observations in the literature suggest. Such cases are of great theoretical importance in discussions of models of variation and change which are based on the notion of *lexical diffusion* (Chen 1976; Wang 1969; Labov 1981, 1994). They underscore the importance of considering various kinds of influence when seeking patterns in variable data.

6.4.2   Conditioning factors

The heart of the linguistic analysis of a variable is uncovering the factors that favor and disfavor the associated variants. Phonological variables are very often influenced by their immediate phonetic context. In the Northern Cities Shift, for example, (ɛ) displays variation in two directions: sometimes backing and sometimes lowering (Gordon 2001b; Eckert 2000). Backed variants are favored when the vowel precedes an /l/ (e.g., *bell*) while lowered variants are more common preceding velars (e.g., *beg, heck*). At the same time, adjacent palatal consonants (e.g., *mesh, yet*) appear to disfavor shifting of (ɛ) in any direction. Such statements about the phonological conditioning of a variable need to be distinguished from the previous discussion (section 6.4.1) about range of a variable's influence. Rather than delineating the variable's scope – what it affects and what it does not affect – the kinds of observations discussed here are meant to describe the relative strength of factors in shaping the variation. These are statements of probability rather than possibility; thus, the observation that adjacent palatals disfavor (ɛ) shifting does not imply that the vowel is never shifted in this context, but only that shifting is less likely here.

In addition to adjacent segments, conditioning may be found in other aspects of the phonological context. Syllable structure, for example, has been found to be an important element shaping vocalic variation in Philadelphia. Labov (1994: 57ff) distinguishes between free (open) and checked (closed) syllables in his analysis of the fronting of the back vowels (uw) and (ow). This distinction also applies in the case of the notoriously complex (æ) variable which only appears as tense in closed syllables.[6] Similar examples are found in Belfast (see Milroy 1992: 105).

Many cases of phonological conditioning have clear phonetic motivations, one such case being the backing of (ɛ) before /l/. Backing appears to be a coarticulatory effect caused by the velarized /l/. Alternatively, it might be explained in acoustic terms: the lowering of F2 frequency in the vowel, which is a correlate of backing, results from the influence of /l/, a consonant characterized by a low F2.[7] Kerswill (1987), following Dressler and Wodak (1982), describes such variation as resulting from connected speech processes. These include phenomena such as deletions and assimilations characteristic of allegro speech. Examples from RP and some other varieties of English are the alternation at syllable boundaries between alveolars and palatals ([dɪdjuː]~[dɪdʒuː], "did you") and alternation in similar contexts between alveolar and bilabial ([hɒt biːnz]~[hɒp biːnz], "hot beans"). In both examples the alveolar is assimilated to the place of articulation of the following segment. Another example is variable deletion of both voiced and voiceless alveolar stops in certain contexts ([fas(t)nɪs], "fastness"; [sɛn(d) miː], "send me").

Despite their apparent "naturalness," these processes are variety-specific. For example, one common process in Durham English is voicing assimilation at syllable boundaries ("scraped [bd] down") while the place of articulation assimilation characteristic of RP is not found (Kerswill 1987: 44). Thus, while conditioning patterns may be phonetically motivated, they are not wholly determined by such processes. Social forces may intervene in ways that directly contradict "natural" phonetic developments. Eckert (1991), for example, reports that the usual backing of (ɛ) among some of her Northern Cities Shift speakers was often replaced by lowering when the vowel appeared before /l/, a context that should favor backing. Eckert suggests that this unusual tendency stems from the group's desire to mark their usage as distinct. Precisely because backing before /l/ is so common, it had apparently lost its ability to carry social meaning, and the speakers had to resort to a phonetically unexpected combination.

Phonological factors are not the only type of linguistic conditioning on variables. Some patterns may be defined in lexical terms. For example, Neu's (1980) analysis of final stop deletion suggests that some words are affected by the process more than others. Thus, for example, inclusion of the frequently occurring item *and*, which shows high frequency deletion, skews the data considerably; for this reason, Labov excluded *and* from his original study of final stop deletion (Labov 1980: xvi). In another example pertaining to final stop deletion, Fasold (1978) has remarked on the idiosyncratic behavior of the item *kept*, where [t] is almost always deleted. Because of the frequent occurrence of *kept*, this causes difficulties in quantitative analysis. The literature on final stop deletion also illustrates the influence of another type of factor: morphological context. As Guy (1980) demonstrates, deletion is more likely in monomorphemic words (e.g., *mist*) than when the consonant cluster is created by the addition of an inflectional morpheme (e.g., *missed*). Even elements of the discourse context have been found in some cases to play a role shaping phonological variation. In their study of glottalization, Docherty et al. (1997) describe how certain speakers seem to utilize alternative realizations of /t/ as part of a conversational strategy for managing turn-taking. Local, Kelly, and Wells (1986) discuss similar examples from this field which they term *phonology of conversation*.

In practice, it may not always be easy to determine the nature of influence on a particular variable. Consider the case of (ɪ), a variable that undergoes centralization as part of the Northern Cities Shift. In his phonological analysis, Gordon (2001b: 159) identified the context of preceding palatals as one that favors shifting of this vowel. However, many of the items counted for that analysis were tokens of the word *children*. It is possible that the relatively high rate of centralization for this word was actually an effect of the /l/ that follows the vowel, since this context was also found to promote shifting. On the other hand, the effect might be lexical – a suggestion that is made more plausible by the behavior of the word *kid*. This semantically similar item was also found to have a centralized vowel at a very high rate. In the case of *kid* a phonological explanation is less plausible; for example, no other words with preceding velars (e.g., *kick*) were produced with a shifted variant. Still, the numbers that this particular analysis dealt with were fairly small in some cases, owing to the infrequency of particular phonological combinations in everyday speech. Ultimately, the questions raised here would probably be resolved with more data.

6.5   The Relationships among Variants: Issues of Interpretation

The distinction presented earlier (section 6.2.1) between discrete and continuous variables is useful as an introduction to different ways of approaching variation. We should remember, however, that both of these categories are methodological conveniences; they offer the investigator a means of analyzing the data, but they may not accurately describe the relationships among the variants involved. We have already hinted at this by noting that binary discrete variables (e.g., (aj) monophthongization) often involve intermediate forms that are ignored or lumped with another variant. We discuss here some of the difficulties inherent in the notion of continuous variables.

The idea of the sociolinguistic variable whose variants are assumed to lie on single co-extensive phonetic and social dimensions has been criticized by (among others) Hudson and Holloway (1977), Romaine (1978), and Knowles (1978). One objection is the loss of potentially important phonological information when phonological elements that vary on more than one dimension are analyzed as varying only on a single dimension. For example, in the Northern Cities Shift (æ) undergoes raising, which is sometimes accompanied by ingliding (e.g., [bɛək] "back"). The scale used by Gordon (2001b) distinguished four degrees of raising (see section 6.2.1) but did not code for the presence or absence of a diphthongal vowel. The same is true of Labov's treatment of (æ) in New York City. Treating the data in this way allowed speakers to be compared in terms of index scores along a continuum; however, any information about the distribution of the diphthongal forms was sacrificed in the process.

Interestingly, the use of instrumental acoustic measurements of vocalic variables like (æ) offers only a minor improvement on this score. The view offered by F1 and F2 frequencies allows for more nuanced displays of variation occupying both the front–back and high–low dimensions. Nevertheless, other distinctions of variants are not easily displayed. It is possible to include information in an F1 by F2 plot about the presence of an accompanying glide for each token measured, though it is often not practical owing to the clutter it would introduce to the picture.[8] For other acoustic elements including fundamental frequency, the frequencies of other formants, and vowel length, there is no simple way of integrating such information with the F1 and F2 data into a single visual representation like figure 6.2. Thus, with these methods too, potentially relevant dimensions of variation may be omitted from consideration unless the investigators look beyond the basic picture (see, e.g., DiPaolo and Faber 1990).

A second, related, objection has been advanced of the assumption that variants of a variable lie along a single *sociolinguistic* dimension of nonstandard to standard, which in turn co-varies with a single phonetic dimension. Labov's treatment of (æ) in New York City (1966) reflected this assumption. Researchers working in, for example, Liverpool, Glasgow, Edinburgh, or Belfast (described by Johnston (1983) as "divergent dialect" areas) experienced difficulties in attempting to adapt Labov's approach because in these areas there is a sharp discontinuity between the local vernacular and any recognizable supralocal spoken norm. One consequence of this discontinuity is a difficulty in identifying the prestige forms that should be placed at the "standard" end of the continuum. While, for example, the influence of Received Pronunciation is consistent and considerable in Norwich, researchers such as Romaine (1978; see also section 6.2.2 above) and Macaulay (1977) encountered difficulties in applying the concept of a *single* prestige norm in Scotland. These cases illustrate some of the difficulties in working with the notion of "prestige" particularly in assuming a uniform and direct connection between prestige and social class (see further sections 4.3 and 5.3).

The multidimensional character of sociolinguistic variation was exemplified earlier with the discussion of Newcastle (o) (section 4.1). The four variants [œ, oː, oə, and ou], are distinguished phonetically in a number of different ways; they involve differences of length, frontness, and diphthongal versus monophthongal quality. There is no clear phonetic scale onto which they could be placed. Socially, too, there seems to be little justification for positing a single continuum for these variants as each form has its own associations. Therefore, the investigators sought to avoid any implication of a continuum by calculating the usage for each variant separately. A further advantage of this method is that it readily illuminates the relationships between particular phonetic forms and particular groups of speakers. Consider, for example, the gender patterns from tables 4.2 and 4.3 where women are shown to prefer overwhelmingly the monophthongal [oː] while men's usage is more divided. The interpretation of the results is made easier by the retention of the phonetic information, the specifics of which would probably have been lost had the variable been treated as continuous. In choosing the widely distributed northern form [oː], the Newcastle women illustrate the general trend toward accent leveling in which local forms are replaced by those with broader regional currency (see Watt and Milroy 1999; also section 5.3).

The general point to take from this discussion is that the way in which investigators conceive of the relationship among variants can have a profound impact on the entire analysis. The same can also be said about the relationship among variables: while many phonological variables seem to operate independently, others seem to be interlinked. Chain shifts represent a prime case in point. The notion of a chain shift implies a series of related sound changes that are causally connected, the most familiar examples involving vowels shifting about in phonetic space. The connections among changes are traditionally seen as being of two types: (1) one vowel encroaches upon the territory of another causing the latter to vacate the space; or (2) a vowel vacates its original space thereby creating an opening into which a nearby vowel shifts to fill. Those of type 1 are known as "push" chains and those of type 2 as "drag" chains. The chain shift model clearly implies that a relationship of some kind obtains among the shifting elements though the nature of the putative connections is the subject of ongoing debate (see Labov 1994; Gordon 2001a, 2001b).

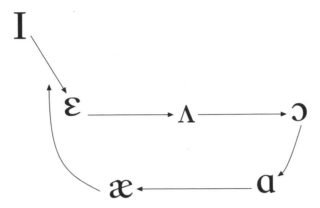

Figure 6.3   The vowel changes of the Northern Cities Shift (after Labov 1994: 191)

To illustrate how the adoption of this model might influence a researcher's analysis we consider the now familiar case of the Northern Cities Shift (NCS). Labov (1994) discusses the NCS as an example of chain shifting and represents the changes roughly as depicted in figure 6.3. The arrows in this figure are meant to indicate the paths followed by the shifting vowels and thus the connections among them. For example, (ɛ) is connected to both (ɪ) and (ʌ). According to Labov's suggested chronology of these changes (see Labov 1994: 195), (ɛ) was originally lowered (not depicted here) to create a drag chain with (ɪ) then later underwent backing to create a push chain with (ʌ).

A researcher investigating the NCS in a given community would naturally listen for the expected variation: lowering of (ɪ), backing of (ʌ), backing and possibly lowering of (ɛ). What, however, should he or she do with forms that are not predicted by the chain shift model, such as backed variants of (ɪ) or lowered variants of (ʌ)? One might exclude such forms from consideration and base the analysis only on the patterns conforming to the chain shift model. In doing so, however, the researcher assumes that the alternative trajectories are unrelated to the "main" directions of shifting – a dangerous and unwarranted assumption that few if any sociolinguists would make. As an alternative, the researcher might include all the evidence in the analysis but ignore or downplay the significance of the unexpected trajectories by grouping those data in with the rest. In this case the assumption is that these are minor tendencies without any sociolinguistic relevance, which, again, is a dangerous assumption. The recommended approach records all the variation to allow for the sociolinguistic analysis of each form. Only with this complete picture can an accurate sense of the relationships among variables be obtained. In a case such as this, the picture may challenge the

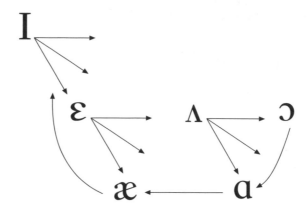

Figure 6.4   Another view of the Northern Cities Shift (after Gordon 2001b: 197)

previous interpretation that the variables are involved in a chain shift. Gordon (2001b: 217), faced with the evidence of the alternative trajectories illustrated in figure 6.4, suggested that the movements of (ε), (ɪ), and (ʌ) were linked, not by chain shifting, but rather by a kind of parallelism whereby a pattern of multidirectional variation had been analogized to these three vowels. The variables are apparently related, just not in the way described by the chain shift model.

A relationship of a rather different sort is illustrated by the case of mergers. Mergers involve the loss of a phonemic contrast. Unconditional mergers result in the loss of the contrast throughout the language as two (or more) phonemes become one. The merger of the low back vowels of *cot* and *caught* – a development characteristic of Scottish dialects that is also very widespread throughout North America (see Labov, Ash, and Boberg, forthcoming) – operates unconditionally. With conditioned mergers, on the other hand, the loss occurs only in particular phonological contexts. For example, in the American South and West the contrast between the tense and lax vowels /i~ɪ/, /u~ʊ/, and /e~ε/ is variably lost when the vowels appear in the context of a following /l/ (*feel = fill, fool = full, fail = fell*) (see Labov 1994; DiPaolo and Faber 1990).

For researchers investigating ongoing mergers the situation is more complicated than the usual phonological account suggests. The loss of contrast affects both production and perception, and researchers must examine both dimensions. When speakers have merged two sounds, it is assumed that they have lost the ability to produce the distinction in their own speech as well as perceive the distinction in the speech of others. Labov has pioneered a number of procedures to investigate the status of mergers in individual speakers (see Labov 1994: 353–6; Gordon 2001a), and this line of research has revealed something quite unexpected: speakers who perceive two sounds as merged but regularly produce the sounds as distinct. How people can produce a distinction they do not hear is a question that remains to be answered. These cases are known as "near" or "apparent" mergers; they are of great theoretical interest as they may help to explain some historical problems (see Labov 1994: 371–90). The general point to be made here is that these cases illustrate a previously unimagined relationship among variables – one that was uncovered by looking beyond the standard accounts.

6.6   Comments about Quantification

We close this chapter by considering some issues related to the quantitative analysis of language data. Much of our discussion has already touched on questions of quantification as this matter is central to any account of sociolinguistic methodology. Since a detailed account of the multifaceted topic of quantification is beyond the scope of this book, we will concentrate in this section on picking out general principles of particular relevance to sociolinguists, referring as appropriate to more specialist treatments. Fuller treatments of many of these issues are offered by Hudson (1996), Fasold (1984), Wolfram (1993b), and Guy (1993). Our discussion will be illustrated with phonological examples though many of the issues are equally relevant to the study of syntactic and other variables.

6.6.1   Counting matters

Behind the apparently straightforward process of assigning numbers to variants of a variable in such a way as to reflect, reasonably faithfully, their phonetic and social relationships with each other there lies a great deal of linguistic, sociological and mathematical abstraction. Labov has commented that

> even the simplest type of counting raises a number of subtle and difficult problems. The final decision as to what to count is actually the solution to the problem in hand; this decision is taken only through a long series of complicated exploratory maneuvers. (Labov 1972b: 82)

The form taken by some of these "exploratory maneuvers" was outlined earlier (sections 6.2.2 and 6.2.3). We discuss here some of "the subtle and difficult problems" associated with the process of counting. As our discussion in the next chapter indicates (see section 7.4.2), many of the problems are even more acute in the study of syntactic variables.

In the analysis of even the most straightforward variables, the researcher faces numerous choices about what and how to count. Moreover, the decisions made have often profound effects on the results and their interpretation. Some of the decisions might be anticipated before the analysis begins though many questions arise as the investigator becomes more familiar with the data.

Consider the procedures followed in the analysis of the Northern Cities Shift (NCS) by Gordon (2001b). Because the NCS changes potentially affect all instances of the six vowels involved (see figure 6.3) – compared to changes that operate with greater phonological or lexical restrictions (e.g., Philadelphia (æ)) – the identification of items to count was relatively simple. If one of the six vowel phonemes occurred in a word, that word was to be included in the analysis. Before coding began, several exceptions to this basic rule were anticipated, including the following:

- Only stressed syllables were coded because of their greater audibility.
- Items pronounced too quickly, too quietly, or with background noise were excluded as not audible enough for reliable coding.
- Words in which the variable appeared before /r/ were excluded because this consonant often influences vowel quality in ways unrelated to the NCS.

During coding, a number of exceptions related to individual lexical items were formulated. For example, the words *milk* and *Illinois* had to be omitted from consideration. They demonstrated variation between [ɪ] and [ɛ], as is expected with the NCS. However, this alternation is fairly widespread in American dialects and its appearance could not be reliably linked to the NCS. In some cases, items had to be omitted because of uncertainty about which variable/phoneme they represented. Thus, tokens of the word *Chicago* were not included in the counts because speakers were found to variably classify the stressed vowel as either /ɑ/ or /ɔ/. If a speaker pronounced this word as [ʃə'kɑgo], it might represent a conservative token of (ɑ) or an innovative token of (ɔ).

Acknowledging the inevitability of such complications during the counting process, Wolfram advises researchers to "make principled decisions, keep a record of each of these decisions, and then follow them procedurally in a consistent way" (1993b: 210). It is also essential that a full account of the procedures be given when the results are reported.

One common decision faced when analyzing phonological variation is whether to limit the number of tokens examined for a particular item. In striving for comparability across speakers, the investigator wants to avoid potential linguistic bias in the speech samples. This bias might be phonologically or lexically based. Recall, for example, the observation that backing of (ɛ) in the Northern Cities Shift is strongly favored in the environment of a following /l/. If the coded speech sample from one speaker contains a high number of tokens of the word *bell* and the sample from another speaker contains no tokens of *bell* or any other items with /ɛl/, then, all else being equal, the first speaker's calculated rate of shifting for this variable is likely to be higher. The difference, however, is a reflection of a phonological pattern and has nothing to do with the speakers. Recall that the principle of accountability, which obliges the researcher to consider all potential occurrences of the variable and not handpick those confirming his or her hypothesis, is designed to reduce the danger of skewed data. Still, this danger is not completely eliminated. There are various reasons why a particular word might be especially common in the section of speech to be analyzed (e.g., the speaker described his *bell* collection). To address this problem, researchers often impose limits on the number of occurrences of a word/morpheme that they will count. Gordon (2001b), for example, only considered the first three tokens of an item in his analysis of each speaker's usage. The same approach was taken by Wolfram (1969) in his approach to final stop deletion in Detroit, but, as Wolfram later notes (1993b), the choice of taking three tokens instead of two or four or five was essentially arbitrary. Investigators should consider the total number of tokens to be coded for each speaker in deciding where to establish lexical limits. Three tokens can introduce more bias into a pool of 20 occurrences than into a pool of 50 or more (see section 6.6.2).

Imposing limits such as these helps to ensure that the description of each subject's speech is based on a lexically varied sample which, in turn, should represent a greater diversity of phonological contexts. In this way, it seeks to equalize the influence of linguistic factors across all speakers so that they can be compared for their social characteristics. For this same reason, such limits may not be appropriate when the investigation is in the stage of linguistic analysis (see Gordon 2001b: 60). The finding that a particular variant is overwhelmingly associated with a particular lexical item across a sample of speakers is relevant to understanding the factors conditioning the variation. If limits are imposed, it will be harder to recognize lexical patterning. Nevertheless, the inclusion of all the available data can present problems of interpretation similar to those discussed earlier with regard to (1) in the NCS (section 6.4.2). It may be difficult to disentangle phonological from lexical patterns if the pool of data is dominated by a limited number of words.

6.6.2 How many tokens are needed?

This question needs to be tackled if we are to be reasonably certain that observed variation reflects a speaker's norm rather than random fluctuation in the data. By implication it is raised, but not dealt with, by Labov's statement of the principle of accountability; simply to note all occurrences of variants without further considering the size of "the section of speech being examined" is plainly insufficient. For example, if we are examining a rather impoverished little text containing only five tokens of (h) of which four are realized as [h] and one as zero, a speaker score of 20 percent on this variable is hardly meaningful, even within a single social context, as a characterization of normal language use. It is likely that if five other tokens were considered from a different section of text gathered in a comparable social context, the score would turn out to be very different – say, 80 per-cent. While this might seem to be stating the obvious, the fact is that this issue has not received a great deal of systematic (as opposed to *post hoc*) discussion in the literature. Exceptions to this generalization are Guy (1980, 1993), Romaine (1980: 190–3), and Wolfram (1993b).

Using a detailed study of final stop deletion to exemplify a more general principle, Guy suggests that 30 tokens per variable is a reasonable objective. As he points out, $N = 30$ is an important dividing line in statistics generally between large and small samples. Different parametric tests of significance are used for samples above and below this figure, which take account of different relationships to the population from which they are drawn (Butler 1985: 79–97). In fact the data presented by Guy seem to conform to general statistical laws; if the number of tokens is lower than 10, there is a strong likelihood of random fluctuation, while a figure higher than 10 moves towards 90 percent conformity with the predicted norm, rising to 100 percent with 35 tokens. These observations usefully demonstrate the hazards of working with fewer than 10 tokens; the ideal appears to be around 30, but if this cannot be attained a figure as much as possible in excess of 10 is a sensible goal. It is, however, assumed that the total N will not be subdivided to examine the effect of (for example) linguistic environment; in that case the ideal figure would be 30 tokens per environment, bringing the total for the variable as a whole to a figure proportionate to the number of environments examined. The same is true of a total which is subdivided for any other pur-pose: for example, to examine the effects of style. In general, more tokens are needed if relationships among several variables at once are to be examined (Erickson and Nosanchuk 1992: 131).

6.6.3   Use of statistical analysis

The traditional approach to statistical analysis is to use one of a range of tools to test for "significance" as a means of indicating whether or not an explicitly formulated hypothesis can be upheld; Fasold (1984: ch. 4) dis-cusses the application of this general method in sociolinguistics. The difficulty with standard significance tests is that their valid and effective use usually depends on the way the data are approached – for example, whether the research has been designed with a specific hypothesis in mind or a less-focused *post hoc* analysis is being carried out with a view to revealing underlying patterns. The logic of significance testing with respect to this type of issue is discussed by Erickson and Nosanchuk (1992: ch. 8), Butler (1985: ch. 6), and Woods, Fletcher, and Hughes (1986: ch. 8). The use of tests also depends upon certain assumptions about the nature of the data, such as whether or not it is normally distributed, is of roughly equal within-group variability, and reflects independent observations. Some tests such as analysis of variance are fairly robust in that they permit violation of such assumptions, while others are not. Butler (1985) and Woods, Fletcher, and Hughes (1986) provide a clear account of the assumptions underlying a number of different tests.

It is relatively easy, with a minimum of statistical or computational knowledge, to use the facilities of a statistical package for computer analysis – such as SPSS (Statistical Package for the Social Sciences) or Minitab – to carry out a wide range of tests. It is, however, important that users of these powerful facilities have adequate knowledge of the principles upon which statistical testing is based. The limitations and advantages of the selected procedure need to be understood, and the purpose of the analysis should be carefully specified. Exactly the same comments apply to powerful programs like David Sankoff's Varbrul, which are designed specifically for sociolinguistic analysis. Both the mathematical assumptions and the assumptions concerning the nature of the linguistic input which underlie the program need to be appreciated before the researcher can decide on its suitability for a particular analytic purpose. Guy (1980, 1993) gives a detailed account of the logic, limitations and applications of Varbrul, while a number of papers in Sankoff (1978) discuss various details of its design and application. Horvath (1985: 59) provides a useful critical account of the advantages and limitations of Varbrul, and a comparison of the Varbrul technique with Principal Components Analysis (see below). A helpful guide on how to use the program is provided as an appendix by Bayley and Preston (1996).

If any benefit is to be derived from statistical analysis, it is important to define the nature of the problem then find the most appropriate way of solving it. Since defining the problem can implicate a whole range of linguistic and social issues such as those discussed in this and earlier chapters, decisions about appropriate methods of statistical analysis cannot be made in isolation. This is perhaps best demonstrated by citing four specific and very different examples, which should also give some indication of the wide range of problems that can be illuminated by an appropriate statistical analysis.

One part of the Belfast analysis was concerned with the relationship between linguistic variable scores and social network scores, the hypothesis being that the two sets of scores were related. The statistical test which measures the strength of the relationship between paired sets of observations of this kind is a *correlation* test, and a large number of these tests were carried out to investigate the relationship (see Milroy 1987; Fasold 1984: 102–8). The decision to investigate this relationship in the first place was bound up with theories of the social function of close-knit networks (see section 5.2).

A rather different problem to which a different statistical analysis was appropriate is reported by Nagy (2001) who examined the merger of the vowels of *father* and *bother* in New England. Nagy hypothesized that a change is in progress among residents of southern New Hampshire who are adopting the merger. To test this hypothesis she divided her survey respondents into two age groups (under and over 50 years old) and used the chi-square test to look for differences between them. This commonly used test looks for interdependence in the distribution of data across the parameters of interest (Fasold 1984: 95). In this case, it demonstrated that presence of the merger was significantly more likely for younger respondents.

A common problem faced when analyzing complex variation is how to weigh the relative influence of several factors. In his social analysis of Northern Cities Shift data, for example, Gordon (2001b) needed to examine potential effects of age, sex, and location (comparing the two towns studied). To do so, a multiway analysis of variance (ANOVA) was performed for each variable. This procedure takes into consideration all factors at once. As Guy (1993: 237) explains, it produces more accurate results than examining each factor individually, "because while computing the effect of one independent variable [e.g., age], it explicitly controls for the effect of all other known independent variables." It also examines possible interactional effects among variables. Such an effect was found in the analysis of (ɪ) for which sex and age showed significant interaction. Shifting of the vowel was more common among women than girls but also more common among boys than men (Gordon 2001b: 100).

A very different approach to statistical analysis is illustrated by the sociolinguistic survey of Sydney, Australia. Here, a technique known as *Principal Components Analysis* (PCA) (Horvath 1985: 53; Horvath and Sankoff 1987) was used to examine the hypothesis that groups of speakers would show certain similarities in their linguistic behavior. The only input to the program was individual linguistic data, and the procedure was particularly suitable in view of the difficulties in Sydney of grouping speakers according to class (see section 2.6). Speaker variables were used to interpret the results of the analysis rather than as an input to it, and in fact speakers did fall into ethnic, status, and age groups (cf. Le Page and Tabouret-Keller 1985: 127ff).

Figure 6.5 illustrates the type of pattern revealed by PCA. Individual speakers are represented by dots, the only input to the program being a

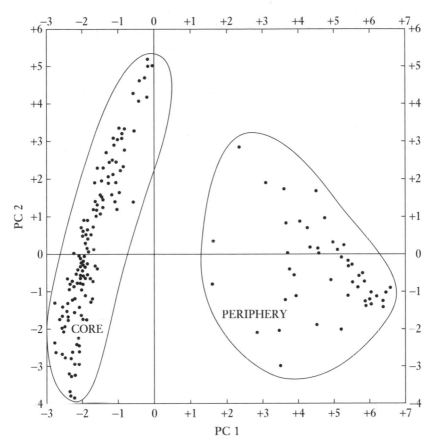

Key: PC = Principal Component

Figure 6.5   The Sydney speech community: core and periphery (after Horvath 1985: 71)

linguistic score on five vowel variables (see further Horvath 1985: 70). The program plots speakers in terms of their scores on two principal components, represented as axes of the graph. These components are interpreted in social terms *after* the analysis by considering the social characteristics of the speakers who have been sorted on the basis of their linguistic behavior into the two groups (periphery and core) which emerge in figure 6.5. In fact, Principal Component 1 divides speakers by ethnic group, distinguishing non-English-accented from Australian English-accented speakers. Principal Component 2, the vertical axis, distinguishes sociolects within the continuum of traditional Australian English accents.

The decision to use PCA in Sydney was related to an awareness of the problems of defining speaker variables (cf. chapters 4 and 5), and in fact the Sydney project is a particularly clear example of the interdependence between different stages of the research. The ultimate analytic method was chosen to take account both of sampling problems in the field and theoretical problems associated with speaker variables.

As these examples have suggested, statistical analysis can be a powerful aid in analyzing sociolinguistic variation. Nevertheless, it is important to maintain perspective and not expect this mechanical aid, however useful, to answer all questions. To illustrate this point we consider briefly the relationship between sample size and probability calculations. The threshold of statistical significance is generally easier to achieve with larger samples since, as noted above, they involve less random fluctuation in their distribution. Davis (1990: 26–9) demonstrates this with a hypothetical example involving deletion of post-vocalic /r/. Imagine two samples of fairly large size, $N = 100$ and $N = 50$, for which the mean rates of r-lessness are 24 and 22 percent respectively. While the percentage difference seems small, it does reach statistical significance at the level of $p < 0.05$. However, if these same means were based instead on smaller samples of 32 and 33, the results are not deemed significant. Nevertheless, should we equate failure to achieve statistical significance with sociolinguistic irrelevance? By the same token, should we assume that significant results reflect salient sociolinguistic patterns? Our general point is that statistical tests, like all quantitative procedures are tools to provide insight into patterning in variation. They must be used critically. As Wolfram (1993b: 203) comments:

> I personally feel that the current emphasis on variable manipulation simply through the production of more powerful computer programs runs the risk of turning variation studies into a type of methodological reductionism, camouflaged by the sophistication of the quantitative management programs. . . . [I]t is important for language variationists to be good linguists and good sociolinguists, not simply good collectors of data or good number crunchers.

This discussion of quantification concludes our exploration in this chapter of a number of issues raised by a quantitative analysis of phonological variation in its social context. We focus in chapter 7 on some special problems associated with analyzing syntactic and other types of variation.

7

Beyond Phonology: Analyzing and Interpreting Higher Level Variation

7.1 Introductory

Labov's account (1969) of contraction and deletion of the English copula extended the scope of the variationist method to morphological variation. He focused on the ranking of internal constraints on variation, thus enabling the cross-variety comparison of variable patterns. Among other things, he observed that some kinds of predicate were more likely than others to favor copula deletion (NP versus Adjective, for example). As well as providing a methodological template, this influential article introduced the copula as a "showcase" variable (Rickford et al. 1991: 103) and launched a variationist tradition in the United States of studying morphological variables in African American English. Recent examples of the enormous amount of such work on this variety are to be found in Mufwene et al. (1998), Rickford (1999), Poplack (2000), and Poplack and Tagliamonte (2001); and Walker (2000) provides a comprehensive review and critique of work on the copula in AAE. Many accounts of grammatical variation at various levels have followed Labov in focusing on constraint rankings rather than on relative frequencies of particular variants, thus differing in procedure and emphasis from much phonological work; as examples cited in the previous three chapters show, frequencies of phonological variables are often compared across speaker groups with relatively little attention to internal constraints on variation. Poplack (2000: 14) discusses the implications for cross-variety comparison of a focus on constraints rather than on frequencies.

While variationist studies of morphological variation are sometimes relatively straightforward, the extension of quantitative methods to higher level grammatical variation raises methodological questions which impinge on broader theoretical concerns. For this reason, Romaine (1984) argues that the concept of the variable cannot usefully be applied to any but low-level morphological variation. It is generally agreed that the pragmatic or semantic considerations which often constrain the occurrence of specific syntactic variants create methodological problems for a quantitative analysis, but some scholars further argue that almost all cases of variation are accounted for by such factors (e.g., Winford 1996: 188). We will consider shortly some work on variability in French interrogative structures that partially supports such positions.

One intrinsic difference between phonological and syntactic systems has far-reaching implications for variationists. Since speakers make use of a sharply limited and therefore frequently recurring inventory of phonological contrasts, realizations of any given variable are likely to show up quite frequently in even a short sample of speech. This is not the case for morphological and more especially higher level syntactic variables, since a sufficient quantity of tokens of a given type of construction cannot usually be guaranteed to appear in a piece of spontaneous discourse. This difficulty is partly a consequence of the non-finite or "leaky" nature of syntactic systems, which in turn is associated with the susceptibility of syntactic choices to pragmatic and semantic constraints. Speakers can exercise considerable choice in the way they use grammatical resources to encode meanings; for example, since there is no isomorphic relationship between function and form, questions are not always realized syntactically as interrogatives and interrogative forms may realize many different functions.

Coveney (1996: 123) discusses in detail the implications of the function/form disjunction for an analysis of the sociolinguistic distribution of different types of interrogative in French. He points out that in order to establish the pool of potential variants from which a speaker might have selected in a given instance, it is necessary first to identify the communicative function of utterances. The precise range of variants available for a particular function then needs to be established, because different ranges of interrogative variants are likely to be available for different communicative functions – requests for information, requests for action, offers, echo questions and so forth. To illustrate the problem, Coveney notes that examples such as (1), uttered by a European French-speaking adult about to take a group of children on a shrimping expedition, do not support the claim of Di Sciullo and St-Pierre (1982) with respect to Montreal French that the expression *s'il vous plaît* can occur in questions which function as requests for action but not in requests for information (Coveney 1996: 131):

(1)   Est-ce que vous savez où sont les épuisettes s'il vous plaît? "Do you know where the (shrimp) nets are please?"

To identify potential variants of a given utterance in a given discourse context, Coveney assigns a communicative function to each interrogative token in his corpus (1996: 123–75). Since communicative functions are notoriously indeterminate, this time-consuming task is far from straightforward. Coveney then proceeds by treating *yes/no* questions (YNQ) and *Wh*-questions (WHQ) as two separate variables. Three variants of (YNQ) are identified, as follows:

(2)   [SV] Vous voulez la tisane? "Would you like herbal tea?"

(3)   [ESV] Est-ce que c'est bon aussi? "And also, is that a good thing?"

(4)   [V-CL] Aurais-tu du feu? "Would you have a light?"

Coveney reports that a very large proportion of (YNQ) tokens is categorically constrained by pragmatic factors – i.e., the speaker appears to have no choice of structure, given the communicative function realized by the variant. Of the three (YNQ) variants distinguished, [SV] is the most common and [V-CL] is extremely rare (at least in informal French as spoken in France, as opposed to Canadian and perhaps Belgian varieties). Coveney further remarks that "the marked [ESV] structure was used only rarely when the speaker expected an answer from the addressee. On the few occasions that it was used, it seemed to be motivated by sociopragmatic considerations, especially politeness" (1996: 297). In a separate study of the (WHQ) variable, Coveney (1995) discusses a range of structural and pragmatic constraints on the realization of just one variant, [SVQ]:

(5)   Tu vas où? "Where are you going?"

Cheshire (1999) observes that, because of their lower frequency, syntactic variables are less available than phonological variables as resources for social evaluation, and so less likely to be socially indexical (see also Hudson 1996: 45). It is probably partly for this reason that work on syntactic variation tends to focus less on social and more on internal, linguistic constraints. Even relatively frequently occurring morphological variables, where pragmatic and semantic issues of the kind discussed by Coveney are less problematic, do not appear to fulfill the same sociolinguistic function as phonological variables. Hence, a contrast has often been noted between the sharp patterns of morphological variation and the gradient patterns of phonological variation. Table 7.1 shows how multiple negation (for example, *I don't want nothing* versus *I don't want anything*), a frequently studied variable in the English-speaking world, is distributed by gender and social class among 32 adolescent speakers in Milton Keynes, England.

The type of so called "sharp stratification" evident here is quite different from the gradient patterns in (for example) tables 4.1 and 4.4, in that multiple negation is distributed in an all-or-nothing fashion with middle-class speakers avoiding it completely. Although tokens of the variable occur relatively infrequently for both girls and boys within the working-class group, the non-standard variant follows the canonical pattern of being used more frequently by boys.

Table 7.1 Frequency of multiple negation in the
Milton Keynes data set (Cheshire 1999: 61)

Speakers	N	%
WC girls	50	20
WC boys	35	60
MC girls	35	0
MC boys	24	0
Total *N*	**144**	

The remainder of this chapter examines some implications of the issues reviewed above. We first discuss data collection problems associated with the study of syntactic variation, considering how interview data might be supplemented by data derived from other sources, and in section 7.3 we review some historical studies that have employed variationist methods. In section 7.4 we move to questions of data analysis, where we consider a range of issues associated with identifying variants and variables. In section 7.5, we discuss analyses of pragmatic and discourse constraints on syntactic variation, and conclude the chapter with a review of work which complements variationist frameworks with other traditions of linguistic research.

7.2   Data Collection Issues

Although it seems intuitively likely that clauses containing negative markers such as *not* or *never* will show up relatively frequently in a sizable corpus of data, Cheshire (1999) notes that 32 individual ethnographic interviews yielded a total of only 144 instances of clausal negation (see again table 7.1). When tokens of variables occur even less frequently than this, it is difficult to obtain sufficient data in any corpus of spontaneous speech. Consider the case of the BÍN/*bin* contrast in African American English where the stressed form of *been* is thought to express remote past meanings "for a long time" or "a long time ago," depending on the type of verb. Its unstressed counterpart is thought to express a more currently relevant perfective aspectual meaning, as discussed by Winford (1998) and Green (1998). This contrast is illustrated in (6) and (7) below, both of which are drawn from the work of Rickford (1999, 21–3) who reports an earlier (1975) investigation of the BÍN variant:

(6)   She ain't tell me that today, you know. She BÍN tell me that ("She told me that a long time ago").

(7)   He *bin* doing it ever since we was teenagers, and he still doing it.

Given that the subtle semantic and pragmatic meanings encoded by BÍN make it unlikely that tokens will show up frequently in a regular interview, Rickford discusses several ways of supplementing audio-recorded interview material. The first of these involves an extended period of observation of speakers of the relevant speech community, when the observer endeavors to record every instance of the relevant variable, noting also linguistic and non-linguistic context. Over a period of time, a sizable corpus of even the rarest variants can be collected in this way. Another procedure is to draw additional examples from corpora of various kinds. A combination of these methods and others is used by Rickford et al. (1995) in their study of variable absence of the verb (*be concerned* or *go*) in *as far as* constructions which function as topic restrictors in English. The following examples (Rickford et al. 1995: 102) illustrate the variable deletion pattern: ·

(8a) *As far as* the organized resistance *is concerned*, that's pretty much taken care of

(8b) *As far as* misunderstanding *goes*, I'd like to focus . . .

(9) *As far as* the white servants Ø, it isn't clear.

Pragmatic and semantic restrictions on the occurrence of topic-restricting expressions made the task of collecting sufficient tokens to examine patterns of variation particularly challenging, and the process of gathering tokens a little in excess of 1,200 from whatever sources the researchers were able to tap extended over an eight-year period. Of this number, 500 came from searches of various computerized corpora – a particularly rich resource for data on grammatical variation. Only a small proportion showed up in socio-linguistic interviews, and the remainder came from observations of many different kinds of spoken and written language activity such as lectures, meetings, media broadcasts, books, newspapers, and e-mail messages.

Another procedure sometimes used to obtain tokens of some types of syntactic variable is an interview question or protocol which encourages the emergence of particular structures. Coveney describes this strategy in his study of variation in the French spoken in the Somme region of Picardy:

> . . . questions about games, craft activities and local recipes often led to descriptions of how to go about these various processes, and these produced large numbers of tokens of the generalised indefinite subject pronouns *on* and *tu* or *vous*. . . . Questions about the informant's plans . . . unsurprisingly succeeded in eliciting instances of the simple and periphrastic future forms of verbs. (Coveney 1996: 16)

We turn now to a somewhat different procedure for supplementing spontaneous spoken language data, namely the elicitation of speakers' judgments on the meaning and acceptability of particular grammatical variants. Labov (1975) pioneered this method, but was sensitive to problems associated with absolute judgments of grammaticality of the kind routinely used by formal linguists. One of the grammatical features investigated was the failure of negative attraction – i.e., the tendency in some dialects of English to attach the negative marker to the quantifier:

(10)   All the men didn't arrive.

(11)   Every man didn't arrive.

(12)   Each of the men didn't arrive.

(13)   Anybody didn't arrive.

Labov had hypothesized "a regular gradient of negative attraction to quantifiers, strongest to *any*, weaker for *each* and *every*, weakest for *all*" (1975: 19), and so asked his subjects to code different levels of confidence by assigning to each sentence one of four judgments of acceptability: *No native speaker would say it*; *Other native speakers might conceivably say it*; *Awkward, but can conceive of saying it*; *Would say it without qualms*. Labov was able to confirm the original prediction of a gradient of acceptability and also describes a number of similar experimental studies. In the context of a detailed demonstration of the mismatch between linguistic intuitions and linguistic behavior, he provides a more recent account of experiments of the same general type (Labov 1996).

Using the same kind of elicitation method, Rickford designed questions such as (14) to establish whether black speakers were more likely than white to assign the "remote" past interpretation to the stressed form BÍN:

(14)   Someone asked, "Is she married? And someone else answered, "She BÍN married". Do you get the idea that she is married now? Yes— No—

In fact, black speakers were very much more likely than white speakers to answer Yes to this question (Rickford 1999: 25).

It is clear that in the absence of prior knowledge derived from observation, basic information about syntactic structure cannot be derived from experimental methods such as those employed by Rickford or Labov. Prior to framing a hypothesis that can be tested experimentally by eliciting responses to carefully worded questions, the experimenter needs to have acquired a good deal of detailed knowledge of the object of investigation. Given this caveat, experimental procedures can provide a highly economical and efficient method of investigating a speaker's responses to particular items. However, a well-known difficulty associated with them is a mismatch between what speakers *claim* when they are directly questioned, and what they actually *do*, as evidenced by linguistic behavior in naturally occurring conversation, particularly when one of the variants under investigation is associated with a stigmatized language or dialect. Consider, for example, Labov's (1973) account of his investigation of constraints affecting so-called "positive *anymore*" sentences in Philadelphia. In standard English *anymore*, along with other items in the *any* series, is in main clauses usually restricted to interrogative or negative constructions, but this restriction does not hold for "positive *anymore*" dialects, as shown in (15) and (16):

(15)   We keep the beer here anymore.

(16)   John's smoking anymore.

Labov (1973) cites the following dialogue to illustrate problems that beset attempts to tap native speaker intuition:

(17)   Interviewer: Can people say round here *We go to the movies anymore?*
         Subject: We say *show*, not *movies.*

This speaker's failure to comment overtly on syntactic structure is open to different interpretations. However, the tendency for prescriptive ideologies to inhibit and distort responses when informants are conscious of a competing set of standard norms became evident when Labov pressed his questions with people who had been heard using the positive *anymore* construction in conversation. The usual reaction was confusion followed by a claim that a "mistake" had been made in not including a negative in the utterance. Henry (1995: 12) reports the same kind of response to instances of the *for to* complementizer in Belfast English, in sentences of the following type:

(18)   For to do that would be foolish.

(19)   I got up early for to paint the kitchen.

(20)   ? I want for to do that.

Henry had suspected that *for to* could not introduce complements of *want*, and one particular native speaker, when questioned, had confirmed this tentative hypothesis only to say a few minutes later in spontaneous conversation:

(21)   I want for to be helpful.

When Henry questioned him further, he agreed that he would use structures such as (21), but added "Of course they wouldn't be right."

In general, responses to direct or indirect questioning about acceptability of variants are likely to be conditioned by speakers' awareness of their indexical value and of normative standards. Labov (1996) documents numerous instances of the consequent mismatch between intuitions and behavior, but Rickford (1987) offers a more optimistic assessment of the reliability of speaker intuitions, with the proviso that they are interpreted in conjunction with observed data.

7.3   Grammatical Variables and Historical Linguistics

Researchers working primarily on contemporary communities sometimes exploit the availability of written texts to add historical depth to analyses of grammatical variation and change. For example, Tottie and Harvie (2000) include information on relative markers at earlier stages of English to support an argument for the close relationship between early African American English (AAE) and dialects of English. Poplack and Tagliamonte (2001) analyze contemporary and earlier spoken and written materials to compare constraints on variable AAE and non-AAE tense and aspect systems. By documenting relationships between AAE and non-AAE varieties, they throw light on the historical antecedents and evolutionary mechanisms that give rise to contemporary AAE. Trudgill (1996) provides details of a language contact situation in sixteenth century Norwich to account for a contemporary pattern of alternation between zero and -*s* present tense third person singular verb forms in contemporary Norwich vernacular. Sankoff and Vincent (1980) report that stylistically stratified patterns of variable deletion of the French negative particle *ne* have hardly changed since the sixteenth century, when deletion was associated with informal styles.[1] They note that *ne* appears now only rarely in conversational contexts, but is favoured in certain formal (particularly written) styles. Romaine (1982) reports a similar stability over time of the relative pronoun system of Middle Scots, where the ranking of stylistic and syntactic constraints on choice of relative pronoun variant appears to have changed little in 450 years; zero marking in subject position was preferred in written Scots in less formal styles, and continues to be a characteristic of the contemporary dialect (see further section 7.4.3 below).

The hybrid subfield of historical sociolinguistics focuses on trajectories of changes completed at early stages of the language, and employs variationist methods to investigate these changes. Romaine (1982) sets out methodological principles for this enterprise, as well as documenting variation and change in the Scots relative pronoun system. Historical linguists work with the uniformitarian principle, which holds that patterns of variation in the past are similar to those observed in contemporary speech communities (see Lass 1997: 26ff), but the methodological challenges which they face in applying this principle have led Labov to describe historical linguistics as "the art of making the best use of bad data" (1994: 11). The "bad-data" problem has several dimensions: data are often patchy as a consequence of the random preservation of some texts and the equally random loss of others; the relationship between data derived from various kinds of written source and the data of spoken interaction which forms the basis of much contemporary sociolinguistic work is unclear; reconstructing the social information needed to interpret patterns of variation in written texts is not always straightforward.

The context of Labov's pessimistic comment is an extended account of principles of phonological change, but given difficulties of obtaining sufficient tokens of grammatical variables, even in contemporary speech communities (see section 7.2 above), it is probably less relevant to accounts of morphological or grammatical change, which usually draw on substantial computerized corpora. Nevalainen (1999) shows that earlier social worlds can to some extent be reconstructed from the detailed findings of social historians, some of which are of considerable sociolinguistic relevance (see, for example, Keene 2000). She is able to present well-motivated accounts of the social trajectories of particular grammatical changes associated with the sixteenth and seventeenth centuries, a period of particularly rapid social change. In a number of publications (e.g., Nevalainen and Raumolin-Brunberg 1996; Nevalainen 2000a, 2000b) her research group has used the resources of various historical corpora compiled by the English Department at the University of Helsinki, which make available different types of text at various periods between 850 and 1740. The Helsinki group has examined a wide range of grammatical variables, and we discuss here some of Nevalainen's (1999) findings on just two of them. The first is the variable use of the older third person present singular verb form -ETH as opposed to the innovatory northern dialect form -(E)S in the sixteenth century (see again Trudgill 1996). These variants were in competition for over two hundred years, before -ES, which had emerged as an alternating variant in the fifteenth century, took over from -ETH, becoming the norm by about 1600 in all but "high registers" (Lass 1999: 162–5). The following example (dated 1585) shows Queen Elizabeth I of England using both variants in a single short stretch of discourse:

(22)   He *knoweth* not the pryse of my bloude, wiche shuld be spilt by the
        bloudy hande of a murtherar . . . I am assured he *knowes* and therefor
        I hope he wil not dare deny you a truthe. (Nevalainen 2000a: 48)

Figure 7.1 shows the social trajectory of the change in the work of male writers between 1540 and 1559, and we can clearly see that the incoming form is preferred by men of lower social rank.

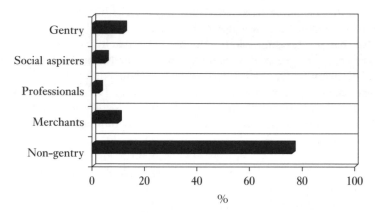

Figure 7.1 The use of -(E)S (%) as opposed to -(E)TH in the third-person
singular in a corpus from 1540–59, excluding HAVE and DO (male writers)
(from Nevalainen 1999: 519)

Another change considered is the decline of multiple negation. Figure 7.2
shows the effect of rank and gender on choice of variant, and demonstrates
a social trajectory in the period 1520–1681 quite different from the one
shown in figure 7.1.

The pattern characteristic of the contemporary English-speaking world is
evident here, in that the decline of multiple negation is most marked in the
writing of the highest and middle social ranks, with persons of low rank being
most resistant to change. Both male and female usage is considered for the
highest social ranks and, interestingly, women lag behind men in promoting
a change that is oriented toward prescriptive norms (cf. table 7.1). While it
is possible that low levels of female literacy are relevant to this unexpected
pattern, Nevalainen points out that men lead changes to incoming prestige
forms with respect to other variables also, even when there is ample evidence
that educated women can read and write (1999: 526). These findings confirm
the need for caution in offering global interpretations of effects of locally
embedded social variables such as status and gender (cf. section 4.4.3).

Pratt and Denison (2000) note that sociolinguistic models are attracting
increasing interest among historians of language who have previously concentrated on language internal accounts of change. Thus, while the work of
the Helsinki group is innovatory and extensive, it constitutes only part of
a substantial and expanding body of sociohistorical work on grammatical
variation. A different tradition is represented by Kroch and his associates
in a series of studies where they combine variationist and generative frameworks to investigate word-order and typological changes in Old English
(e.g., Pinzuk and Kroch 1989; Kroch and Taylor 1997).

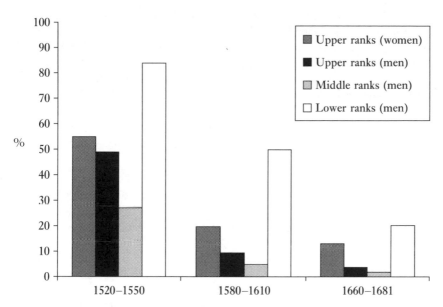

Figure 7.2 Multiple negation according to social rank. Upper ranks: royalty, nobility, gentry; middle ranks: professionals, merchants, social apirers; lower ranks: other ranks below the gentry (from Nevalainen 1999: 523)

7.4 Syntactic Analysis and the Sociolinguistic Variable

7.4.1 Some early work

Sankoff (1980b) provides a collection of influential early work on syntactic variation by Gillian Sankoff and her associates on a range of variables drawn from the Montreal French speech community and from the Tok Pisin speech community of Papua New Guinea. Taken together, the chapters employ a wide range of approaches and at various points include discussions of theoretical and practical issues that are still highly relevant.[2] Sankoff's article "Above and beyond phonology in variable rules" (1980c) demonstrates the methods and principles involved in extending to syntax the notion of the linguistic variable with three examples: variable placement of the future marker *bai* in Tok Pisin; variable deletion of the complementizer *que* in Montreal French; variation in the use of the French indefinite pronoun *on*. This seminal work shows the tendency noted earlier to focus on internal rather than social constraints. Only internal constraints are discussed for the *bai* and *que* variables; in the case of *bai* structure of the non-pronominal subject NP of the sentence; and in the case of *que* preceding and following phonological environments. The influence of social factors (age and gender) is discussed only for the *on* variable. In another chapter, Laberge and Sankoff (1980) describe their use of a computerized corpus in analyzing *on* versus *tu/vous* realizations of the indefinite personal pronoun. The input to this analysis was "4,300 tokens, each one of which has been carefully studied as to its syntactic and discursive role . . ." (Laberge and Sankoff 1980: 287). This investigation is an early demonstration of the value of computerized corpora in addressing pragmatic and discoursal dimensions of syntactic variation.

The English language version of Sankoff and Thibault's substantial analysis of variation between the auxiliaries *avoir* and *être* in Montreal French, first published in French in 1977, is an important contribution to the volume. This chapter addresses several important methodological issues, such as defining the scope and relevant contexts of the syntactic variable and problems associated with the low frequency of particular verbs. Also discussed are problems in deciding whether variation can be said to be between semantically equivalent forms which carry social meaning, or to encode an aspectual distinction; this latter issue is treated in the context of a (non-quantitative) analysis of the semantic distinctions underlying tense and aspect marking. Finally, several quantitative analyses are carried out, including a variable rule analysis of the effect of linguistic market indices on variation (cf. section 4.3.2).

As might be inferred from the discussion in section 7.1, Sankoff's extension of the notion of the linguistic variable from phonology to various levels of morphology and syntax was not free from controversy. In the remainder of this chapter we discuss issues of analysis and interpretation that have regularly emerged in the literature. The first concerns the application of the *principle of accountability* to the study of variable syntax, and the second how far variants of variables might be considered to be *semantically equivalent*.

7.4.2   *The principle of accountability and the envelope of variation*

Recall the requirement of the principle of accountability (cf. section 6.1 above) that "all occurrences of a given variant are noted, and where it has been possible to define the variable as a closed set of variants, all non-occurrences of the variant in the relevant circumstances" (Labov 1982a: 30). However, noting the rigor of this requirement, Labov (1982a: 87) proposes the following modification:

> There are a number of variables that can be studied now by noting only each occurrence, but not each non-occurrence, *since it has not yet been possible to*

close the possible set of variants [our emphasis]. Studies of the aspect markers of the Black English Vernacular, like invariant *be* are still at this stage. The same is true for the distribution of relative clauses, where we can't yet define the set of possible choices that the relative is selected from. Here, quantitative work is confined to tracing the relative frequency of occurrence in some globally defined section of speech, controlled for length by an independent measure like number of sentences, pages, or hours of speech.

Accordingly, Wolfram and Christian (1976) report simple frequencies of the surface form *done* in such contexts as (23)–(25), rather than attempting to calculate them as a proportion of *possible* occurrences:

(23)   We thought he was done gone.

(24)   The doctor done give him up.

(25)   I done forgot when it opened.

Rickford's BÍN variant is handled in the same way, as are the Hiberno-English perfective aspect markers discussed by Harris (1984; see further section 7.5 below).

Somewhat different difficulties can arise in defining a closed set of possible choices in a variable system when it is not clear what counts as a variant. Recall the procedure adopted in defining the scope of a *phonological* variable, where tokens occurring in contexts which do not allow variation are eliminated from the analysis. Usually this presents no particular problem (see section 6.2.3). In studies of grammatical variation such "don't count" forms (the term is taken from Blake 1997) are eliminated from the analysis for several practical and theoretical reasons. For example, particular contexts may make a candidate variant difficult to hear reliably in the stream of speech. Coveney (1996: 66) discusses such an instance in his account of the variable omission of the French negative particle *ne*. Following Sankoff and Vincent (1980) and Ashby (1976, 1981) he excluded all tokens where the subject pronoun *on* was followed by a vowel, since both liaison and a reduced form of *ne* were realized in such contexts in a similar way as [n] and could not be reliably distinguished in rapid speech:

(26)   mais on (n'?) avait pas faim? "But we weren't hungry?"

Potential variants were eliminated from the analysis also in instances where it was not possible to determine whether a token of *ne* was present because the preceding word ended with [n]:

(27)   rien (n'?) est ouvert quoi "Nothing is opened up, like" (a comment on letters received by teenagers at the vacation camp).

Reasons for specifying particular forms as "don't count" are often more complex than this, as we shall see from examples provided by three different studies: Tottie and Harvie's (2000) account of variation in relative markers in early AAE; the analysis of Rickford et al. (1995) of the (*be concerned* or *go*) variable in *as far as* constructions; Blake's (1997) review of analytic practices adopted by a number of different studies of variable copula deletion.

The variants of interest to Tottie and Harvie (2000) were *that*, *what*, and *zero* in subject and non-subject function in a range of different construction types which constrained probability of occurrence. Noting the heterogeneity of earlier work on relative constructions with respect to methods both of data collection and classification, they confine their analysis to "restrictive, non-adverbial relative clauses. . . . Firstly because most of the variability occurs in this context and, secondly this is the preferred site for zero relatives" (2000: 207). Thus, examples such as (28) were included, while non-restrictive relatives where the antecedent is already a fully determined NP head, as in (29), were not considered (Tottie and Harvie 2000: 206–7):

(28)   That's for cold, or anything Ø you have around your body.

(29)   Anderson *who* was then you know [incomprehensible] a old president. . . .

Also excluded were instances of whiz-deletion (i.e., deletion of both relative marker and auxiliary) since whiz-deleted clauses are complicated by auxiliary deletion and, by definition, allow only zero relative markers:

(30)   And there's a lot of people Ø [who are] gonna be hungry this winter.

Non-headed relatives constituted another construction excluded as invariant:

(31)   That's *who* brought me up.

Also placed in the "don't count" category were ambiguous utterances not clearly analyzable as relative clauses. For example, (32) could be paraphrased either as "I don't want any crow who/that/Ø comes around and tells me" (relative clause interpretation) or "I don't want any crow to come around and tell me" (non-finite subordinate clause interpretation):

(32)   I don't want no crow Ø come around telling me . . .

Specification of "don't count" forms for this study clearly required considerable prior analysis.

Rickford et al. (1995) encountered a different set of problems in specifying instances of the (*be concerned* or *go*) variable in *as far as* constructions;

recall the authors' interest in topic-restricting sentences, as exemplified by (8) and (9) above. They report, however, that some tokens that have the same superficial form as such sentences are found to have a different semantic function in that the *as far as* clause does not restrict the topic of the NP but rather refers to the point of view of the referent of the NP. These perspective clauses are invariant as they require a verb, and this verb must be *be concerned* rather than *go*. A further characteristic of perspective clauses is that the referent is always human (or a group of humans) and can be realized as a personal pronoun or a full NP:

(33) *As far as I'm concerned,* we've won.

(34) *As far as the faculty was concerned,* reaccreditation was beyond question. (Rickford et al. 1995: 107–8)

Perspective clauses were identified and eliminated from the analysis on the grounds of their invariance and semantically different behavior.

Blake's (1997) discussion of research on copula contraction and deletion in AAE points out that an important application of variationist analysis is cross-variety comparison, with attention to the relative strength of constraints in different varieties – for example, between AAE, other varieties of American English, and African and Caribbean varieties of English. Poplack (2000) focuses on such comparisons with respect to a range of morphological and syntactic variables, including the copula. However, despite the massive quantity of research on the copula, researchers have often disagreed on such basic matters as which forms to count and how to count them, as discussed by Rickford et al. (1991). Blake notes that indeterminate tokens (such as the French examples (26) and (27)) constitute a substantial subset of "don't count" forms, another large subset being tokens in contexts where they are invariant; thus, for example, the copula can be neither contracted nor deleted in clause final position, but always appears in its full form:

(35) That's what he is /*he's/*he Ø (Blake 1997: 58)

Other tokens generally agreed to be invariant are preterite forms (*was/wasn't*), which are thought to be categorically present. However, there is considerable disagreement on procedures for treating a further range of structures, such as all forms of *am* (*am, 'm, Ø,* as in "I'm tired") and variants of *what is, it is,* and *that is*. The justification for excluding this latter set is their near invariant behavior and their status as idioms:

(36) *Tha's* my daily routine/*wha's* your name again/*i's* a real light yellow color. (Blake 1997: 60)

Blake reports that since half the studies which she surveyed counted these disputed forms and half did not, comparison across different populations was extremely difficult. Walker's (2000) comprehensive review of the literature on the copula supplements Blake's methodological critique.

Cheshire (1999) addresses the issue of what counts as a variant of a variable from a somewhat different perspective, beginning with the observation that the same syntactic variables tend to get analyzed repeatedly by sociolinguists – various non-standard verb forms, subject–verb agreement, multiple negatives and non-standard negative forms such as *ain't*. This is because the saliency of these forms to laypersons and linguists alike makes them a target for prescriptive comment. Furthermore, the envelope of variation is usually specified to reflect prescriptively identified patterns, in that the variants selected for study are non-standard forms alternating with the prescribed standard form (as in the examples of negative concord or copula deletion). Cheshire suggests that attention to the alternations derived from prescriptive ideologies rather than to the structure of spoken grammars might lead not only to a neglect of important features of spoken language but also to misidentification of variants. This point is illustrated with reference to existential *there* constructions where a plural noun phrase complements some form of BE. Although absence of agreement between BE and the following noun phrase has motivated scholars like Schilling-Estes and Wolfram (1994) and Tagliamonte and Hudson (1999) to treat such constructions as non-standard variants, social distributions reported by several researchers suggest that speakers do not treat existential constructions such as (37) in the same way as other non-standard concord variants such as (38) and (39):

(37)   There was no roads.

(38)   You was only away a bit.

(39)   All their belongings was taken to the cattle market.

For example, Tagliamonte and Hudson report that young women in York, England, use non-standard *was* in non-existential constructions like (38) and (39) less than females in any other age group, but on the other hand use non-standard existential constructions like (37) at very much higher relative frequencies. The tendency for singular forms to appear almost categorically in existential constructions has also been noted in data collected in Ocracoke; Schilling-Estes and Wolfram suggest that *there was* effectively functions as a lexical unit in both single and plural contexts (1994: 285). Cheshire similarly reports that in the Milton Keynes data set (see section 7.1 above) *there's* and *there was* operate as a lexical unit. Thus, instead of a sharp pattern of stratification by social class of the kind shown in Table 7.1 invariant existential *there* constructions are used by male and female speakers in both social groups almost categorically. Noting the existence of similar invariant structures in French and German (*il y a* and *es gibt*) Cheshire concludes that constructions like (37) should be excluded from the set of non-standard variants in studies of subject–verb agreement. She further proposes that existentials are more appropriately treated as one of a set of similarly invariant constructions, all of which function to introduce topics in informal spoken English (1999: 72). This discussion raises important general issues about the way in which grammatical variation in spoken English should be addressed – particularly, the forms that constitute "non-standardness," apart from forms that are prescriptively defined as such.

7.5 Semantic Equivalence and the Discourse Context

We turn now to a notorious difficulty briefly mentioned earlier in this chapter in extending the notion of the linguistic variable to the analysis of syntactic variation. In an influential commentary on Weiner and Labov's (1983) study of variable agent omission strategies, Lavandera argued against extending the concept in this way on the grounds that variants of so-called "syntactic variables" were not semantically equivalent in the same way as phonological variables; "*Laughing and laughin'* or [gaːd] and [goːd] can more convincingly be shown to be used to say referentially the same thing than any pair of postulated synonymous syntactic constructions such as *the liquor store was broken into* versus *they broke into the liquor store*" (1978b: 175). Further, Romaine (1984) remarked that the notion of semantic equivalence (i.e., saying "referentially the same thing") was not at all straightforward, since numerous complexities were introduced by the discourse context. We consider the issues underlying this debate with reference to the work of Laberge and Sankoff (1980), Lavandera (1978a, 1982), Silva-Corvalán (1994), and a small body of recent work on the discourse marker and quotative expression *like*.

Laberge and Sankoff's (1980) account of the indefinite pronoun in Montreal French concentrates on the alternation between *on* on the one hand, and *tu/vous* on the other, in their function as indefinite personal pronouns. However, since *on* can alternate also with first and third person pronouns, which like their second person counterparts can also have *definite* reference, it is not easy to specify tokens of the alternating class (Laberge and Sankoff 1980: 272ff). An extended analysis of the functions of *on* with respect to all these alternating categories is therefore carried out prior to the main (quantitative) analysis of syntactic variation. The *discourse* constraints that favor indefinite reference turn out to be complex; the formulation of morals and truisms is one example discussed by the authors (see (40) below), and in this discourse function *on* is overwhelmingly preferred. Also considered are purely surface syntactic constraints, as in (41): "indefinite *tu* or *vous* cannot be used in contexts where there is a definite 'you' immediately to the left, for fear of confusion with the latter" (p. 289):

(40)   Mais je me dis, des enfants c'est des enfants, *on* peut pas les faire penser comme des adultes, *on* peut pas. "I tell myself, children are children; one can't make them think like adults – one just can't."

(41)   *Vous* [+def.] me demandez de vous raconter une partie de ma vie là, mais il y a des choses qu'on [–def.] peut pas expliquer pourtant. "You (the interviewer) ask me to tell you part of my life, but there are things that one just can't explain."

Laberge and Sankoff assign probabilistic weightings to constraints of the types exemplified in (40) and (41), to determine differences in their social distribution. Utilizing a combination of quantitative and discursive modes of analysis, they observe that their analysis leads to a very broad consideration of the place of the constructions in discourse and of a number of other constructions serving similar discourse functions. The study as a whole addresses a range of still largely unresolved problems of defining and constraining the scope of an account of syntactic variation where pragmatic and semantic issues are implicated. Coveney's (2000) account of the alternation in spoken European French between the first person plural pronoun *nous* and the pronoun *on* (used with definite reference to mean "we") provides a more recent discussion of many of the same issues.

   Lavandera's work (1978a, 1982, 1984) is also characterized by close attention to issues of semantic equivalence and discourse context. One article (Lavandera 1978a) examines variation in *cocoliche*, the reduced form of Spanish spoken by Italian immigrants to Argentina, while in other work Lavandera (1982, 1984) proposes a reanalysis of the alternation among verb forms along the dimensions of tense, mood, and aspect (TMA). She had studied these alternants in Buenos Aires Spanish, exemplified by (42)–(45), as semantically equivalent syntactic variants in *si* clauses, one of their possible environments (Lavandera 1975). According to Lavandera, all of them might be roughly translated as "If I have time, I'll go."

(42)   Si *tuviera* tiempo, iría (imperfect subjunctive).

(43)   Si *tendría* tiempo, iría (conditional).

(44)   Si *tengo* tiempo, iría (present indicative).

(45)   Si *tenía* tiempo, iría (imperfect indicative).

A quantitative analysis of these alternants based on 30 one-hour interviews of 15 men and 15 women had revealed a preference for the indicative and conditional forms in lower-status groups and by all speakers in less careful styles, so that the overall frequency of subjunctive forms was relatively low. However, Lavandera noted that the frequency of subjunctive forms in all environments in the speech of 50 *cocoliche* speakers was even lower than in the Buenos Aires Spanish corpus. This low frequency did not seem simply to reflect a poor command of Spanish by the immigrants, since a careful examination of the 50-hour *cocoliche* corpus did not reveal a higher overall frequency of the non-subjunctive alternants, but rather an absence of appropriate discourse contexts for the subjunctive. Lavandera points out a tendency for *cocoliche* speakers to avoid indirect speech, which in certain types of Spanish clause is an obligatory context for the subjunctive. Spanish speakers alternate between present and imperfect subjunctive in sentences of the following type:

(46)   Nos dijo que nos *quedemos/quedáramos* quietos hasta que el *vuelva/volviera*. "He told us to stay quiet until he came back."

While *cocoliche* speakers show an independently established ability to handle the subjunctive, they "simply refrain from using indirect discourse, and use direct discourse instead, i.e., quotations preceded by a form of the performative 'to say' (*digo, dice*)" (Lavandera 1978a: 399). What appears to be involved here is a group-specific discourse and stylistic preference (cf. Gumperz 1982a).

Lavandera notes that variationist analysis typically starts not with the discourse contexts in which forms are used, but with the forms themselves. Frequencies of the imperfect subjunctive are then calculated in relation to all contexts where its occurrence is possible. But such a procedure in the case of the *cocoliche* speakers would be likely to lead to the conclusion that the investigator had failed to elicit environments where the variable could be studied, and would miss the point that speakers were making use of a different range of choices for stylistic purposes. The standard solution to this assumed data-collection problem would be the one adopted by Lavandera herself in her original 1975 study, of structuring interview questions to encourage the appearance of linguistic contexts that required the subjunctive – a strategy discussed in section 7.2 above. But this strategy, however successful, would not reveal the ability of *cocoliche* speakers to converse fluently without recourse to those contexts. Lavandera's response to these complexities was to examine initially discourse function rather than surface grammatical form, and then to consider the functions served by particular forms. Such an approach, as demonstrated by *cocoliche* speakers' avoidance of indirect speech, permits the important insight that the function performed by the subjunctive in Spanish is performed in *cocoliche* by quite different means.

Silva-Corvalán (1994) uses both quantitative and qualitative procedures to address problems of the kind discussed by Lavandera. The issue that she examines is the attrition of grammatical morphemes expressing distinctions of tense, mood, and aspect (TMA) in relation to the Spanish language competence of Spanish/English bilingual speakers in Los Angeles. Consider the following alternations between indicative/subjunctive and preterit/imperfect forms:

(47)   No te creo que *viene* (Ind)/*venga* (Sub) mañana. "I don't believe you that he's coming/he may come tomorrow."

(48)   Mi país *fue* (Pret)/*era* (Imp) hermosa antes. "My country was/used to be beautiful before."

Silva-Corvalán points out that two quite different conclusions might be drawn from a speaker's choice of indicative rather than subjunctive and preterit rather than imperfect. The first is that the imperfect and subjunctive, which are vulnerable to attrition, have disappeared from the speaker's simplified TMA system. The second is that he or she is communicating by these choices a higher degree of assertiveness (in 47) and (in 48) expressing a view of the situation as "a dynamic, unanalyzed whole and not as temporally suspended in its existence" (1994: 23). Silva-Corvalán addresses these interpretative ambiguities by considering the morphological attrition explanation in different kinds of obligatory and optional context, and comparing the behaviors of speakers of different Spanish language ability across contexts. Thus, for example, utterances which evaluate narrative events are obligatorily coded as preterit by first-generation immigrants to Los Angeles, but only variably by speakers who were born and educated in America. Similarly, subjunctive forms appear regularly in utterances which express hypothetical information, and since they are evident in this favorable context only in the speech of first generation immigrants, it is assumed that their consistent absence in the conversations recorded with the American-born and -educated speakers indicates attrition rather than an expression of a subtle semantic or pragmatic distinction (Silva-Corvalán 1994: 24–5).

Similar semantic, pragmatic and discourse issues emerge in a body of recent work on non-standard *like*. This lexical item appears both as a discourse marker with a focuser function as in (49) and in the form *be like* as a quotative, as in (50):

(49)   and he found it *like* at the bottom of his backpack.

(50)   we *were* all *like* "if that was meant to be a joke it isn't very funny."

Both functions of *like* are currently associated with casual speech, with young people, and with women more than men. Dailey O'Cain (2000: 61) describes focuser *like* as "a pragmatic or discourse marker, similar to *you know* or *well*." Quotative *like* on the other hand is one of a quite different set of variant constructions which introduce reported speech or thought. In an early study of *like*, Romaine and Lange (1991) argue that the advance of quotative *like* is a case of grammaticalization in progress – that is, the progressive use of a lexical item as a grammatical marker, in this case a particle for introducing direct speech. They also note that *be like* is largely limited to first person subjects and is not strictly equivalent to other quotative verbs, since it often introduces reports of thoughts rather than direct speech (as in (50)). For this reason, they do not attempt to set up *be like* as one of a closed set of semantically equivalent variants of a variable (see again section 7.4.2 above). Their analysis is based on 80 instances of *be like* obtained from observations and recordings of teenagers and adults in Washington, DC, supplemented by various media sources.

Although Romaine and Lange discuss the issues raised by *be like*, they do not attempt the systematic quantitative analysis that was conducted by Ferrara and Bell (1995) and Tagliamonte and Hudson (1999). Ferrara and Bell (1995) is a real-time study, reporting analyses of three corpora collected in 1990, 1992, and 1994 of tape-recorded narratives from 405 Texas informants ranging in age from 6 to 86, who produced a total of 284 instances of *be like*. An important conclusion is that *be like* has dramatically expanded its functions in the 1994 corpus, with many more tokens occurring with third person (as opposed to first person) subjects.

Tagliamonte and Hudson (1999) extracted from their two corpora of British and Canadian speech around 1,300 quotative verbs collected in Canada in 1995 and in Britain in 1996. The chief quotative variants identified are *say*, *go*, *be like*, *think*, and *zero* (e.g., "She looked at him: 'who do you think you are?'"). Their goal was an accountable variationist description and cross-variety comparison of British and Canadian quotative systems, with attention to major linguistic and social constraints proposed in earlier studies – sex of speaker, grammatical person (first or third), and content of quote. This final constraint refers to whether the dialogue contains direct speech, internal dialogue (as in (50)), or non-lexicalized sound (e.g., "He's like AARGH"). The effect of each of these constraints is reported for both British and Canadian corpora, and many suggestions of earlier studies are confirmed. *Be like* emerges as a preferred variant for women, although more clearly in Britain than in Canada. Interestingly, both British and Canadian speakers show a preference for first person subjects at a level comparable with Ferrara and Bell's 1990 and 1992 Texan recordings, but do not show the expansion of function into third person use reported for their 1994 corpus. The content of quote constraint attempts to determine the accuracy of claims that *be like* is more likely to introduce reported thought or to be used for dramatic effect to introduce non-lexicalized speech sounds than to introduce direct speech, and here Tagliamonte and Hudson's findings are complex. In both varieties *say* is found to be particularly associated with direct speech and *go* with non-lexicalized sound, but in other ways the uses of *go* are very different between varieties, since in Britain this form is favored for direct speech and in Canada for internal dialogue. *Be like*, on the other hand, is preferred for non-lexicalized sound and internal dialogue across varieties, but is much less likely to be used for direct speech. As a result of such distributional differences *be like* as an introducer of internal dialogue competes with *think* in Britain, but with both *think* and *go* in Canada (Tagliamonte and Hudson 1999: 164).

Tagliamonte and Hudson attempt to explain these quantitative findings with a qualitative analysis of different styles of narration in Britain and Canada, touching also on mechanisms of global diffusion that might account for the rapid transnational expansion of *be like* among young speakers of English. Their work is a good example of an accountable quantitative study which addresses problems both in defining the envelope of variation and in specifying relevant semantic and pragmatic constraints. Taken as a whole, the body of research on (*be*) *like* not only documents a vigorous change in progress, but also addresses problems recurrent in syntactic analysis.

7.6   Variationist Analysis and Syntactic Theory

In this section we consider the relationship between variationist and formalist traditions of research. Twenty-five years ago Labov drew attention to the undesirable consequences of the considerable gulf between them: ". . . introspective linguists continuing to construct divergent models on the basis of non-existent idiolects; sociolinguists studying isolated cases of variation without any coherent grammar to place them in" (1975: 56). Variationists are typically critical of the unwillingness of formal linguists to accommodate variability as a central feature of language with important implications for linguistic theory (including theories of change). They also perceive formalist treatment of data as selective and unaccountable, manifested in appeals to native speaker intuition as a major source of evidence (cf. section 7.2 above). However, the two traditions of research are not now as polarized as Labov suggested in 1975, and two decades later he reviews recent work by formal linguists which addresses the role of speaker intuitions in linguistic theory (Labov 1996). Variationists for their part make use of theoretical frameworks to varying degrees, as evidenced by such work as Pinzuk and Kroch (1989), Kroch and Taylor (1997) and Rickford et al. (1995), all cited earlier in this chapter.

In their search for theories capable of illuminating variationist findings, researchers draw on a range of different frameworks. This eclectic approach is exemplified by Cameron (1996, 1997) in his account of the phenomenon of pro-drop in Latin American and Iberian Spanish. He notes that second person singular pronoun forms functioning as sentence subjects are variably ellipted, and when overtly realized take a number of different forms. Also, alternations between null and overt realizations are constrained by whether reference is specific or non-specific. These constraints are differently ranked in Latin American and Iberian dialects.

Cameron employs functionalist frameworks developed by Givón to explore discourse and pragmatic explanations for variation. To explain his findings in terms of a workable linguistic theory, he follows Prince (1988) in arguing for an expansive conception of speaker competence, such that "the linguistic competence of any speaker includes his ability to model the limit of his hearer's memory and shifting focus of attention as well as to instantiate this model through the selection of syntactic and referential forms" (1996: 13). He also makes extensive use of Ariel's Accessibility Theory (1990, 1991), a cross-disciplinary, psycholinguistically based theory of discourse structure, to explain the rankings of interrelated constraints on the variable expression of personal pronominal or null subjects in particular contexts. His findings are presented as evidence for a theory of competence which accounts for real world constraints of memory and attention and the need to communicate with an addressee.

Some researchers close the gap between variationist and formal traditions of work in a somewhat different way, by considering and challenging the theoretical implications of a variationist analysis. In an article first published in 1984 and reprinted in 1996, Harris notes that an assumption of equivalence of meaning between variants carries a further assumption that they are embedded in structurally similar grammars. However, as the amount of research on non-standard syntax increases, it has become evident that differences between standard and non-standard varieties reflect radical structural diversities rather than low-level variation. Arguing this point, Harris attributes the tense and aspect patterns of Irish English to influences both from Irish as a substratum language and from older forms of English that have survived in a geographically peripheral speech community. However, since contemporary Standard (Anglo) English and Irish English syntactic forms do not mark the same temporal and aspectual distinctions, they cannot be assumed to be embedded in the same underlying grammar. Similar comments might be made about tense and aspect distinctions of AAE (and some Southern white dialects of the United States) such as perfective *done*, and remote past *bin* (see section 7.4.2 above). Although scholars are clearly aware that semantic distinctions expressed by these forms cannot be mapped directly on to any set of standard English forms and so pose problems for a variationist analysis, the theoretical implications of these structural asymmetries are seldom considered. Such asymmetries may be particularly likely to arise when the non-standard dialect has developed historically in a contact situation involving structurally different languages such as Irish and English (see Harris 1986).

Harris (1984) demonstrates non-equivalence between semantically related sets of Irish English and standard English sentences which exemplify the range of perfect constructions. The six left-hand sentences below are unremarkable examples of standard British English present-perfect sentence types, all with present-tense marked forms of *have*. However, all occur only variably even in relatively standardized varieties of Irish English, and could be "translated" by a range of commonly occurring Irish English forms as follows (see further Kallen and Kirk 2001):

(51)   I've just seen my father = I'm after seeing my father.

(52)   He has finished his course = He has his course finished.

(53)   I've known him since he was a small boy = I know him from he was a wee fella.

(54)   Have you ever been to Bellaghy? = Were you ever in Bellaghy?

(55)   I've been waiting here for ten minutes = I'm waiting here ten minutes.

(56)   Have you sold your car? = Did you sell your car?

The striking lack of correspondence between the two sets of equivalents is both formal and semantic, going far beyond differences in surface realization. For example, Irish English (56) is equivalent not only to standard English (56) but to the same standard English surface form, so that Irish English does not mark syntactically the semantic distinction expressed by the verb form in standard English between "Have you sold your car?" and "Did you sell your car?" The Irish English present form (55) overlaps in the same way into an area of temporal reference that is covered by an identical standard English form. On the other hand, an action completed in the recent past is expressed in Irish English by a construction of the type exemplified by (51), while standard English does not mark that semantic category (the *hot news* perfect) in the verb form at all. Thus, the scope of temporal reference covered by the standard English present-perfect is expressed in Irish English by no fewer than the six forms shown above, of which two overlap into areas of temporal reference expressed by the same standard English forms (Harris 1984: 313).

Although Harris collected tokens from 15 hours of speech by 24 speakers in order to carry out a limited quantitative analysis of this variation, his procedure was different from any discussed so far. Rather than counting the variants of a postulated underlying syntactic variable, he examined variation in the surface exponence of four semantic categories: *hot news, resultative, extended now,* and *indefinite anterior,* exemplified by (51), (52), (55), and (56). While standard English uses perfect *have* forms in all cases, these four distinctions are expressed by six different Irish English forms.

Observing that such structural divergences underlie differences between varieties intuitively thought to be "dialects of the same language," Wilson and Henry (1998) point out the relevance to variationists of the generative notion of *parameters.* Developed specifically to deal with variability between languages, it is potentially applicable to variability between dialects. In an extended analysis of grammatical variation within the framework of a Principles and Parameters theory (the version set out by Chomsky 1992), Henry (1995) examines the relationship between standard and non-standard grammars with reference to five features of the Belfast dialect of English: subject–verb agreement; overt subject imperatives; for-to infinitives; inversion in embedded questions; and subject contact relatives. These non-standard forms with their standard equivalents are exemplified in (57)–(61) below:

(57)   The eggs is cracked/ The eggs are cracked.

(58)   Go you away!/ (You) go away!

(59)   I want them for to win/ I want them to win.

(60)   She asked had anyone called/ She asked whether anyone had called.

(61)   We had a window looked out on that side/ We had a window which looked out on that side.

Constructions like (57) and (61) have, of course, been examined quantitatively by variationists, and we shall consider shortly the contribution to variationist research of Henry's formal analysis. Crucially, it is based on systematically observed rather than introspectively constructed data.

Readers are referred to Henry (1995) for a lucid exposition of the theory and details of the analysis, which cannot be summarized adequately here. The essence of her argument however is that differences between Belfast dialect and standard English, far from being low-level surface alternations (the point stressed by Harris), involve different parameter settings and are therefore structurally comparable to differences between languages. She notes as an example that languages vary in whether or not they have verb raising to C(omplementizer), a difference giving rise to the verb second effect in some Germanic languages. She observes that the same kind of parametric difference is exemplified by variation in the Belfast imperative system (1995: 68). In addition to the standard form shown in (58) where an (optional) overt subject must precede the verb, Henry distinguishes two specifically Belfast English dialects characterized by (*inter alia*) different patterns of overt subject imperative. In both of these, the subject follows the verb. Dialect A, the more restricted, is used by younger speakers. The construction occurs in this variety only with a subclass of unaccusative verbs of motion, namely those with the feature [+telic] (see Wyngaerd 2001). Furthermore, the verb always follows a sentential adverb when one appears, as in (62) (Henry 1995: 60):

(62)   Always come you here when I call you.

(63)   Eat you your dinner.

Dialect B, used by older speakers, allows the overt subject imperative with all verbs as in (63). In light of these contrasting overt subject imperative patterns and a range of other linguistic issues which they raise, Henry argues that three possible grammars exist in the community, all of which admit optionality; standard English, dialect A and dialect B. The first two differ from each other in that in dialect A the subject need not raise out of VP in imperatives, while in standard English subject raising is obligatory (1995: 63). However, Henry argues that dialects A and B differ in the availability of verb raising; while in dialect A the verb remains in VP, in dialect B it may raise to C, as in those Germanic verb second languages where movement to C is obligatory in all matrix clauses. Henry notes that this movement triggers other properties found in these languages such as object shift, obligatory for weak pronouns, which moves the object in front of adverbs; see also Wilson and Henry (1998: 9). Such a pattern is apparently always found in speakers who regularly use the overt subject imperative:

(64)   Give you them always your full attention. (*Give you always them your full attention.)

Henry's procedure with all constructions analyzed is to establish the distribution of the non-standard construction in question before describing it in terms of the Principles and Parameters framework. At this point, distributional restrictions sometimes emerge which are highly relevant to a variationist analysis but have not been noted in the literature. For example, a considerable amount of research has been carried out on the subject–verb agreement of the type exemplified in (57) which is associated chiefly with Scottish and Ulster dialects and is also found in areas settled by Scottish and Ulster migrants to the United States, as well as in early African American English. The so-called Northern Subject Rule is evident in written texts as early as the thirteenth century, and is discussed in some detail by Harris (1993: 155) and Smith (2000: 42), and by Tagliamonte and Smith (2000: 153) who cite Murray's succinct formulation:

> When the subject is a noun, adjective or relative pronoun, or when the verb and subject are separated by a clause, the verb takes the termination -*s* in all persons. (Murray 1873: 211)

This rule produces such sentences as (57), which Murray is at pains to stress "are not vulgar corruptions but strictly grammatical in the northern dialect" (1873: 211). It also predicts that *They is cracked* will not occur. The two constraints identified by Murray (i.e., type of subject and adjacency of subject and verb) are widely reported in much more recent accounts – see, for example, Wolfram, Hazen, and Schilling-Estes (1999) and Montgomery (1996). In dialects where the Northern Subject Rule applies bare plural pronoun subjects are seldom followed by a singular verb, and it is this restriction which distinguishes these dialects from other varieties of non-standard English where forms such as *we was* and *you was* regularly occur (Tagliamonte and Hudson 1999: 155; Tagliamonte and Smith 2000; Smith 2000: 37–75).

In addition to restrictions on subject–verb concord in the urban dialect of Belfast where the Northern Subject Rule is clearly evident, Henry's procedures identify associated constraints not (as far as we are aware) reported in the sociolinguistics literature. For example, she notes that adverb position between subject and verb is not available in sentences where the rule applies, and therefore sentences like the following do not occur:

(65)   *Them eggs really is cracked.

Henry further argues that the Belfast non-standard concord patterns are best analyzed as absence of agreement marking, and one particularly interesting consequence of this analysis (for variationists) is that it permits the occurrence of negative polarity items (NPIs) in subject position (cf. section 7.2 above):

(66)   Any student didn't apply for the job.

As far as we know, such constructions have not hitherto been associated with "singular concord," the term used by Henry and other researchers for the Northern Subject Rule as it appears in Belfast English:

> That there is a link between singular concord and NPI – licensing seems clear from the fact that the two phenomena seem to go together in speakers'

grammars; those speakers who allow singular concord also permit NPIs in subject position, and conversely non-users of singular concord find NPIs in that position strongly ungrammatical. This is a clear case where careful examination of dialects or subdialects can help to show whether proposed connections are real or not, and where it is important to check what co-occurrence constraints there are on dialect features. (Henry 1995: 30)

Thus, the Principles and Parameters theory provides in this case a unified account of apparently unrelated features co-occurring in particular dialects.

Some of Henry's more general points are also of interest to variationists, such as her discussion (with reference to overt subject imperatives) of the range of different grammars available to children acquiring the dialect. However, she does not follow the variationist procedure of modeling variation as overlapping portions of a continuum (cf. Silva-Corvalán's (1994) description of variation and change in the tense–mood–aspect system of Los Angeles Spanish). Rather, variation is conceived as involving three different grammars, as in the account of imperative constructions reviewed above. Faced with this varied input, Henry hypothesizes that the main task of the learner is "not to hypothesize or select, or even set the parameters corresponding to a grammar which can generate all the data in the input; rather, it is to determine which grammar, from among the limited range made available by UG, can accommodate the majority of the data in the input" (1995: 79). Combined with an assumed preference for the simplest possible grammar, this strategy provides for the possibility of a child developing a grammar without verb inversion in imperative constructions, despite encountering frequent examples of inverted structures. It is clear that such an acquisition strategy allows for linguistic change and, indeed, Henry succeeds in documenting patterns of change within a Principles and Parameters framework.

7.7   Concluding Remarks

This chapter concludes our review of variationist frameworks for analyzing and interpreting interspeaker variation. Chapters 4 and 5 concentrated on social dimensions of variation, and this chapter and chapter 6 focused on linguistic issues. Chapter 6 reviewed phonological frameworks and models, and this chapter complements the material discussed there by considering a wide range of research which addresses morphological, syntactic, semantic, and discourse-related variation.

Recalling that variationist methods and theories originally developed the concept of the linguistic variable to examine phonological variation, we observed that research on higher level variation differs from the work considered in chapter 6 in a number of ways. Partly because of the relative rarity of tokens, the task of data collection and quantification often proves problematic in ways not reported by analysts of phonological variation. Thus, a wider range of quantitative and qualitative methods are commonly employed. Nor is it always clear at the stage of data analysis how the concept of the sociolinguistic variable might be applied. Sometimes it is not easy to specify what elements might be said to constitute variants of an underlying variable, and in the case of syntax and discourse-related variation, the extent to which variants might be said to be semantically equivalent is also unclear. Partly as a consequence of such considerations, the emphasis of work on higher level variation tends to be somewhat different from work of the kind discussed in chapters 4, 5, and 6. All variationists are acutely aware of the relationship between language variation on the one hand and social structure and social practices on the other. But research of the kind considered in this chapter is often concerned largely with language internal constraints on variation, while much phonological work continues to address and refine conceptions of the relationship between language variation and the social world.

8

Style-Shifting and Code-Switching

8.1 Introductory

Since analyses of style are fundamentally concerned with the choices made by individual speakers, they are often understood to relate to intraspeaker dimensions of variation rather than the interspeaker or intergroup patterns that have been the focus of earlier chapters. However, community linguistic repertoires which provide raw materials for speakers' choices are of various kinds. Monolingual and monodialectal speakers who do not have a clear sense of different codes in the community repertoire are usually said to shift between styles. Bilingual (or multilingual) speakers, speakers from diglossic communities, and bidialectal speakers on the other hand have access to community repertoires which are perceived (and usually named) as different languages or as different dialects of the same language, and such speakers are said to switch between codes. In their influential account of patterns of switching between standard and dialect codes in northern Norway, Blom and Gumperz (1972) point out that social actors' perceptions of code discreteness do not necessarily correlate with analyst notions of linguistic discreteness. They show that morphological and phonological forms characteristic of Bokmål (the standard) and Ranamål (the dialect) can be analyzed quantitatively as variables lying on a continuum between these two reference points in much the same way as the variables implicated in monolingual style-switching.

Bilingual or bidialectal switching is usually a more visible process than monolingual style-shifting, and there are certainly some crucial differences between style-shifting and code-switching processes with respect to factors such as levels of speaker awareness, the linguistic practices in which speakers engage, and the linguistic materials which they can access for social-symbolic purposes. Nevertheless, there are many commonalties in the psychosocial dynamics underlying these different kinds of intraspeaker variation.

Linguistic repertoires commonly allow speakers to deploy both the stylistic resources typical of monolingual style-shifting and the bilingual resources typical of code-switching, as is the case with the different groups of English/ Spanish speakers described by Mendoza-Denton (1997) and Zentella (1997). Certainly, speakers from monolingual and bilingual communities express by their linguistic choices similar contrasts in social meanings, and indeed some frameworks address both types of phenomenon. For example, Myers-Scotton's markedness model (1993) was designed originally to explicate code-switching in bilingual communities but has also been applied to the analysis of stylistic choices which exploit the resources of different kinds of repertoire (Barrett 1998; Bernsten 1998). Consider also Rampton's (1995) analysis of the phenomenon of *crossing*, where monolingual speakers treat as a stylistic resource elements of other languages which, crucially, they do not "own" (see also Cutler 1999; Hill 1999). The motivation for treating style-shifting and code-switching separately at some points in this chapter is therefore not primarily theoretical but rather a matter of organizational convenience, since these phenomena have most commonly been studied with reference to different frameworks.

A great many types of context-sensitive linguistic variation may be described as stylistic, ranging from the small-scale phonological variables studied by Labov (1972b) and Eckert (2000) to Biber and Finegan's (1994) work on registers – i.e., global language varieties associated with different occasions of use (see also Biber 1995). Stylistic analysis is also understood to include work on conversational patterns (Tannen 1994), politeness strategies (Brown and Levinson 1987; Holmes 1995), address systems (Fasold 1990, ch. 1; Mühlhäusler and Harré 1990) and linguistic routines such as greetings, partings, and phatic behavior generally (Laver 1981). Much work on style employs qualitative and discursive rather than quantitative modes of analysis, as is evident from contributions to the collections edited by Rampton (1999) and Eckert and Rickford (2001) and from the work of Tannen, among others. Furthermore, assumptions of the dynamics underlying style-shifting which researchers bring to their work are very different. For example, Labov (1972b, 2001a) and Bell (1984) treat stylistic choice as responsive, determined by components of the communicative context. Similarly, much early ethnographic work on style of the kind pioneered by Hymes (1972, 1974) employed large taxonomies designed to characterize "rules of speaking" – that is, the various situational factors that influence code choice. More recently, style has been treated less as a response to a set of contextual variables than as strategic, proactive use of available linguistic resources to construct social meaning. Linguistic choices are interpreted as part of a larger set of strategies and practices whereby speakers not only associate themselves with particular social groups and index distinctiveness from others, but also construct by means of these practices social categories such as "whiteness," "masculinity," "jock," "burnout" and so forth (Buchholz 1999; Eckert 2000; 2001; Schilling-Estes 1998; Bell 2001).

Thus far, we have outlined some different approaches to style, and in the sections that follow we focus chiefly, but not exclusively, on analyses within a variationist framework. Discussion is organized around two basic approaches contrasted above: style as socially responsive and style as proactive and strategic. In section 8.4 we consider issues emerging from research on code-switching in bilingual and bidialectal communities.

8.2　Style as a Response to Situation

8.2.1　*Stylistic variation as a function of attention paid to speech*

Labov's early approach to stylistic variation located two types of conversational style (casual and formal) and three types of reading style (elicited by a passage of continuous prose, a word list, and a minimal pair list) on a unidimensional continuum from most casual to most careful speech. This procedure was motivated by the axiom that "styles can be arranged along a single dimension, measured by the amount of attention paid to speech" (Labov 1972b: 208). Thus, casual style, or the style nearest to the vernacular, was said to be the product of the smallest amount of conscious self-monitoring, while minimal pair style, produced while speakers were reading pairs of words that were homophonous in the vernacular system, was the product of the maximum degree of self-monitoring. Stylistic variation defined in this way intersects with interspeaker variation, since speakers in their more careful styles approximate progressively to the norm of higher-status social groups. Because the same phonological variables operate simultaneously on both inter- and intraspeaker dimensions, Labov suggested, in a memorable phrase, that it might be difficult to distinguish "a casual salesman from a careful pipefitter" (1972b: 240). Speakers thus display awareness of linguistic exonorms in their style-shifting behavior, and it is this intersection between the stylistic and the social that makes style, for Labov, a crucial sociolinguistic concept. Armstrong (2001) discusses implications of the social/stylistic relationship in his analysis of variation in two cities of northern France.

Labov has recently been careful to point out that his view of style as co-varying unidimensionally with the amount of attention paid to speech does not amount to a theory of stylistic variation; it is "not intended as a general description of how style-shifting is produced and organized in everyday speech, but rather a way of organizing and using the intraspeaker variation that occurs in the interview" (2001a: 152). His current conception of style appears, therefore, to be largely methodological, the goal being to develop procedures for eliciting comparable subsamples of speech across different speakers in order to achieve a bird's eye view of the large-scale social patterning of sociolinguistic variables.

Rickford and McNair-Knox (1994) note that, for the most part, researchers have not attempted to follow Labov in distinguishing careful and casual speech, probably because procedures for drawing this distinction are difficult to implement. They also summarize different objections to the idea of studying style as a function of the amount of attention paid to speech. The most radical of these is that speakers make stylistic choices not in response to normative pressures which induce attention to speech production, but as one of a set of social practices in which actors engage to construct social meaning. As we shall see, it is certainly true that speakers do not reliably follow the predicted pattern of using progressively lower frequencies of vernacular variants as they move into reading and word-list tasks, precisely because they are able to use variable linguistic resources proactively and strategically. Also problematic are:

- the generally undertheorized relationship between speaking and reading, as displayed in the assumption that speech and reading are comparable types of behaviour which can be located straighforwardly at different points on a single continuum (Milroy 1987: 100–7);
- the claim that the production of speech oriented to a standard exonorm requires more attention than performances of a speaker's vernacular (Schilling-Estes 1998);
- the validity of attention paid to speech as an explanatory variable rather than the nature of the speaker's response to different audiences (Bell 1984).

To illustrate the consequences of some of these problems for a piece of research which adopted in a slightly modified form, Labov's original model of stylistic variation, consider table 8.1 where frequencies of vernacular variants for the Belfast variables (th) and (a) in the speech of 13 speakers are presented. Reading from left to right, the columns show frequencies for Spontaneous Style, Interview Style and Word List Style. The first two categories correspond roughly to Labov's Casual Speech and Careful Speech, referring respectively to discourse which is initiated by the informant and discourse which is directly responsive to an interview question. The figures for (th) represent percentage deletion of /ð/ in intervocalic contexts (as in *mother*, *brother*), and those for /a/ relative degrees of backness of the vowel (as in *man*, *grass*).

The first two columns under (th) in table 8.1 are consistent with Labov's predictions in suggesting that, in unscripted speech, deletion operates variably and gradually; speakers vary considerably in the amount of deletion, but always tend to delete more frequently in spontaneous conversation than in

Table 8.1   Frequency scores for two variables in three styles for 13 Belfast speakers

	(th) (% score)[a]			(a) (index score)		
	SS	IS	WLS	SS	IS	WLS
Donald B	56.25	90.00	0.00	3.00	2.66	3.00
George K	88.89	55.56	0.00	4.15	3.40	4.62
Mary T	50.00	7.14	0.00	2.05	1.40	1.00
Elsie D	25.00	33.33	0.00	2.65	1.60	2.31
Millie B	66.67	53.85	0.00	2.80	1.85	2.69
Brenda M	33.33	33.33	0.00	2.80	2.15	2.69
James H	100.00	100.00	0.00	3.30	2.75	2.92
Terence D	94.74	69.23	0.00	2.90	3.35	3.15
Brian B	93.75	75.00	75.00	3.65	2.65	3.00
Stewart M	75.00	66.67	0.00	4.05	2.80	3.00
Alice W	25.00	22.22	0.00	2.55	2.20	2.69
Lena S	20.00	0.00	0.00	2.40	1.92	2.46
Rose L	0.00	40.00	0.00	1.35	1.55	1.50

[a] Figures show percentage of zero variants
Key: SS = Spontaneous style; IS = Interview style; WLS = Word-list style.

responses to questions. The word-list pattern shows a sharp contrast, in that even speakers who use the vernacular variant at high levels in spontaneous conversation avoid it when they read word lists. However, as Brian B's behavior shows, there is nothing to prevent a speaker using the zero form of (th) in all styles – and indeed the contrast between 18-year-old Brian's use of this variant in the word list and other speakers' total avoidance of it invites a clear inference of the social meaning expressed by Brian's choice. He habitually uses this variant at the high level characteristic of young working–class Belfast men, and maintains that pattern in reading the word list contrary to what other speakers appear to treat as the unmarked choice for that activity (see Myers-Scotton 1998).

It also seems likely that the striking *uniformity* of (th) scores in word-list style (with the exception of Brian's list) is attributable not exclusively to attention to speech, but to a low-level rule of the English spelling system which consistently uses *th* to represent [ð] in intervocalic positions. Although spelling clearly cannot always be used to account for patterns of stylistic variation, it seems likely that a speaker who is aiming for a pronunciation appropriate to reading aloud (the one that he or she consciously views as "correct") will be guided when possible by clearly rule-governed aspects of the spelling system.

The pattern for (a) in table 8.1 is harder to interpret but also poses difficulties for Labov's model. Speakers certainly tend to modify in Interview Style the high level of use of vernacular variants characteristic of Spontaneous Style, but do not continue this movement away from the vernacular in Word List Style. Possible reasons for this pattern have been discussed elsewhere (Milroy 1987: 105), the chief being that the standard exonorm on which Labov's model depends is not evident from the linguistic practice of the speech community, although speakers certainly have a clear sense of the norms of their own vernacular and modify vernacular forms in interaction with socially distant addressees. And although orthography provides a reliable guide in the case of the variable (th), it is not helpful in suggesting a normatively correct vowel pronunciation. Researchers in Scotland, such as Romaine (1978) and Macaulay (1977), have reported difficulties in identifying a single standard norm, and Johnston (1983) suggests that a pattern of stylistic contrast similar to that shown for (a) in table 8.1 is characteristic of divergent dialect communities – that is, communities where there is a considerable disparity between localized and standard norms. In any event, the patterns in table 8.1 highlight difficulties in applying Labov's model of stylistic variation, whatever their explanation.

At a purely operational level, Milroy (1987) and Baugh (2001) have noted difficulties in using instruments such as reading passages and word lists in communities where literacy skills and reading fluency cannot be assumed. In his most recent discussion, Labov (2001a) does not refer to the role of reading passages or word lists in extending the stylistic continuum, and in fact it is quite rare now to find such readings treated as simulations of increasingly formal styles. However, in a reaffirmation of the methodological value of distinguishing careful and casual styles, Labov proposes a taxonomy of several different styles which might be assigned fairly mechanically to these categories. Eckert (2001) queries both the validity and feasibility of such a procedure, noting also that the proposed taxonomies are something of a mixed bag. Two of them, *response* (assigned to careful style) and *tangent* (casual style) are related to discourse structure – a response being fitted to a preceding question while a tangent by definition involves the speaker taking control of the discourse with an initiating move (cf. the distinction between Spontaneous Style and Interview Style described above). On the other hand *narrative* (casual speech) along with the oratorical style *soapbox* (careful speech), where the speaker expresses generalized opinions, are both defined in terms of genre. Eckert points out the difficulty of automatically assigning soapbox style to careful speech, given that people get onto soapboxes for different reasons, some of which call for "in your face" displays of vernacular speech (Eckert 2001: 120–1). This criticism highlights a more general problem of analyses of style which do not recognize the speaker's ability to exploit the resources of variability in different and sometimes unpredictable ways.

8.2.2   *Style as audience design*

Bell's influential audience design model is critical of the idea that stylistic variation is a function of attention to speech, but resembles it in treating style primarily as responsive to situation (Bell 1984, 2001). His fundamental point is that "at all levels of language variability, people are responding primarily to other people. Speakers are designing their style for their audience" (1984: 197). The link between stylistic and social variation is attributed to an association of linguistic features with particular social groups, and to processes of social evaluation whereby style carries these associations. In this way, stylistic variation derives from intergroup language variation. Nor do speakers design language only for addressees, but react also to auditors and overhearers, which are other categories of audience. Style is thus seen explicitly as a response to persons, rather than a consequence of speaker awareness of social norms or attention mechanisms. Bell further argues that because particular topics and settings are associated with specific types of addressee, the situational variables of topic and setting are subservient to the addressee variable. Thus, for example, a setting such as a workplace is often associated with a more socially distant kind of addressee than a domestic setting, and the "danger of death" question that Labov used to elicit casual speech mentions a topic associated with an intimate addressee (see section 3.3.3 above).

In support of his claim for the primacy of audience, Bell cites comparative levels of intervocalic /t/ voicing in the speech of four New Zealand newscasters broadcasting from two different stations, A and B. Station A contrasts with station B in catering to a somewhat elite older audience, and /t/ voicing in New Zealand is associated with casual speech and younger or lower status speakers. As figure 8.1 shows, the style adopted by each of the

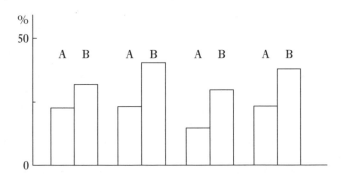

Figure 8.1   Percentage of intervocalic /t/ voicing by four newscasters on two New Zealand radio stations, A and B (adapted from Bell 1984: 171)

four newscasters strikingly corresponds with the language patterns of the target audience, for whom they might be said to be designing a speech style (Bell 1984: 171). This interpretation is more plausible than one based on different levels of attention to speech, since a considerable amount of attention is necessarily paid to speech by all newscasters.

The claim that the critical motive driving variation is audience design rather than attention to speech has the advantages of aligning the quantitative study of stylistic variation with related work on intraspeaker variation. Particularly, Bell points out that his model is congruent with the accommodation theory of social psychology (Giles 1984; Thakerar, Giles, and Cheshire 1982), which attempts an explanatory account of stylistic variation in terms of speaker response to the addressee. It is also congruent with approaches to bilingual code-switching, discussed further in section 8.4, where audience has always been recognized as a crucial factor in language choice. Similarly, variation in interactive behavior of the kind evident in politeness phenomena or choice of address terms is usually analyzed with reference to addressee characteristics (see Fasold 1990: ch. 1).

Although Bell's 1984 article is notable for its attempt to present a comprehensive and predictive theory of stylistic variation, he was not the first to propose that addressee was the primary factor controlling stylistic variation. For example, Dressler and Wodak (1982) criticized Labov's presentation of stylistic variation as overly simplistic, arguing that a series of specific findings could be accounted for in terms of attention to the addressee but not in terms of attention to speech. Also congruent with Bell's framework is the work of Coupland (1980, 1984), where the speech patterns of addressee clients are shown to correspond to variation in the speech of an assistant in a travel agency. Similarly, Trudgill's analysis of patterns of /t/ glottalization correlates variation in his own production (as an interviewer) with his informants' variable levels (1986: 8). It is also evident that much early sociolinguistic work on stylistic variation which is interpreted implicitly or explicitly in terms of attention to speech can equally well be treated with reference to audience design. Certainly variation in the Belfast variables (a) and (th) reported in section 8.2.1 can be accounted for in this way, since Spontaneous Speech scores are generally derived from utterances addressed to friends and intimates while Interview Style is by definition produced in response to the interview questions of an outsider. Douglas-Cowie's (1978) findings in Northern Ireland, where a change of interviewer resulted in radically different styles in the speech of the villagers of Articlave, in Co. Derry, are particularly amenable to an analysis in terms of response to addressee.

Rickford and McNair-Knox (1994) report an explicit attempt to test the predictive power of Bell's claims in the form of an analysis of stylistic variation in the speech of Foxy Boston, an 18-year-old African American woman resident in East Palo Alto, California. Their study, which forms part of a larger assessment of work on style within the variationist framework, is designed as a naturalistic experiment where Foxy's speech is recorded in two different interviews. The first interview is with Faye McNair-Knox, a 41-year-old African American, accompanied by her daughter Roberta who is close in age to Foxy. Foxy was already well acquainted with Faye, who had carried out earlier interviews with her. The second interview, one year later, is with Beth, a 25-year-old white woman who was a stranger to her. Stylistic variation is examined with reference to the distribution across both interviews of several morphological features salient in African American English (zero copula, invariant BE, 3rd person singular -*s* and possessive -*s*). Their findings generally confirm Bell's predictions both of the effect of audience and the primacy of addressee over topic. However, when the investigation is extended to interviews recorded with Faye and Roberta some years earlier, one of these is found to be further from the vernacular than Bell's model would predict for an African American addressee. In this interview, Foxy's demeanor is somewhat remote and distant, and that remoteness and distance is signaled also by her stylistic choices which are closer to those used in the interview with Beth. Since few researchers would want to claim that individuals have one fixed style which they always use with particular categories of addressee – in this case African American speakers with African American addressees – this variation needs to be accounted for. Rickford and McNair-Knox therefore propose further development of Bell's notion of "initiative style-shift" – a style designed not in response to a change in the situation but which itself initiates a situational change. This dimension of stylistic choice was treated as little more than marginal in Bell's 1984 paper, but captures the capacity of speakers to treat language variation as a resource on which they are able to draw to define their role in the situation and to construct particular social identities. Thus, provided she is socially positioned to make her choice meaningful, Foxy or any other speaker can creatively exploit available linguistic resources to construct for herself a particular persona or to construct an encounter as intimate, distant, friendly or otherwise. Let us consider now some recent work on style which explicitly treats the speaker as active initiator rather than passive respondent.

8.3   Style as Initiative and Strategic

Schilling-Estes' (1998) case study investigation of the self-conscious speech of Rex, a resident of the remote island of Ocracoke, incorporates criticisms of presentations of style-shifting as essentially responsive either to social context or to audience. Rex has developed ways of speaking to outsiders (including sociolinguistic investigators) that highlight salient dialect features, particularly the pronunciation of /aj/ with a raised and backed nucleus, as in the stereotyped phrase *hoi toiders* ("high tiders"). Contrary to assumptions motivating Labov's emphasis on the primacy of casual, unself-conscious speech as sociolinguistic data, Schilling-Estes shows that performance speech is not a fake, unsystematic variety, but that its characteristic features are phonologically conditioned and quite systematic.

An examination of the discourse contexts in which Rex shifts into performance style leads Schilling-Estes to suggest that he is role-playing for an absent body of linguists who he knows will analyze his tape-recorded speech. Far from trying to sound like or unlike those for whom he is performing (the options offered by an audience design theory) Rex "opts to assume the role of the quintessential quaint islander rather than the role of someone who speaks 'better' than outsiders often assume" (p. 75). Sociolinguists who assume an attention to speech model commonly believe the latter choice, which Rex does not make, to be the likely one. But precisely because Rex can choose how to present himself linguistically, his style-shifting needs to be treated as proactive rather than reactive or responsive, and performance speech as a distinctive style constructed by Rex as he positions himself socially, rather than as sociolinguistic detritus.

Taking into account such criticisms and findings, Bell's (2001) updated account of style-shifting upgrades the importance of initiative design (also called "referee design") which is now seen as a dimension complementary to responsive style-shifting. Speakers engaging in initiative style-shift are able to use resources of different dialects and languages, or vernacular or archaic forms of their own dialects, to express identification with particular groups, which may be socially or geographically distant. Bell's examples of research documenting initiative shifting include not only Schilling-Estes (1998) but also the use of dialects in television advertisements (Bell 1999), Rampton's (1995) analysis of the phenomenon of crossing, where white London adolescents use elements of Panjabi, Creole and Indian English, and Yaeger-Dror's (1991; 1993) study of variation in the language of Israeli singers.

Johnstone's (1999) ethnographic and discourse analytic account of the use made by Texas women of what she describes as "Southern-sounding" speech particularly emphasizes the proactive dimension of stylistic choice. Crucial to the analysis is the complex and somewhat ambiguous relationship of Texas with the American South, which means that it may be thought of as both a Western and a Southern state. Although for much of its history it has been important for Texas to position itself as distinctive from the South, Texan speech is characterized by a number of pan-Southern features. Southern speech is thus part of the sociolinguistic world of Texan speakers and Southern features are available as a stylistic resource. Unlike Rampton's white adolescents who engage in ethnolinguistic crossing, they are therefore not appropriating elements of a code which unambiguously "belongs" to a distinguishable other group when they adopt such features. One of the Texan women studied by Johnstone (a telephone sales agent) reports that considerable economic advantage accrues from her "Southern drawl" – a composite of discourse, phonological and prosodic features which allow her to construct a stereotyped "Southern Belle" persona (for details see Johnstone 1999: 51).

Penelope Eckert goes further than any researcher discussed so far in locating style as a central sociolinguistic phenomenon: "a clustering of linguistic resources, and an association of that clustering with social meaning" (2001: 212). Particular linguistic practices are associated with other social practices (such as choices of dress, adornment and demeanor) and by means of these practices social actors construct and define mutually distinctive social categories. Eckert's approach can be illustrated by her analysis of the linguistic distinctiveness created by the group which she calls "the burned-out burnouts." Recall the contrasts between burnout and jock ideologies and practices (see section 5.2.1); the burnouts are involved in local urban-oriented networks and engage in a range of practices which display their opposition to authority, while jocks are involved in suburban networks and orient to the institutional world of the high school and to corporate institutions generally. Linguistically, burnouts orient to local and jocks to standard norms, and burnouts lead in sound changes associated with urban variables. The burnouts cover a considerable range not only in their use of key linguistic variables, but in their characteristic social practices. Particularly, the girls are reported to construct an important social division between regular burnouts and burned-out burnouts. Burned-out burnouts are more extreme than burnouts in all aspects of social practice, including language, and define "for the entire community the quintessential burnout" (Eckert 2001: 214). Relevant here is the tendency of girls generally to locate themselves more firmly than boys in whatever social category they orient to, further discussed in section 8.4.3 below (see also section 4.4.3). In table 8.2, Eckert shows that in their extreme raising, centralization and even

Table 8.2　Correlation of raising of (aj) with combined sex and social category, separating two clusters of burnout girls (figures are Varbrul scores) (Eckert 2001: 125)

Input = 0.008	Female jocks	Male jocks	Main female burnouts	Burned-out burnouts	Male burnouts
Sig. = 000	0.248	0.328	0.357	0.906	0.664

backing of the nucleus of (aj), a salient variable in the urban community, burned-out burnouts lead all other subgroups (including male burnouts) by a considerable margin.

In this view, style is not conceived to be the range of variation available to individuals that is constrained by the social groups to which those individuals priorly belong but, conversely, as one of a set of interrelated social practices that construct (and eventually define) groups as distinctive. Johnstone observes that such a conception of style makes it difficult to maintain the traditional distinction between stylistic and social variation that was outlined earlier in this chapter (Johnstone 2000a: 418). In creating an association of particular forms with particular social groups, style becomes central to an understanding of how linguistic changes spread through the community. The kind of distribution shown in table 8.2, interpreted in conjunction with the insights derived from long-term ethnographic observation of social practice, leads Eckert to conclude that "changes do not simply spread through the population person by person, but get taken up and manipulated by communities of practice in the construction of social meaning" (1996: 57). Eckert (2001) further points out that as particular styles begin to be used to identify individuals as members of particular social categories (like "New York Jew," "Valley Girl," or indeed at a local level as "jock" or "burnout"), they become resources for individuals who can incorporate them to construct their own styles. The chief constraint on this proactive linguistic behavior, which accurately describes the practices of Johnstone's Texan women, is the individual's capacity to position herself in relation to a particular style in order to render her choices socially meaningful.

8.4 Code-switching

8.4.1 Introductory

The term "code-switching" can describe a range of language (or dialect) alternation and mixing phenomena whether within the same conversation, the same turn, or the same sentence-utterance. It is clear from, for example, the contributions to Milroy and Muysken (1995) that several different terms are used in the literature, not always consistently, to describe these different phenomena and that code-switching behavior is approached from many perspectives other than the social one considered here. We limit our discussion in this book to those issues that show parallels between style-shifting in monolingual communities and code-switching in bidialectal or bilingual communities. Our focus is thus on the social dynamics of switching rather than, for example, the specification of the linguistic (as opposed to situational) factors which constrain it. Poplack and Meecham (1995) provide a good example of this latter type of work where the distinction between code-switching and *borrowing* is important (see also Poplack 1993; Poplack and Meecham 1998; Poplack, Sankoff, and Miller 1988).

Although psychosocial motivations underlying monolingual style-shifting and bilingual code-switching are generally agreed to be similar, the latter process is more visible. Conversational participants are not necessarily aware of the code-switching behaviors of themselves and their interlocutors, but often display a more subtle meta-pragmatic awareness of two or more named codes in their repertoires. These codes may may be structurally similar (Panjabi and Urdu; Standard Italian and Sicilian dialect) or quite different typologically (Irish and English). Typically, but by no means categorically, each code is associated with different sets of social values and used with different interlocutors – in effect following the patterns predicted by Bell's audience design model. For example, in County Donegal in the west of Ireland the first author has on numerous occasions observed Irish/English bilinguals switching to English not only to address an English-speaking monolingual, but in the presence of a monolingual auditor – a person ratified as a participant in the interaction (Bell 1984: 172). Similar patterns are reported by Dorian in east Sutherland (1981: 79) and Gal in Oberwart (1979: 24), among bilingual speakers of Scots Gaelic/English and Hungarian/German respectively. Grosjean (2001) discusses the implications for language processing inherent in these different language behaviors with monolingual and bilingual interlocutors. He argues that, in response to such social constraints, speakers move into different *language modes* – that is, different levels of activation of different codes in the repertoire. Given the powerful effect of interlocutor (and perhaps of situation more generally) on language choice, socially oriented research on code-switching usually employs ethnographic procedures designed to take account of the language competence and language practices of the observer. Milroy, Li Wei, and Moffatt (1995) discuss the special challenges encountered by researchers in bilingual communities and Li Wei (2000: 475–86) provides a fuller assessment of relevant methodological issues.

The enhanced meta-pragmatic awareness of distinguishable codes in the community repertoire which appears to be characteristic of bilingual speakers makes it feasible for researchers to ask speakers to *report* behavior, in addition to observing it themselves. Accordingly, much early work on language choice such as that of Parasher (1980) and Rubin (1968) utilizes self reports. Informative as much of this work is (see further below) it is important to be aware that self-reports, like other kinds of metalinguistic discourse, are often mediated through stereotypical views of language which reflect perceptions of salient social groups, including the speaker's own group (see Giles and Powesland 1975; Irvine and Gal 2000). Hence, speakers do not always report accurately on their own language behaviour and indeed may not be able to. A common pattern of response is to claim use of a language or variety which commands high prestige and to deny knowledge or use of a code that is stigmatized or associated with localized interactions. Thus, young men in Attica and Biotia deny knowledge of Arvanitika because they want to be viewed as Greek-speaking (Trudgill 1983: 140) and London Jamaican speakers deny knowledge of Creole, because they view themselves as English speakers (Le Page and Tabouret-Keller 1985). However, Li Wei, Milroy, and Pong Sin Ching (2000: 198) report that the results of Pong Sin Ching's questionnaire study confirm the chief findings of Li Wei's 1994 participant-observation study of patterns of language use in 20 three-generational Chinese families in northern England. Self-report is therefore not necessarily unreliable, but is best used in conjunction with observation. It is likely that a correspondence between self-report and observed patterns of use depends partly on methods of eliciting evaluative judgments and partly on the community's particular language ideologies.

The practice of mixing codes in the same utterance is often reported to be particularly stigmatized, probably as a consequence of underlying ideologies of linguistic purity and structural autonomy (Milroy and Muysken 1995: 8), and terms for such practices abound. We find "Nuyorican," "Spanglish," "Tex-Mex" in the United States for Spanish/English mixes; "tuti futi" in Britain for Panjabi/English; "Chinglish" in Hong-Kong for Chinese/English, and many more. The following example of Panjabi/English code-mixing by a British man illustrates several of the issues discussed in this section – the kinds of mixed code encountered by researchers; the attitude of the speaker to mixing; the mismatch between his attitudes and behavior, and his inability to monitor his own language mixing behavior:

(1) I mean . . . I'm guilty in that sense ke zIada esĩ English i bolde ɛ̃ fer ode nal edã hɔnda ke tɔ hadi jeṛi zɔban ɛ, na? odec hər Ik sentence Ic je dɔ tIn English de word hɔnde ɛ . . . but I think that's wrong, I mean, mɛ̃ khɔd canã ke mɛ̃, na, jedo Panjabi bolda ɛ, pure Panjabi bolã esĩ mix kərde rɛne a, I mean, unconsciously, subconsciously, kəri jane ɛ, you know, pər I wish you know ke mɛ̃ pure Panjabi bol səkã.

Translation:

I mean . . . I'm guilty as well in the sense that we speak English more and then what happens is that when you speak your own language you get two or three English words in each sentence . . . but I think that's wrong, I mean, I myself would like to speak *pure* Panjabi: Whenever I speak Panjabi. We keep mixing [Panjabi and English] I mean unconsciously, subconsciously, we keep doing it, you know, but I wish, you know, that I could speak *pure* Panjabi. (Chana and Romaine 1984: 450)

Data like these vividly illustrate potential limitations of self-reports. Bilinguals are often unable to remember which language was used in any particular exchange, leading Gumperz to suggest that asking them to report on incidence of switching is no more rational than asking a monolingual to report on incidence of future tense (1982a: 62). Bearing in mind the general issues reviewed in this introductory section, we look next at different socially-oriented approaches to code-switching.

8.4.2   *"Allocational" and "interactional" paradigms*

Much research on the social determinants of language choice and on language maintenance and shift is informed directly or indirectly by the work of Joshua Fishman. Fishman typically concentrates on the effects of institutions on language behavior in creating large-scale patterns of language dominance which regularly lead to overt or covert language conflict. His concept of domain attempts to show how such effects play out in the language choices of individuals in different contexts such as work, family, church, and neighborhood. The language/domain link is seen as a consequence of larger scale social, political, and economic factors, and language choices are said to be predicted by the domain in which they occur (Fishman 1972, 1980). Thus, for example, Spanish speakers in the United States are predicted to use English in formal, work-related domains and Spanish in family domains because of the associations of English with institutionally driven activities and of Spanish with personal and intimate life. Researchers such as Parasher (1980) and Rubin (1968) assume a domains analysis. Parasher reports questionnaire information collected from 350 speakers in two Indian cities on the use of their mother tongue in seven ordered domains: family, neighborhood, friends, transactional, government, employment, education. The highest levels of mother tongue use are reported in the family domain, with a progressive decline through the others, culminating with the lowest level of use in the education domain. In her study of Spanish/Guaraní bilingualism in Paraguay, Rubin uses the formal device of a decision tree (1968: 109) to represent language behaviors as the outcome of an ordered series of binary choices determined by the social context.

Myers-Scotton has referred to work of this general type as the "allocational paradigm" to distinguish it from the "interactional paradigm" (1993: 49). The allocational paradigm treats social structure as broadly determining language behaviors, and particular speech activity types of the kind distinguished by Parasher or Rubin are said to trigger the use of one language or another. The interactional paradigm, on the other hand, treats individuals as making rational, intersubjectively understood language choices to achieve specifiable interactional goals. Auer (1995) spells out the difficulties of extending a Fishman-style domains analysis to bilingual conversations, which often display language alternation within a single domain. As both Auer and Myers-Scotton point out, such alternation appears to be patterned, purposeful and rationally motivated by individual communicative goals and strategies, rather than to fall out predictably from higher level institutional conditions and constraints. Researchers sometimes attempt to draw a distinction between two types of switching behavior of the kind which is captured by the allocational/interactional paradigm contrast. The first type can be related with varying degrees of transparency to macro-level factors – the symbolic value of each of the languages in the world outside the conversation – and the second to the interactants' strategic deployment of code choice. While the distinction drawn by Gumperz between "situational" and "metaphorical" code-switching (1982a: 61) and by Myers-Scotton between "unmarked" and "marked" code choice (1993: 75) in no sense map directly onto one another, both refer to the disjunction between these two major types of switching.

In a considered account of sociolinguistic research on code-switching, Myers-Scotton (1993: 45–74) notes that unmarked code choices reflect the link between language and situation captured by Fishman's domains analysis (the allocational paradigm) where, for example, Spanish might be the language of business and English the language of the home. She also notes that, in some types of speech community, switching between languages may itself be an unmarked choice (1993: 117–31), social meaning being carried by this continuous pattern of switching rather than by individual switches. Unmarked choices are socially unremarkable, reflecting a pre-existing set of social rights and obligations indexed by each language. Marked choices, on the other hand, by flouting expectations, trigger inferences and so implicate such meanings as intimacy or distance, irony or hostility. Speakers can therefore make marked choices strategically. To illustrate how Myers-Scotton's markedness model works, consider the following example where a passenger on a bus in Nairobi, Kenya, engages in interaction with the conductor in Swahili, the unmarked choice in such public contexts. A dispute develops over the conductor's tardiness in handing over the passenger's 50 cents change. The switch to English (a marked choice) in the final two turns draws attention to itself and in the context implicates an authoritative and angry stance derived partly, according to Myers-Scotton, from the status of English as a colonial language:

(2) PASSENGER: Nataka kwenda Posta
     "I want to go to the post office."

     CONDUCTOR: Kutoka hapa mpaka posta nauli ni senti hamsini.
     "From here to the post office, the fare is 50 cents."
     (Passenger gives the conductor a shilling, from which he should get 50 cents in change.)

CONDUCTOR: Ngojea *change* yako.
"Wait for your change."
(Passenger says nothing until some minutes have passed and the bus is nearing the post office where the passenger plans to get off.)

PASSENGER: Nataka *change* yangu.
"I want my change."

CONDUCTOR: *Change* utapata, Bwana.
"You'll get your change."

PASSENGER: *I am nearing my destination.*

CONDUCTOR: *Do you think I could run away with your change?*
(Myers-Scotton 1993: 133)

Bell has noted recently (2001) that his own distinction between audience design and initiative design (see section 8.1 above) is of the same general type as the unmarked/marked distinction; indeed much recent work on code-switching runs parallel to the work reviewed earlier on style-switching in emphasizing strategic motivation rather than situational influence. Myers-Scotton (1993, 1998) describes the details of her theory, which is intended to account comprehensively for code- and style-switching behavior in both and bilingual and monolingual communities.

8.4.3   *Language choice and code-switching: three case studies*

In this section we review three influential studies with very different goals, all of which illustrate the social significance of particular language choices, and hence of code-switching. Gal (1978, 1979), Zentella (1997), and Woolard (1997) all present analyses which appeal in different ways to the social world outside the interaction and to the strategic choices of the speaker. Gal focuses primarily on the processes of language shift in Oberwart, Austria, where the community is becoming monolingual in German after several hundred years of German/Hungarian bilingualism (see section 5.2.3). While, as expected, younger speakers use more German than their elders, it is specific language choices in particular situational contexts that give rise to a gradual process of language shift across three generations. Like Bell, Gal concludes that participant is the critical variable to which the other dimensions of context (such as topic and setting) are subservient. She is able to order her data implicationally to show that while the effect of age of speaker is paramount, some addressees are more likely than others to be spoken to in German, or in a mixture of German and Hungarian. For example, prayers are always in Hungarian, and grandparents are addressed in Hungarian except by the youngest speakers, who use a mixture of German and Hungarian. At the other extreme, the doctor is addressed in German except by a handful of elderly speakers who use Hungarian (Gal 1978: 231). Gal also notes the strategic deployment of German in a Hungarian conversation where the effect of a switch to German is often to cap a point and close an argument. This kind of bilingual practice is displayed by an angry participant in a mealtime dispute who achieves the last word in this way (Gal 1979: 117).

Despite a general sense that Spanish in the United States is resistant to shift, Zentella notes evidence of a three-generational shift pattern[1] of the kind documented by Gal and others in her account of a Puerto Rican community in New York City (*el bloque*). She describes a number of features characteristic of language behavior on *el bloque*. While choice of code is heavily network-dependent, as noted in section 5.2.3, several varieties of both Spanish and English available in the community repertoire give rise to multiple codes. Thus, the linguistic resources of *el bloque* residents provide for more than a simple choice between Spanish and English, and patterns of code choice from this multidimensional repertoire are systematically associated with a range of distinctive gender- and age-related networks, as shown in table 8.3. Thus, children and teenagers use primarily Puerto Rican English but have access to other codes. The primary code of mature males and females on the other hand is non-standard Puerto-Rican Spanish, with additional access to a somewhat different range of codes than the children.[2] Many of the children speak very little Spanish, mixing Spanish into English to produce the code which Zentella describes as "Spanglish."

Residents of *el bloque* appear to make use of the rich linguistic resources at their disposal to construct styles characterized by elements from various Spanish and English sources, and these styles form part of the social practices

Table 8.3 Networks and codes of *el bloque*

Network	Primary code	Other code
Children	PRE	NSPRS, AAVE
Teens	PRE	NSPRS, AAVE, SE
Young dudes	AAVE	PRE, NSPRS, SE
Young mothers	PRE	NSPRS, AAVE, SE
Mature females	NSPRS	SPRS, HE
Mature males	NSPRS	SPRS, HE, SE

Source: Zentella (1997: 48).
Key:
PRE   = Puerto-Rican English   SPRS = Standard Puerto-Rican Spanish
AAVE = African American Vernacular English   SE   = Standard English
NSPRS = Non-Standard Puerto-Rican Spanish   HE   = Hispanicized English

of particular network groups. Thus, the styles constructed by younger speakers all have elements of AAVE, some more than others, depending on the ties and language practices of their everyday lives (Zentella 1997: 113–14). The presence of English-speaking siblings promotes English-dominant patterns in some children, while single children are immersed in Spanish-speaking networks (Zentella 1997: 212).

Continuing ties with Puerto Rico may partly explain why a mixed Spanish–English code is associated with young people, as reported by Zentella and others, since these speakers have shifted substantially to English mono-lingualism but still need to find a way of communicating with Spanish monolinguals. Zentella examines details of Spanglish, the precise patterns of which she ascribed to different kinds of factors – structural constraints on mixing, age and language proficiency of the speaker, and socially motivated discourse strategies (Zentella 1997: 80–136).

Woolard's (1997) account of speakers' social purposes in deploying linguistic resources focuses on gender-specific practices in a very different kind of bilingual setting, where bilingualism is historically stable and both languages are highly valued in the linguistic market. She argues that differences in the way male and female high school students use Castilian and Catalan in the Barcelona area emerge from different peer group structures. Peer group structure is examined in a number of different ways – such as the incidence of cliques ("a highly cohesive subset of actors within a network": p. 544), and patterns of who names whom as a friend, both reciprocally and non-reciprocally. Girls' networks are found to be more cohesive and more ethnically and linguistically homogeneous than those of boys, while boys' contacts are looser with larger networks that are more ethnically mixed and internally differentiated. Girls and boys appear to have different views of the etiquette and ideology of friendship – girls' friendships, in particular, set stronger constraints upon behavior, including linguistic behavior. Woolard suggests that gender differences of this general type are replicated elsewhere, particularly noting parallels with Eckert's findings on the relation between social category and gender. Recall that Eckert's girls were more concerned than boys to maintain symbolic (including linguistic) differentiation between the jock/burnout categories.[3] Woolard notes an important stylistic consequence of the tendency to police category boundaries in this way – namely, that the Barcelona girls are much less likely than the boys to code-switch between languages.

8.4.4 Bilingual conversations

Although speakers in Oberwart, New York, Barcelona, and elsewhere deploy bilingual resources to construct social meaning, little has been said so far about the details of code-switching strategies in specific conversations – that is, how socially motivated choices play out at the interactional level. Recall that this is the chief issue addressed by Myers-Scotton's theory of markedness (see again section 8.4.2), where she argues that choice of a marked code in a particular context has the capacity to trigger inferences that lead social actors to assign meaning to an act of switching. In this section, we shall look at a strand of research which focuses explicitly on individual switches with some attention to community norms and values but more particularly to the discourse meanings that derive from the sequential positioning of the switch in the conversation. Much of this work develops Gumperz's treatment of "conversational code-switching" (1982a: 59) (i.e., utterance internal switching) as network- and community-specific discourse strategies, with choice of specific languages being related to the relative value of the codes on the linguistic market. The changing language practices of the Slovenian/German bilingual community of Austria's Gail Valley described by Gumperz (1982b; see also in section 5.2.3 above) are analyzed in this way, as are the practices of speakers from many other communities. In the Gail Valley, Slovenian is associated with local values and German, the language of wider communication with more sophisticated, cosmopolitan values.

Gumperz focuses on speakers' use of linguistic resources (discourse strategies) and the inferences that their conversational partners are able to draw from particular contextualization cues, the communicative purpose of which is understood by "insider" addressees but often not by "outsiders." Conversational code-switching is one such cue which flags a meaning at a particular point in the discourse, but resources available to monolinguals such as prosody, pause patterns and lexicalized discourse markers such as *well, but, now, you know* may also be employed, as shown in (3) below. Schiffrin (1987) discusses the interactional meaning of these and other items, and their role in structuring discourse. The first of the examples cited below shows two switches from English to Spanish in the conversation of two Chicano professionals, both of which reiterate and emphasize a portion of the utterance. Gumperz reports this emphatic function of code-switching as a discourse strategy understood and widely used in bilingual communities. The second example demonstrates the significance of an initial choice of African American English by a man who opened the door to an African American interviewer who had made an appointment to interview the man's wife:

(3)   The three old one spoke nothing but Spanish, nothing but Spanish. *No hablan ingles* (they did not speak English).
             [Later in the same conversation]
      A: I was I got to thinking *vacilando el punto* (mulling over that point) you know?

(4)   HUSBAND: So y're gonna check out ma ol lady, hah?
           INTERVIEWER: Ah, no. I only came to get some information. They
           called from the office.
           (Husband, dropping his smile, disappears without a word and calls
           his wife.) (Gumperz 1982a: 133)

Gumperz explains the source of the evident communicative problem in (4)
as follows:

> The student reports that the interview that followed was stiff and quite
> unsatisfactory. Being black himself, he knew that he had "blown it" by failing
> to recognize the significance of the husband's speech style in this particular
> case. The style is that of a formulaic opening gambit used to "check out"
> strangers, to see whether or not they can come up with the appropriate
> formulaic reply. Intent on following the instructions he had received in his
> methodological training and doing well in what he saw as a formal interview,
> the interviewer failed to notice the husband's stylistic cues. Reflecting on the
> incident, he himself states that, in order to show that he was on the husband's
> wave-length, he should have replied with a typically black response like
> "Yea, I'ma git some info" (I'm going to get some information) to prove
> his familiarity with and his ability to understand local verbal etiquette and
> values. Instead, his Standard English reply was taken by the husband as an
> indication that the interviewer was not one of them and, perhaps, not to be
> trusted.

In an influential analysis of code-switching by young Italian/German
bilingual speakers in the town of Konstanz, Germany, Peter Auer (1984)
departs from Gumperz's model in a number of ways, particularly from
those parts of his work that stress the relationship between code-switching
patterns and the social values assigned to particular languages. Chiefly
because of doubts about their empirical adequacy and explanatory capacity,
Auer (1995) is critical both of Fishman's account of code-switching, which
attempts to link particular acts of switching with the domains appropriate to
each language, and of Gumperz's analyses of conversational code-switching
in terms of a set of functions – such as reiteration, emphasis, or quotation.
However, he develops Gumperz's notion of contextualization cues within
a conversation analytic framework, which is designed to explicate the way
conversationalists express and interpret the meanings of particular conversational moves locally – that is, on a turn by turn basis – with reference to
their sequential position in the discourse (see Psathas 1995 and Ten Have
1999 for accounts of the basic principles of CA). Auer's application of
this framework emphasizes code-switching as a conventionalized, network-
specific discourse practice which structures the conversation independently
of the global values associated with contributory languages or situational

norms of language choice. When code-switching is "participant-related" – i.e., explicable in terms of the language competence or preference of inter-locutors – language choice and the direction of switching are relevant. "Discourse-related" switching on the other hand structures the discourse to contextualize some aspect of the conversation, and the contrast displayed by the switch appears to be more important than the direction of the switch. Giacalone-Ramat (1995: 50–1) provides clear examples of both types of switching. Switches between the dialect of the Italian province of Piacenza and standard Italian in a service encounter in a village store are participant-related, in that the unmarked code is the dialect but a child is addressed in standard Italian. Quite different is the discourse-related switch between two university researchers in Sicily who discuss business matters in standard Italian, but switch into dialect to "bracket off" a comment on the weather. Similarly, Shin and Milroy (2000) distinguish participant- and discourse-related switching patterns of 6- and 7-year-old Korean/English bilingual children in New York City.

We shall concentrate here chiefly on discourse-related switching, as this constitutes the most influential contribution of Auer's approach. Consider the following example, where an Italian adolescent in Konstanz reports a quarrel with German class-mates:

(5) wenn ae Italiener kommt gell – sofort aeh: *guardate* Ittakerstinker und so
     [when Italians come you know – immediately they say *look* spaghetti
     heads and so on]. (Auer 1995: 119)

Here, the student's turn is in German with a single word switch to Italian. Rejecting an interpretation of the significance of this switch with reference to the symbolic value or use of Italian in the world outside the conversation, Auer notes that the reported German speakers are unlikely to use Italian when insulting their Italian class-mates. Rather it appears that the function of the switch is to contextualize the reported speech, which is not otherwise marked by any overt quotative device. Code alternation provides a contrast – effectively a boundary – between the reported speech and the surrounding discourse, thus functioning in much the same way as other quotative devices (cf . section 7.5 above).

Several contributions to Auer (1998) apply this conversation-internal analysis of discourse-related switching in different bilingual communities. The examples below are taken from Li Wei (1998: 160), who argues that Cantonese/English bilingual speakers are able to use a code-switching strat-egy to contextualize topic changes in the ongoing interaction. In (6), two teenage girls are discussing a teacher whom A evaluates as boring, and on the first line of (7) a man (A) and a woman (B), both in their twenties, end their discussion of a topic that they want to keep secret from a friend.[4]

(6)   A.   . . . he's bor[ing
      B.   [mm
      A.   I don't know (.) don't like him
           (2.0)
>   A.   *Ah ngaw jau di mafaan gelak*
           (I'LL HAVE SOME TROUBLE)
      B.   *Dimgai a?*
           (WHY?)
      A.   Yesterday right. . . .

(7)   A.   . . . *m hou gong koei tengji*
           (BETTER NOT TELL HIM YET)
           (2.0)
>   Did you see Kim yesterday?
      B.   Yeah
      A.   *Mou* [*mat si . . .*
           (NOT SERIOUS)
      B.   [*Yau di tautung je. Mou mat si ge.*
           ((SHE) ONLY HAS A LITTLE HEADACHE. NOT SERIOUS)
      A.   *Ngaw jing yiu man nay*
      B.   (I WAS JUST ABOUT TO ASK YOU)

Li Wei notes the structural similarities between these two conversations. In both cases, code-switching (into Cantonese in (6) and English in (7)) takes place following a short gap which marks the end of a conversational episode, as discussed by Jefferson (1989). Although it is not clear in (6) what A wants to talk about, it seems that after she switches back to English she does not continue discussing the teacher. Effectively, the paired Cantonese turns mark a boundary between two (English) conversational episodes. In (7), the post-pause switch is in the opposite direction, from Cantonese to English. Again, the utterance "Did you see Kim yesterday" is not built upon an earlier contribution; rather, it is a question that sets up the preconditions for a subsequent enquiry about a friend's health. Such pairs sequences as this – a request for information followed by a brief response – are recognizable as presequences, a structural type built to prefigure following talk, which is well described in the conversation analytic literature (for a clear account, see Levinson 1983: 346). The presequence in (7) is marked as such not only by its pair structure and sequential placement but also by a code alternation, and subsequent discussion of Kim's health is in Cantonese, as is the conversation preceding the two-second pause. The point here is that resources available to bilingual speakers that have the effect of contextualizing topic are rather different from those available to monolingual speakers to do the same conversational "work."

Such an analysis contrasts with Myers-Scotton's markedness model of code-switching, which depends upon the specification of situational norms of language use. Against the background of these norms linguistic resources are strategically manipulated by the speaker. Commenting specifically on Myer-Scotton's claims of universality for her socially-oriented model of code-switching, Li Wei notes that it is difficult to relate examples such as (6) and (7) to the contrasting social values assigned to each language or to the set of rights and obligations indexed by these languages. Particularly, the direction of switching does not appear to have the same relevance as the rhetorical contrast provided by the code alternation. Li Wei suggests that in both cases the code alternation has the effect of attracting the addressee's attention and effectively restarting a lapsed conversation. He follows Auer in arguing that switches such as these are difficult to understand with reference to macro-level values associated with the two languages; indeed, the assignment of such values can itself be problematic. Rather, their function is understood with reference to their sequential implicativeness – that is, the nature of the interactional moves that precede and follow them. Myers-Scotton and Bolonyai (2001: 21) offer an alternative analyses of some of Li Wei's Cantonese/English data within the framework of Myers-Scotton's markedness model, where they argue that motivations for particular switches are more plausibly explained with reference to the rights and obligations indexed by specific languages.

Interactionally oriented approaches to code-switching thus seem to be divided between those that refer to the external symbolism of the two codes and those that treat specific instances of shifting primarily as devices for structuring the ongoing discourse. We suggest that these accounts should not be treated as mutually exclusive, but that both are needed for a satisfactory analysis of code-switching. It certainly seems to be true, as Auer and Li Wei suggest, that instances of code-switching such as those discussed above are difficult to explain with reference to global values assigned to codes in a repertoire. However, it is equally clear that Myers-Scotton's markedness model is particularly helpful in explaining a large proportion of code-switching instances when speakers have a normative sense of the code(s) appropriate for particular situations. For example, Goetz (2001) shows that Dai/Chinese bilingual speakers in the Dehong Delta of southwest China, near the Burmese border, orient to a clear set of norms in using Dai, as opposed to Chinese, and that a large part (but not all) of the switching in her data can be accounted for with reference to the markedness framework. However, Goetz also shows that a sequential analysis like that discussed for (6) and (7) illuminates instances of switching that are resistant to explanation in terms of the markedness model. Similarly, Shin and Milroy (2000) report that English is best treated as the unmarked language of the classroom for the children whom they studied. Consequently, the rarity of code-switching in this setting renders it highly marked. This markedness gives it a prominence that invites analysis of its use by even very young children as a resource for organizing discourse. In a similar vein, Jørgensen (1998) notes that both "global" (large-scale social) and "local" (discoursal) factors need to be taken into account for a satisfactory analysis of the code-switching behavior of Esen, a Turkish/Danish bilingual girl.

8.5   Concluding Remarks

In this chapter, we highlighted similarities between the dynamics under-lying monolingual style-shifting and those underlying bidialectal or bilingual code-switching. Early variationist approaches treat style-shifting as essen-tially responsive either to the formality of the situation or to the social iden-tity of the audience. However, a variety of recent approaches treat style as proactive and strategic. Sometimes it is seen as the site where new varieties are constructed, and thus an important locus of linguistic change. While socially-oriented research on code-switching is generally carried out within different frameworks, we find the same contrast between approaches that treat switching behavior as a response to pre-existing social and linguistic norms, and those that emphasize the strategic, proactive dimensions of lan-guage alternation behavior.

9

Epilogue

We noted in the preface that although we began this project with the intention of simply updating a book published 15 years ago, changes in the field ensured the emergence of something very different and much more ambitious. By way of conclusion, we reflect briefly on some important ways in which the field has changed and expanded. We also attempt to identify issues that are currently attracting the attention of researchers and invite some careful reconceptualization.

First, it is clear that the scope of the field has changed and that variationists now employ a very much wider range of methods than in 1987. Large-scale urban studies that sample many speakers across a social class continuum and collect data primarily in overtly structured sociolinguistic interviews are much less common than they were, although it was work of this kind, following Labov's New York City study, that set the original standard for the field. Smaller scale studies that target particular communities and make use of a range of data collection methods are now more prominent. Still, interest in survey-level studies has by no means disappeared. As discussed in chapter 1, technological advances have been of benefit to much recent dialectological work that has increasingly employed quantitative methods. The boundaries between dialectology and variationist sociolinguistics have subsequently blurred, to the benefit of both fields. For example, Labov has taken insights from the study of sound change in progress and applied them to his Telsur dialect mapping project which covers the entire North American continent. This work is also significant methodologically in its reliance on acoustic data and its examination of coordinated shifts to which entire vowel systems, rather than isolated phonological features, are subject. The same approach to vowel variation is adopted in analyses of the sociolinguistic structure of small speech communities or communities of practice. Methodological flexibility is also evident in a willingness to use different types and sources of data in cases where sociolinguistic interviews prove insufficient. Consider, for example, the procedures employed by Rickford et al. (1995) in their analysis of the *as far as* construction, described in chapter 7.

Technological advances have had very general and far-reaching effects on analytic methods. For example, software packages designed to facilitate instrumental acoustic analysis (see chapter 6) are now readily available, allowing scholars to carry out work on personal computers which at one time would have required the resources of a fully equipped phonetics laboratory. Moreover, as noted by Docherty and Foulkes (1999), a very much wider range of phonetic phenomena can now be studied, allowing variationists to work at a higher level of phonetic sophistication. As a result, we will surely see a considerable expansion of "sociophonetics," as this area is sometimes described. Advances of a somewhat different kind in computer technology have given rise to an increased interest in corpus-based studies. A prominent example discussed in chapter 7 is the socio-historical work of Nevalainen and her colleagues.

In analyzing and interpreting their data, it is evident that analyses of variation now draw upon a very much wider range of linguistic and social theories than previously. For example, Nagy and Reynolds (1997) examine word-final deletion within an Optimality Theory framework, and Cameron (1996, 1997) draws upon Ariel's Accessibility Theory to account for variability in Spanish pronouns. Sometimes we find a particularly advanced *rapprochement* between variationist and other theoretical frameworks – for example, Henry's (1995) account of syntactic variation in the urban dialect of Belfast within a Minimalist framework. This increased attention to appropriate theoretical frameworks is particularly evident with respect to social theories. As discussed in chapters 4 and 5, social categories such as class, ethnicity, and gender are no longer accepted as previously given, unproblematic measures allowing straightforward correlation with linguistic data, and researchers draw on frameworks from adjacent disciplines as they attempt to theorize them appropriately. An important outcome of this reconceptualization is to view social categories as locally constructed rather than global, stable, and unproblematic. Moreover, in their effect on language they also inevitably interact with other locally relevant social factors, which in turn need to be discovered by careful research in the speech community, rather than be assumed. These themes are particularly prominent in Eckert's recent work (e.g., Eckert 2000).

It is probably safe to predict that the field will continue along the road of enriching variationist theory by integrating insights from both linguistic and social theory. There are, however, a number of other issues that have been to varying degrees underdeveloped or undertheorized, and are likely to be prominent in the future. One clear example is provided by an increasingly influential body of research on dialect contact which Trudgill (1986) began to incorporate into the variationist literature. This work addresses problems that result from restricting the analytical focus to intra-varietal variation and change – a restriction that Labov (2001b: 20) stated explicitly but is implicit in much variationist analysis. A conception of the speech community as a construct that does not provide for contact between communities results in a tendency to treat not only minority groups, but also speakers of putatively localized dialects, as if they were isolated from contact with others. In response to such concerns, scholars such as Kerswill (e.g., 1996, 2002) have developed methods that address the effects of contact on language variation and change. Similarly, Milroy (2002) provides a varied collection of work by British and North American scholars which incorporates into a variationist analysis perspectives derived from processes such as koineization, dialect leveling and second dialect acquisition. Given the pervasiveness of mobility in the contemporary world, it seems likely that scholars will be increasingly reluctant to treat speech communities as sociolinguistic islands and will continue to develop the potential of dialect contact frameworks.

One issue likely to become prominent in future research is the conceptualization of differently structured speech communities, and of associated ways in which particular patterns of linguistic variation and change are organized and linked to social organization and linguistic repertoires. For example, Dubois and Horvath (1999) show in some detail that generalizations about variation and change made originally on the basis of observations in the New York City speech community cannot be usefully applied to the Cajun community in Louisiana. There is now an impressive body of literature from the Arabic-speaking world that shows this problem to be particularly acute. As noted in chapter 4, where we discuss work by Haeri (1997) and Al-Wer (1997), patterns of variation somewhat different from those described in New York City can be linked to different social practices. Moreover, the diglossic character of Arabic-speaking communities is likely to give rise to patterns of stylistic variation that are quite different from those in New York City and require a more careful conception of the standard to which speakers can be shown to orient. Walters (2002: 154) cites the observation of an Arab linguist that "Sociolinguists often fail to understand that many shops in the Arab world do not have a fourth floor." This point implied here is quite general: although the speech communities of, for example, Louisiana, Tyneside, and Belfast may present themselves as somewhat less exotic than those of Cairo or Tunis, they are no more amenable to being studied in accordance with the model developed in New York City. While many sociolinguists are more aware of this set of issues than the comment of Walters' friend implies, very little systematic attention has been given to the way in which different relationships among linguistic variables might be associated with different kinds of speech community and different social practices.

We comment finally on an area that was partially neglected 15 years ago, but is currently attracting an increasing amount of research attention. As noted in chapter 8, stylistic variation has moved very much closer to the center of the variationist stage, and a number of different perspectives have been adopted which go far beyond the early conception of stylistic variation as a consequence of varying degrees of attention to speech. For example, Eckert (2000) has argued that the urge of social groups to construct stylistic distinctiveness with respect to many kinds of social practices gives rise to intergroup distinctiveness of various kinds and hence provides a catalyst for linguistic change. Several scholars – for example, Bell (2001) and Schilling-Estes (1998) – have moved away from a conception of style as primarily responsive to situation, and have developed frameworks that allow speakers to be seen as rational social actors who employ linguistic resources for strategic purposes (such as persona management). As Rampton (1995) and Johnstone (1999) show, speakers may also deploy resources that "belong" to other speech communities as long as they can socially position themselves to do so. Eckert and Rickford (2001) provide a collection of recent work on stylistic variation which embodies a range of different perspectives.

Our comments in this short conclusion are in no sense intended to constitute a complete list of innovations in the field or an exhaustive account of the likely future shape of variationist research. We have simply selected those issues that seem particularly salient to us. However, variationist sociolinguistics has emerged for us in the course of our writing as an increasingly exciting field. We hope that readers will agree with us, and that our work will stimulate them to identify gaps in the research literature of the kind discussed here, and so to move off in their own new directions.

Bon voyage!

Notes

Chapter 2   Locating and Selecting Subjects

1   In this respect developments in urban sociolinguistics apparently reflect those in sociology where detailed and systematic studies of class are less common than they once were. For example, in a first chapter entitled "The rise and fall of class," Cannadine (1998: 1) suggests that class is no longer widely assumed to be the key to understanding social life and social history in Britain. In their study of inequality in Detroit, which focuses chiefly on race, Farley et al. (2000) make no more than a very general distinction between blue-collar and white-collar workers. They use neighborhood as an indicator of class, in much the same way as Milroy et al. (1999) and Poplack, Sankoff, and Miller (1988).

Chapter 3   Data Collection

1   This technique ignores, for example, possible differences between the perception and production of the merger. Respondents may perceive a difference between the vowels but be unable to produce it consistently in their own speech, and vice versa (see Gordon 2001a).

2   Basically, the two classes stem from different Middle English vowel phonemes, but various types of evidence suggest that these two classes merged during the early modern period. This apparent merger is problematic because the present situation, in which MEAT and MATE are separate classes, implies that the merger has been undone. This scenario would contradict the general principle that mergers cannot be reversed.

3   In fact, sociolinguists have been criticized for promoting such an image of African American English even in their scholarly discussions (see Morgan 1994; Rickford 1997b).

Chapter 4   Language Variation and the Social World

1   As a procedure for checking reliability, tokens of the HOME vowel were analyzed independently by Dominic Watt and Lesley Milroy. Although agreement on the

values of the large number of tokens examined was extremely close, the two sets of figures were not identical. The figures cited here are taken from Milroy (1999) and differ slightly from those cited by Watt and Milroy (1999).

2   Giddens accordingly understands racism as the false attribution of undesirable inherited characteristics to someone of a particular physical appearance, but the term further refers to ideologies and behaviors which serve to perpetuate inequalities arising from racial and ethnic distinctions.

Chapter 5   Social Relationships and Social Practices

1   This is the publication date of research which had been available in working paper form for many years prior to the publication of *Discourse Strategies* (1982a).

2   In an extended discussion of sociolinguists' use of the network concept, Murray (1993) is sharply critical of the quantitative analysis employed by Labov (1972a) and Milroy (1987) on grounds which are not always clear and are more controversial than he suggests. Moreover, a subsequent editorial clarification (Butters 1995: 20) points out that specific criticisms of Milroy's statistical procedures and results rest on an implausible misreading of the text.

3   However, it is clear that the racist attitudes reported by Zentella make it difficult for people of a certain phenotype to integrate, however intense the pressures.

4   Tuten (1998) provides an extended discussion of the leveling/standardization distinction with reference to developments in medieval Spanish.

5   However, Dorian discusses variation in Gaelic only in a small Gaelic/English bilingual community but does not examine the possibility that social meaning in bilingual communities is expressed in the use of both languages (cf. Dubois and Horvath 1999; Mendoza-Denton 1997; Zentella 1997).

Chapter 6   Investigating Phonological Variation

1   Labov's focus on vocalic variation is demonstrated by the dominant role of the topic in his discussion of general principles of linguistic change (1994).

2   Fronting of (o) is certainly heard in other varieties of English (e.g., in California, and the American South (Labov 1994)), but these are apparently independent developments and are thus historically separate from the Newcastle case.

3   We are grateful to Paul Foulkes for pointing out this example.

4   The vowel may, in fact, be raised higher to near [ɪ] (see Labov 1994), though such extreme variants were not common among Gordon's subjects (2001b).

5   A number of software systems for acoustic analysis are available at no cost over the internet, including WASP (www.phon.ucl.ac.uk), Wavesurfer (www.speech.kth.se/wavesurfer), Speech Analyzer (www.sil.org), and Praat (www.praat.org).

6   In fact, the situation is even more complex since tense (æ) can appear in open syllables provided that the opening is created by the addition of an inflectional suffix. Thus, the vowel is tense in *man*, lax in *manner*, but tense in *manning* (e.g., *no one is manning the door*) (Labov 1994: 431).

7 While formants are principally associated with vowels, some types of consonants may also show a formant structure.
8 When information about glides is included, mean values for several tokens are usually given (e.g., Thomas 2001).

Chapter 7 Beyond Phonology

1 More recent research on the early history of *ne* deletion suggests, however, that the feature was not widespread in seventeenth-century French, neither in France nor in Quebec (see Martineau and Mougeon 2001).
2 Although versions of all the papers in the collection have been published elsewhere (but not always in English), they are cited here in these easily available versions except where the date or other details of the original publications are particularly relevant.

Chapter 8 Style-Shifting and Code-Switching

1 The three-generational shift pattern is clearly by no means inevitable in minority or immigrant bilingual communities but seems to be a consequence of social and ideological pressures to monolingualism exerted in the course of the twentieth century by modern developed nation states, particularly through school systems (Cashman 2001: ch. 2).
2 It is sometimes hard to understand the basis on which varieties which differ along a continuum are assigned by Zentella to one variety or another. We are indebted to Holly Cashman for a discussion of this problem, which relates to a more general difficulty with the notion of a "standard" English or Spanish as Zentella uses the term.
3 Woolard expresses some reservations however with respect to Eckert's explanation of these differences in terms of the relative importance of persona for girls and action for boys.
4 In these examples, italics are used for Cantonese and capitals for English translations. Also, [indicates simultaneous talk; (.) a micropause and (2.0) the length of pause in seconds. The symbol > draws attention to the segment of talk under discussion.

References

Abd-El-Jawad, H. R. (1987) Cross dialectal variation in Arabic: Competing prestigious forms. *Language in Society*, 16 (3), 359–68.

Abu-Haidar, F. (1989) Are Iraqi women more prestige conscious than men? Sex differentiation in Baghdadi Arabic. *Language in Society*, 18 (4), 471–82.

Abu-Lughod, L. (1986) *Veiled Sentiments: Honor and Poetry in a Bedouin Society*. Berkeley, CA: University of California Press.

Adank, P., Van Heuven, V., and van Hout, R. (1999) Speaker normalization preserving regional accent differences in vowel quality. In J. J. Ohala, Y. Hasegawa, M. Ohala, D. Granville, and A. C. Bailey (eds.), *Proceedings of the XIVth International Congress of Phonetic Sciences: ICPhP 99*. Berkeley: Dept of Linguistics, University of California, pp. 1593–6.

Al-Wer, E. (1997) Arabic between reality and ideology. *International Journal of Applied Linguistics*, 7 (2), 251–65.

Amuda, A. (1986) Language Mixing by Yoruba Speakers of English. Unpublished doctoral dissertation, University of Reading.

Anderson, B. (1999) Source-language transfer and vowel accommodation in the patterning of Cherokee English /ai/ and /oi/. *American Speech*, 74 (4), 339–68.

Anderson, B. (2002) Dialect leveling and /ai/ monophthongization among African American Detroiters. *Journal of Sociolinguistics*, 6 (1), 86–98.

Anderson, B. and Milroy, L. (1999) Southern sound changes and the Detroit AAVE vowel system. Paper presented at NWAVE 28, Toronto.

Ariel, M. (1990) *Accessing Noun-Phrase Antecedents*. London: Routledge.

Ariel, M. (1991) The function of accessibility in a theory of grammar. *Journal of Pragmatics*, 16, 443–63.

Armstrong, N. (2001) *Social and Stylistic Variation in Spoken French: A Comparative Approach*. Amsterdam and Philadelphia: Benjamins.

Armstrong, N. and Unsworth, S. (1999) Sociolinguistic variation in southern French schwa. *Linguistics*, 37 (1), 127–56.

Ashby, M. (1976) The loss of the negative morpheme *ne* in Parisian French. *Lingua*, 39, 119–37.

Ashby, M. (1981) The loss of the negative particle *ne* in French. *Language*, 57, 674–87.

Auer, P. (1984) *Bilingual Conversation*. Amsterdam: Benjamins.

Auer, P. (1995) The pragmatics of code-switching: A sequential approach. In L. Milroy and P. Muysken (eds.), *One Speaker, Two Languages*. Cambridge: Cambridge University Press, pp. 115–35.

Auer, P. (ed.) (1998) *Code-Switching in Conversation: Language, Interaction and Identity*. London: Routledge.

Babbitt, E. H. (1896) The English of the lower classes in New York City and vicinity. *Dialect Notes*, 1, 457–64.

Bailey, G. and Dyer, M. (1992) An approach to sampling in dialectology. *American Speech*, 67, 3–20.

Bailey, G., Wikle, T., and Tillery, J. (1997) The effects of methods on results in dialectology. *English World-Wide*, 18 (1), 35–63.

Bailey, G., Wikle, T., Tillery, J., and Sand, L. (1991) The apparent time construct. *Language Variation and Change*, 3, 241–64.

Bailey, R. (1996) *Nineteenth Century English*. Ann Arbor, MI: The University of Michigan Press.

Barrett, R. (1998) Markedness and styleswitching in performances by African drag queens. In C. Myers-Scotton (ed.), *Codes and Consequences*. Oxford: Oxford University Press, pp. 139–61.

Baugh, J. (2001) A dissection of style shifting. In P. Eckert and J. Rickford (eds.), *Style and Sociolinguistic Variation*. Cambridge: Cambridge University Press, pp. 192–205.

Bayley, R. and Preston, D. R. (eds.) (1996) *Second Language Acquisition and Linguistic Variation*. Amsterdam and Philadelphia: Benjamins.

Beckford, A. (1999) A Sociophonetic Analysis of Jamaican Vowels. Unpublished doctoral dissertation, University of Michigan.

Bell, A. (1984) Language style as audience design. *Language in Society*, 13 (2), 145–204.

Bell, A. (1999) Styling the other to define the self: a study in New Zealand identity making. *Journal of Sociolinguistics*, 4 (3), 523–41. [Theme issue *Styling the Other*, ed. B. Rampton.]

Bell, A. (2001) Back in style: Reworking audience design. In P. Eckert and J. Rickford (eds.), *Style and Sociolinguistic Variation*. Cambridge: Cambridge University Press, pp. 139–69.

Bernsten, J. (1998) Marked versus unmarked choices on the auto factory floor. In C. Myers-Scotton (ed.), *Codes and Consequences*. Oxford: Oxford University Press, pp. 178–91.

Biber, D. (1995) *Dimensions of Register Variation: A Cross-Linguistic Comparison*. Cambridge: Cambridge University Press.

Biber, D. and Finegan, E. (eds.) (1994) *Sociolinguistic Perspectives on Register*. New York: Oxford University Press.

Blake, R. (1997) Defining the envelope of linguistic variation: The case of "don't count" forms in the copula analysis of African American Vernacular English. *Language Variation and Change*, 9 (1), 57–80.

Bloomfield, L. (1926) A set of postulates for the study of language. *Language*, 2, 153–64.

Bloomfield, L. (1933) *Language*. London: Allen & Unwin.

Blom, J. P. and Gumperz, J. J. (1972) Social meaning in linguistic structures: Code-switching in Norway. In J. Gumperz and D. Hymes (eds.), *Directions in Sociolinguistics*, New York: Holt, Rinehart & Winston, pp. 407–34.

Boal, F. W. and Poole, M. A. (1976) Religious Residential Segregation and Residential Decision Making in the Belfast Urban Area. Unpublished report to the Social Science Research Council, London.

Boberg, C. and Strassel, S. M. (2000) Short-a in Cincinnati: A change in progress. *Journal of English Linguistics*, 28, 108–26.

Boissevain, J. (1974) *Friends of Friends: Networks, Manipulators and Coalitions*. Oxford: Blackwell.

Bortoni-Ricardo, S. M. (1985) *The Urbanization of Rural Dialect Speakers: A Sociolinguistic Study in Brazil*. Cambridge: Cambridge University Press.

Bourdieu, P. (1984) Capital et marché linguistique. *Linguistische Berichte*, 90, 3–24.

Bourhis, R. Y. and Marshall, D. F. (1999) Language and ethnic identity in the United States and Canada. In J. Fishman (ed.), *Language and Ethnic Identity: Before and After the Ethnic Revival*. Oxford and New York: Oxford University Press, pp. 244–64.

Briggs, C. L. (1984) Learning how to ask: Native meta-communicative competence. and the incompetence of fieldworkers. *Language in Society*, 13 (1), 1–28.

Briggs, C. L. (1986) *Learning How to Ask: A Sociolinguistic Appraisal of the Role of the Interview in Social Science Research*. Cambridge and New York: Cambridge University Press.

Britain, D. (1992) Linguistic change in intonation: The use of high-rising terminals in New Zealand English. *Language Variation and Change*, 4, 77–103. [Reprinted in Trudgill, P. and Cheshire, J. (eds.) (1998) *The Sociolinguistics Reader*. London: Arnold, pp. 213–39.]

Britain, D. (1997) Dialect contact and phonological reallocation: "Canadian Raising" in the English Fens. *Language in Society*, 26 (1), 15–46.

Britain, D. (2002) Diffusion, levelling, simplification and reallocation in past tense BE in the English Fens. *Journal of Sociolinguistics*, 6 (2), 16–43.

Brown, P. and Levinson, S. (1987) *Politeness*. Cambridge: Cambridge University Press.

Buchholz, M. (1999) You da man: Narrating the racial other in the production of white masculinity. *Journal of Sociolinguistics*, 3 (4), 443–60.

Butler, C. (1985) *Statistics in Linguistics*. Oxford: Blackwell.

Butters, R. (1995) Editorial clarification. *American Speech*, 70 (1), 20.

Butters, R. (2000) Conversational anomalies in eliciting danger-of-death narratives. *Southern Journal of Linguistics*, 24, 69–81.

Callary, R. E. (1975) Phonological change and the development of an urban dialect in Illinois. *Language in Society*, 4, 155–69.

Cameron, D. (1995) *Verbal Hygiene*. London: Routledge.

Cameron, D., Frazer, E., Harvey, P., Rampton, M. B. H., and Richardson, K. (1992) *Researching Language: Issues of Power and Method*. London: Routledge.

Cameron, R. (1996) Accessibility theory and specificity of reference in Spanish. In L. McNair, K. Singer, L. Dobrin, and M. Aucoin (eds.), *CLS 32: Papers from the Parasession on Theory and Data in Linguistics*. Chicago: Chicago Linguistics Society, 13–28.

Cameron, R. (1997) Accessibility theory in a variable syntax of Spanish. *Journal of Pragmatics*, 28, 29–67.

Cannadine, D. (1998) *Class in Britain*. London: Penguin.

Carver, C. M. (1987) *American Regional Dialects: A Word Geography*. Ann Arbor, MI: University of Michigan Press.

Cashman, H. (2001) Doing being Bilingual: Language Maintenance, Language Shift and Conversational Codeswitching. Unpublished PhD dissertation, University of Michigan.

Cedergren, H. (1973) The Interplay of Social and Linguistic Factors in Panama. Unpublished doctoral dissertation, Cornell University.

Cedergren, H. (1987) The spread of language change: Verifying inferences of linguistic diffusion. In P. H. Lowenberg (ed.), *Language Spread and Language Policy: Issues, Implications, and Case Studies, Georgetown University Round Table on Languages and Linguistics 1987*, Washington, DC: Georgetown University Press, pp. 45–60.

Chambers, J. K. (1992) Dialect acquisition. *Language*, 68 (3), 673–705.

Chambers, J. K. (1994) An introduction to dialect topography. *English World-Wide*, 15 (1), 35–53.

Chambers, J. K. (1995) *Sociolinguistic Theory*. Oxford: Blackwell.

Chambers, J. K. (1998a) Inferring dialect from a postal questionnaire. *Journal of English Linguistics*, 26 (3), 222–46.

Chambers, J. K. (1998b) Social embedding of changes in progress. *Journal of English Linguistics*, 26 (1), 5–36.

Chambers, J. K. and Trudgill, P. (1998) *Dialectology* (2nd edn.). Cambridge: Cambridge University Press.

Chana, V. and Romaine, S. (1984) Evaluative reactions to Panjabi-English code-switching. *Journal of Multilingual and Multicultural Development*, 5, 447–53.

Chelliah, S. L. (2001) The role of text collection and elicitation in linguistic field-work. In P. Newman and M. Ratliff (eds.), *Linguistic Fieldwork*. Cambridge: Cambridge University Press, pp. 152–65.

Chen, M. Y. (1976) Relative chronology: Three methods of reconstruction. *Journal of Linguistics*, 12, 209–58.

Cheshire, J. (1982) *Variation in an English Dialect: A Sociolinguistic Study*. Cambridge: Cambridge University Press.

Cheshire, J. (1999) Taming the vernacular: Some repercussions for variation and spoken grammar. *Cuadernos de Filologia Inglesa*, 8. Departamento de Filologia Inglesa de la Universidad de Murcia, pp. 59–80.

Chomsky, N. (1965) *Aspects of the Theory of Syntax*. Cambridge, MA.: MIT Press.

Chomsky, N. (1986) *Knowledge of Language: Its Nature, Origin and Use*. New York: Praeger.

Chomsky, N. (1992) A minimalist program for linguistic theory. *MIT Occasional Papers in Linguistics*, 1.

Coates, J. (1986) *Women, Men and Language*. London: Longman.

Coates, J. (ed.) (1998) *Language and Gender: A Reader*. Oxford: Blackwell.

Cochran, M., Larner, M., Riley, D., Gunnarsson, L., and Henderson, C. R., Jr. (1990) *Extending Families: The Social Networks of Parents and their Children*. Cambridge: Cambridge University Press.

Cohen, A. (ed.) (1982) *Belonging*. Manchester: Manchester University Press.

Congalton, A. A. (1962) *Social Standings of Occupations in Sydney*. Sydney: School of Sociology, University of New South Wales.

Congalton, A. A. (1969) *Status and Prestige in Australia*. Melbourne: Cheshire.

Cook, V. J. and Newson, M. (1996) *Chomsky's Universal Grammar: An Introduction*. Oxford: Blackwell.

Corneau, C. (2000) An EPG study of palatalization in French: Cross-dialect and inter-subject variation. *Language Variation and Change*, 12, 25–49.

Cornips, L. (1998) Syntactic variation, parameter, and social distribution. *Language Variation and Change*, 10 (1), 1–21.

Coupland, N. (1980) Style-shifting in a Cardiff work-setting. *Language in Society*, 9, 1–12.

Coupland, N. (1984) Accommodation at work: Some phonological data and their applications. *International Journal of the Sociology of Language*, 46, 49–70.

Coveney, A. (1995) The use of the QU-final interrogative structure in spoken French. *French Language Studies*, 5, 143–71.

Coveney, A. (1996) *Variability in Spoken French: A Sociolinguistic Study of Interrogation and Negation*. Exeter, England: Elm Bank Publications.

Coveney, A. (2000) Vestiges of *nous* and the 1st person plural verb in informal spoken French. *Language Sciences*, 22, 447–81.

Crystal, D. and Davy, D. (1969) *Investigating English Style*. London: Longman.

Cukor-Avila, P. (1997) An ethnolinguistic approach to the study of rural southern AAVE. In C. Bernstein, T. Nunnally, and R. Sabino (eds.), *Language Variety in the South Revisited*. Tuscaloosa: University of Alabama Press, pp. 447–62.

Cukor-Avila, P. and Bailey, G. (1995) An approach to sociolinguistic fieldwork: A site study of rural AAVE in a Texas community. *English World-Wide*, 16 (2), 159–93.

Cutler, C. (1999) Yorkville crossing: White teens, hip hop and African American English. *Journal of Sociolinguistics*, 4 (3), 428–42. [Theme issue *Styling the Other*, ed. B. Rampton.]

Dabène, L. and Moore, H. (1995) Bilingual speech of migrant people. In L. Milroy and P. Muysken (eds.), *One Speaker, Two Languages*. Cambridge: Cambridge University Press, pp. 17–44.

Dailey O'Cain, J. (2000) The sociolinguistic distribution of and attitudes towards focuser *like* and quotative *like*. *Journal of Sociolinguistics*, 4 (1), 60–80.

Dannenberg, C. and Wolfram, W. (1998) Ethnic identity and grammatical restructuring: Be(s) in Lumbee English. *American Speech*, 73 (2), 139–59.

Davis, L. M. (1990) *Statistics in Dialectology*. Tuscaloosa: University of Alabama Press.

Dennis, N., Henriques, F. M., and Slaughter, C. (1957) *Coal is Our Life*. London: Eyre & Spottiswoode.

Diesing, M. (1992) *Indefinites*. Cambridge, MA: MIT Press.

Di Sciullo, A.-M. and St-Pierre, M. (1982) Les actes de requête dans les énoncés de forme impérative et interrogative en français de Montréal. In C. Lefebvre (ed.), *La Syntaxe Comparée du Français Standard et Populaire: Approches Formelle et Fonctionelle* (t 2). Québec: Office de la Langue Française.

Disner, S. F. (1980) Evaluation of vowel normalization procedures. *Journal of the Acoustical Society of America*, 67 (1), 253–61.

DiPaolo, M. and Faber, A. (1990) Phonation differences and the phonetic content of the tense-lax contrast in Utah English. *Language Variation and Change*, 2, 155–204.

Ditmarr, N. and Schlobinski, P. (eds.) (1988) *The Sociolinguistics of Urban Vernaculars*. Berlin: de Gruyter.

Ditmarr, N., Schlobinski, P., and Wachs, I. (1988) The social significance of the Berlin urban vernacular. In N. Ditmarr and P. Schlobinski (eds.), *The Sociolinguistics of Urban Vernaculars*. Berlin: de Gruyter, 19–43.

Dixon, R. M. W. (1984) *Searching for Aboriginal Languages*. St. Lucia: University of Queensland Press.

Docherty, G. J. and Foulkes, P. (1999) Derby and Newcastle: Instrumental phonetics and variationist studies. In P. Foulkes and G. J. Docherty (eds.), *Urban Voices*, London: Arnold, pp. 47–71.

Docherty, G. J., Foulkes, P., Milroy, J., Milroy, L., and Walshaw, D. (1997) Descriptive adequacy in phonology: A variationist perspective. *Journal of Linguistics*, 33, 275–310.

Dorian, N. (1981) *Language Death*. Philadelphia: University of Pennsylvania Press.

Dorian, N. (1994) Varieties of variation in a very small place: Social homogeneity, prestige norms and linguistic variation. *Language*, 70, 631–96.

Douglas-Cowie, E. (1978) Linguistic code-switching in a Northern Irish village: Social interaction and social ambition. In P. Trudgill (ed.), *Sociolinguistic Patterns in British English*. London: Arnold, pp. 37–51.

Dressler, W. U. and Wodak, R. (1982) Sociophonological methods in the study of sociolinguistic variation in Viennese German. *Language in Society*, 11 (1), 339–70.

Dubois, S. and Horvath, B. M. (1998) Let's tink about dat: Interdental fricatives in Cajun English. *Language Variation and Change*, 10 (3), 245–61.

Dubois, S. and Horvath, B. M. (1999) When the music changes you change too: Gender and language change in Cajun English. *Language Variation and Change*, 11 (3), 287–313.

Dyer, J. (2000) Language and Identity in a Scottish–English community: A Phonological and Discoursal Analysis. Unpublished doctoral dissertation, University of Michigan.

Dyer, J. (2002) We all speak the same around here: Dialect levelling in a Scottish–English community. *Journal of Sociolinguistics*, 6, 99–116.

Eckert, P. (1989a) *Jocks and Burnouts: Social Categories and Identity in the High School*. New York: Columbia University Teachers College.

Eckert, P. (1989b) The whole woman: Sex and gender differences in variation. *Language Variation and Change*, 1, 245–68.

Eckert, P. (1991) Social polarization and the choice of linguistic variants. In P. Eckert (ed.), *New Ways of Analyzing Sound Change*. San Diego: Academic Press, pp. 213–32.

Eckert, P. (1996) (ay) goes to the city: Exploring the expressive use of variation. In G. R. Guy, C. Feagin, D. Schiffrin, and J. Baugh (eds.), *Towards a Social Science of Language*. Amsterdam and Philadelphia: Benjamins, pp. 47–68.

Eckert, P. (1997) Age as a sociolinguistic variable. In F. Coulmas (ed.). *The Handbook of Sociolinguistics*. Oxford: Blackwell, pp. 151–67.

Eckert, P. (1998) Gender and sociolinguistic variation. In J. Coates (ed.), *Language and Gender: A Reader*. Oxford: Blackwell, pp. 64–75.

Eckert, P. (2000) *Linguistic Variation as Social Practice*. Oxford: Blackwell.

Eckert, P. (2001) Style and social meaning. In P. Eckert and J. Rickford (eds.), *Style and Sociolinguistic Variation*. Cambridge: Cambridge University Press, pp. 206–19.

Eckert, P. and McConnell-Ginet, S. (1994) Think practically and look locally: Language and gender as community-based practice. *Annual Review of Anthropology*, 21, 461–90.

Eckert, P. and Rickford, J. (eds.) (2001) *Style and Sociolinguistic Variation*. Cambridge: Cambridge University Press.

Edwards, V. (1986) *Language in a Black Community*. Clevedon, Avon: Multilingual Matters.

Edwards, W. (1992) Sociolinguistic behaviour in a Detroit inner city black neighbourhood. *Language in Society*, 21, 93–115.

Edwards, W. and Diergardt, N. (2000) *Detroit AAVE and the Northern Cities Shift*. Paper given at NWAV 29, Michigan State University.

Erickson, B. H. and Nosanchuk, T. A. (1992) *Understanding Data*. Toronto: University of Toronto Press.

Farley, R., Danziger, S., and Holzer, H. (2000) *Detroit Divided*. New York: The Russell Sage Foundation.

Fasold, R. (1978) Language variation and linguistic competence. In D. Sankoff (ed.), *Linguistic Variation: Models and Methods*. New York: Academic Press, pp. 85–96.

Fasold, R. (1984) *The Sociolinguistics of Society*. Oxford: Blackwell.

Fasold, R. (1990) *The Sociolinguistics of Language*. Oxford: Blackwell.

Ferrara, K. and Bell, B. (1995) Sociolinguistic variation and discourse function of constructed dialogue introducers: The case of *be + like*. *American Speech*, 70, 265–90.

Fischer, J. N. L. (1958) Social influences on the choice of a linguistic variant. *Word*, 14, 47–56.

Fishman, J. (1972) The link between macro- and micro-sociology in the study of who speaks what to whom and when. In J. Gumperz and D. Hymes (eds.), *Directions in Sociolinguistics*. New York: Holt, Rinehart & Winston, pp. 435–53.

Fishman, J. (1980) Bilingualism and biculturalism as individual and societal phenomena. *Journal of Multilingual and Multicultural Development*, 1 (1), 3–15.

Fought, C. (1999) A majority sound change in a minority community: /u/ fronting in Chicano English. *Journal of Sociolinguistics*, 3 (1), 5–23.

Fridland, V. (1999) The southern shift in Memphis, Tennessee. *Language Variation and Change*, 11 (3), 267–85.

Gal, S. (1978) Variation and change in patterns of speaking: Language shift in Austria. In D. Sankoff (ed.), *Linguistic Variation: Models and Methods*. New York: Academic Press, pp. 227–38.

Gal, S. (1979) *Language Shift: Social Determinants of Linguistic Change in Bilingual Austria*. New York: Academic Press.

Gans, H. J. (1962) *The Urban Villagers: Group and Class in the Life of Italian-Americans* (2nd edn.). New York: Free Press.

Gardner-Chloros, P. (1997) Code-switching: Language selection in three Strasbourg department stores. In N. Coupland and A. Jaworski (eds.), *Sociolinguistics: A Reader*. New York: St. Martins, pp. 361–75.

Gauchat, L. (1905) L'unité phonétique dans le patois d'une commune. In *Festschrift Heinrich Morf: aus Romanischen Sprachen und Literaturen*. Halle: M. Niemeyer, pp. 175–232.

Giacalone-Ramat, A. (1995) Code-switching in the context of dialect/standard language relations. In L. Milroy and P. Muysken (eds.), *One Speaker, Two Languages*. Cambridge: Cambridge University Press, pp. 45–67.

Giddens, A. (1989) *Sociology*. Cambridge: Polity.

Giles, H. (ed.) (1984) The dynamics of speech accommodation. *International Journal of the Sociology of Language*, 46.

Giles, H. and Powesland, P. F. (1975) *Speech Style and Social Evaluation*. London: Academic Press.

Girard, D. and Larmouth, D. (1993) Some applications of mathematical and statistical models in dialect geography. In D. R. Preston (ed.), *American Dialect Research*. Philadelphia: Benjamins, pp. 107–31.

Givón, T. (1979) *On Understanding Grammar*. New York: Academic Press.

Goetz, R. (2001) Investigating Language Maintenance: Social Correlates of Language Choice among the Dehong Dai. Unpublished doctoral dissertation, University of Michigan.

Gordon, E. (1991) The development of spoken English in New Zealand. In G. McGregor and W. Williams (eds.), *Dirty Silence: Aspects of Language and Literature in New Zealand*. Auckland: Oxford University Press, pp. 19–29.

Gordon, M. J. (2000) Phonological correlates of ethnic identity: Evidence of divergence? *American Speech*, 75, 115–36.

Gordon, M. J. (2001a) Investigating mergers and chain shifts. In J. K. Chambers, P. Trudgill, and N. Schilling-Estes (eds.), *Handbook of Language Variation and Change*. Oxford: Blackwell, pp. 244–66.

Gordon, M. J. (2001b) *Small-Town Values and Big-City Vowels: A Study of the Northern Cities Shift in Michigan*. Publication of the American Dialect Society, 84. Durham, NC: Duke University Press.

Grabe, E., Post, B., Nolan, F., and Farrar, K. (2000) Pitch accent realization in four varieties of British English. *Journal of Phonetics*, 28, 161–86.

Grace, G. (1990) The "aberrant" (vs. "exemplary") Melanesian languages. In P. Baldi (ed.), *Linguistic Change and Reconstruction Methodology*. Berlin: Mouton de Gruyter, pp. 155–73.

Grace, G. (1992) How do languages change? (more on "aberrant" languages). *Oceanic Linguistics*, 31 (1), 115–30.

Granovetter, M. (1973) The strength of weak ties. *American Journal of Sociology*, 78, 1360–80.

Granovetter, M. (1982) The strength of weak ties: A network theory revisited. In

P. Marsden and N. Lin London (eds.), *Social Structure and Network Analysis*. Beverly Hills, CA: Sage, pp. 105–30.

Green, L. (1998) Remote past and states in African American English. *American Speech*, 73 (2), 115–38.

Gregg, R. J. (1964) Scotch–Irish urban speech in Ulster. In B. Adams (ed.), *Ulster Dialects: A Symposium*. Hollywood, Co. Down: Ulster Folk Museum, pp. 163–91.

Grosjean, F. (1982) *Life with Two Languages*. Cambridge, MA: Harvard University Press.

Grosjean, F. (2001) The bilingual's language modes. In J. Nicol (ed.), *One Mind, Two Languages: Bilingual Language Processing*. Oxford: Blackwell, pp. 1–22.

Gumperz, J. J. (ed.) (1982a) *Discourse Strategies*. Cambridge: Cambridge University Press.

Gumperz, J. J. (1982b) Social network and language shift. In J. J. Gumperz (ed.), *Discourse Strategies*. Cambridge: Cambridge University Press, pp. 38–58.

Gunn, B. (1990) The Politic Word. Unpublished doctoral dissertation, University of Ulster at Jordanstown.

Guy, G. R. (1980) Variation in the group and the individual: The case of final stop deletion. In W. Labov (ed.), *Locating Language in Time and Space*. New York: Academic Press, pp. 1–36.

Guy, G. R. (1993) The quantitative analysis of linguistic variation. In D. R. Preston (ed.), *American Dialect Research*. Amsterdam and Philadelphia: Benjamins, pp. 223–49.

Guy, G. R. (1997) Violable is variable: Optimality theory and linguistic variation. *Language Variation and Change*, 9 (3), 333–47.

Guy, G. R. and Boberg, C. (1997) Inherent variability and the obligatory contour principle. *Language Variation and Change*, 9, 149–64.

Guy, G. R., Horvath, B., Vonwiller, J., Daisley, E., and Rogers, I. (1986) An intonational change in progress in Australian English. *Language in Society*, 15, 23–52.

Haeri, N. (1997) *The Sociolinguistic Market of Cairo: Gender, Class and Education*. London and New York: Kegan Paul International.

Halsey, A. H. (1995) *Change in British Society* (4th edn.). New York and Oxford: Oxford University Press.

Hammersley, M. and Atkinson, P. (1995) *Ethnography: Principles in Practice* (2nd edn.). London: Routledge.

Harman, L. D. (1988) *The Modern Stranger: On Language and Membership*. Berlin: Mouton de Gruyter.

Harrington, J. and Cassidy, S. (1994) Dynamic and target theories of vowel classification: evidence from monophthongs and diphthongs in Australian English. *Language and Speech*, 37, 357–73.

Harris, J. (1984) Syntactic variation and dialect divergence. *Journal of Linguistics*, 20 (2), 303–27. [Reprinted in Singh, R. (ed.), *Towards a Critical Sociolinguistics*. Amsterdam and Philadelphia: Benjamins, pp. 31–58.]

Harris, J. (1986) Expanding the superstrate: Habitual aspect markers in Atlantic Englishes. *English World-Wide*, 7 (2), 171–99.

Harris, J. (1991) Ireland. In J. Cheshire (ed.), *English Around the World: Sociolinguistic Perspectives*. Cambridge: Cambridge University Press.

Harris, J. (1993) The grammar of Irish English. In J. Milroy and L. Milroy (eds.), *Real English: The Grammar of English Dialects in the British Isles*. London: Longman, pp. 139–86.

Harris, Z. S. (1951) *Methods in Structural Linguistics*. Chicago: University of Chicago Press.

Hartley, L. C. and Preston, D. R. (1999) The names of US English: Valley girl, cowboy, yankee, normal, nasal and ignorant. In T. Bex and R. Watts (eds.), *Standard English: The Widening Debate*. London: Routledge, pp. 207–38.

Harvey, P. (1992) Bilingualism in the Peruvian Andes. In D. Cameron, E. Frazer, P. Harvey, M. B. H. Rampton, and K. Richardson (eds.), *Researching Language: Issues of Power and Method*. London: Routledge, pp. 65–89.

Hay, J., Jannedy, S., and Mendoza-Denton, N. (1999) Oprah and /ay/: Lexical frequency, referee design and style. In J. J. Ohala, Y. Hasegawa, M. Ohala, D. Granville, and A. C. Bailey (eds.), *Proceedings of the XIVth International Congress of Phonetic Sciences: ICPhP 99*. Berkeley: Department of Linguistics, University of California, pp. 1389–92.

Hazen, K. (2000) *Identity and Ethnicity in the Rural South: A Sociolinguistic View Through the Past and Present 'be'*. Publication of the American Dialect Society, 83. Durham, NC: Duke University Press.

Healey, A. (1974) *Handling Unsophisticated Linguistic Informants*. Canberra: ANU, Research School of Pacific Studies.

Heath, C. D. (1980) *The Pronunciation of English in Cannock, Staffordshire*. Oxford: Blackwell.

Henry, A. (1995) *Belfast English and Standard English: Dialect Variation and Parameter Setting*. Oxford: Oxford University Press.

Herman, D. (1999) Toward a socionarratology: New ways of analyzing natural-language narratives. In D. Herman (ed.), *Narratologies: New Perspectives on Narrative Analysis*. Columbus, OH: Ohio State University Press, pp. 218–46.

Hewitt, R. (1982) White adolescent creole users and the politics of friendship. *Journal of Multilingual and Multicultural Development*, 3, 217–32.

Hibiya, J. (1996) Denasalization of the velar nasal in Tokyo Japanese: Observations in real time. In G. Guy, C. Feagin, D. Schiffrin, and J. Baugh (eds.), *Towards a Social Science of Language: Papers in Honor of William Labov, Vol. 1*. Amsterdam and Philadelphia: Benjamins, pp. 161–70.

Hill, J. (1999) Styling locally, styling globally: What does it mean? *Journal of Sociolinguistics*, 4 (3), 542–56. [Theme issue *Styling the Other*, ed. B. Rampton.]

Hindle, D. (1978) Approaches to vowel normalization in the study of natural speech. In D. Sankoff (ed.), *Linguistic Variation: Models and Methods*. New York: Academic Press, pp. 161–71.

Holmes, J. (1995) *Women, Men and Politeness*. London: Longman.

Holmes, J. (1997) Setting new standards: Sound change and gender in New Zealand English. *English World-Wide*, 18 (1), 107–42.

Horvath, B. M. (1985) *Variation in Australian English*. Cambridge: Cambridge University Press.

240 *References*

Horvath, B. M. and Sankoff, D. (1987) Delimiting the Sydney speech community. *Language in Society*, 16, 179–204.

Houck, C. L. (1968) Methodology of an urban speech survey. *Leeds Studies in English*, 11, 135–28. Department of English, University of Leeds.

Hudson, R. A. (1996) *Sociolinguistics* (2nd edn.). Cambridge: Cambridge University Press.

Hudson, R. A. and Holloway, A. F. (1977) *Variation in London English*. Report to the Social Science Research Council.

Hurford, J. R. (1967) The Speech of One Family. Unpublished doctoral dissertation, University of London.

Hymes, D. (1972) On communicative competence. In J. B. Pride and J. Holmes (eds.), *Sociolinguistics*. Harmondsworth: Penguin, pp. 269–93.

Hymes, D. (1974) *Foundations in Sociolinguistics: An Ethnographic Approach*. Philadelphia: University of Pennsylvania Press.

Hymes, D. and Fought, J. (1980) *American Structuralism*. The Hague: Mouton.

Irvine, J. and Gal, S. (2000) Language ideology and linguistic differentiation. In P. Kroskrity (ed.), *Regimes of Language*. Santa Fe, NM: School of American Research Press, pp. 35–58.

Jabeur, M. (1987) A Sociolinguistic Study in Tunisia: Rades. Unpublished doctoral dissertation, University of Reading.

Jahangiri, N. and Hudson, R. A. (1982) Patterns of variation in Tehrani Persian. In S. Romaine (ed.), *Socio-historical Linguistics: Its Status and Methodology*. Cambridge: Cambridge University Press, pp. 49–63.

Jefferson, G. (1989) Preliminary notes on a possible metric which provides for a "standard maximum" silence of approximately one second in conversation. In D. Roger and P. Bull (eds.), *Conversation: An Interdisciplinary Perspective*. Clevedon, England: Multilingual Matters, pp. 156–97.

Johnson, J. C. (1994) Anthropological contributions to the study of social networks: A review. In S. Wasserman and J. Galaskiewicz (eds.), *Advances in Social Network Analysis: Research in the Social and Behavioral Sciences*. Thousand Oaks, CA: Sage Publications, pp. 113–51.

Johnson, K. (1997) *Acoustic and Auditory Phonetics*. Oxford: Blackwell.

Johnston, P. (1983) Irregular style variation patterns in Edinburgh speech. *Scottish Language*, 2, 1–19.

Johnstone, B. (1996) *The Linguistic Individual*. New York and Oxford: Oxford University Press.

Johnstone, B. (1999) Uses of southern-sounding speech by contemporary Texas women. *Journal of Sociolinguistics*, 4 (3), 505–22. [Theme issue *Styling the Other*, ed. B. Rampton.]

Johnstone, B. (2000a) The individual voice in language. *Annual Review of Anthropology*, 29, 405–24.

Johnstone, B. (2000b) *Qualitative Methods in Sociolinguistics*. New York and Oxford: Oxford University Press.

Johnstone, B. and Bean, J. M. (1997) Self-expression and linguistic variation. *Language in Society*, 26 (2), 221–46.

Jørgensen, J. N. (1998) Children's acquisition of code-switching for power wielding.

In P. Auer (ed.), *Code-Switching in Conversation: Language, Interaction and Identity*. London: Routledge, pp. 237–60.

Kallen, J. L. and Kirk, J. M.(2001) Convergence and divergence in the verb phrase in Irish Standard English: a corpus-based approach. In J. M. Kirk and D. P. Ó'Baoill (eds.), *Language Links: The Languages of Scotland and Ireland*. Belfast: Cló Ollscoil na Banríona, pp. 59–79.

Keene, D. (2000) Metropolitan values: Migration, mobility and cultural norms, London 1100–1700. In L. Wright (ed.), *The Development of Standard English, 1300–1800*. Cambridge: Cambridge University Press, pp. 93–114.

Kent, R. D. and Read, C. (1992) *The Acoustic Analysis of Speech*. San Diego: Singular.

Kerswill, P. (1987) Levels of linguistic variation in Durham. *Journal of Linguistics*, 23 (1), 25–50.

Kerswill, P. (1996) Children, adolescents and language change. *Language Variation and Change*, 8 (2), 177–202.

Kerswill, P. (2002) Koineization and accommodation. In J. K. Chambers, P. Trudgill, and N. Schilling-Estes (eds.), *The Handbook of Language Variation and Change*. Oxford: Blackwell, pp. 669–702.

Kerswill, P., Llamas, C., and Upton, C. (1999) The first SuRe moves: Early steps towards a large dialect project. In C. Upton and K. Wales (eds.), *Leeds Studies in English, New Series*, XXX, 257–69. School of English, University of Leeds.

Kerswill, P. and Williams, A. (1999) Mobility versus social class in dialect levelling: Evidence from new and old towns in England. *Cuadernos de Filologia Inglesa*, 8. Departamento de Filologia Inglesa de la Universidad de Murcia, pp. 47–57.

Kerswill, P. and Williams, A. (2000) Creating a new town koine: Children and language change in Milton Keynes. *Language in Society*, 29 (1), 65–115.

Kiesling, S. F. (1997) Power and the language of men. In S. Johnson and U. H. Meinhof (eds.), *Language and Masculinity*. Oxford: Blackwell, pp. 65–85.

Kingsmore, R. (1995) *Ulster Scots Speech: A Sociolinguistic Study*. Tuscoloosa: University of Alabama Press.

Knack, R. (1991) Ethnic boundaries in linguistic variation. In P. Eckert (ed.), *New Ways of Analyzing Sound Change*. San Diego: Academic Press, pp. 251–72.

Knowles, G. (1978) The nature of phonological variables in Scouse. In P. Trudgill (ed.), *Sociolinguistic Patterns in British English*. London: Arnold, pp. 80–90.

Kotsinas, U.-B. (1988) Immigrant children's Swedish: a new variety? *Journal of Multilingual and Multicultural Development*, 9, 129–40.

Kretzschmar, W. A., Jr. (1996) Quantitative aerial analysis of dialect features. *Language Variation and Change*, 8, 13–39.

Kretzschmar, W. A. and Schneider, E. W. (1996) *Introduction to Quantitative Analysis of Linguistic Survey Data: An Atlas by the Numbers*. Thousand Oaks, CA: Sage.

Kretzschmar, W., Schneider, E., and Johnson, E. (eds.) (1989) *Journal of English Linguistics* (*Special Issue: Computer Methods in Dialectology*), 22, 1–170.

Kroch, A. S. (1996) Dialect and style in the speech of upper class Philadelphia. In G. R. Guy, C. Feagin, D. Schiffrin, and J. Baugh (eds.), *Towards a Social Science of Language*. Amsterdam and Philadelphia: Benjamins, pp. 23–46.

Kroch, A. and Taylor, A. (1997) Verb movement in Old and Middle English: Dialect variation and language contact. In A. van Kemenade and N. Vincent (eds.), *Parameters of Morphosyntactic Change*. Cambridge: Cambridge University Press, pp. 297–325.

Kurath, H. (1949) *Word Geography of the Eastern United States*. Ann Arbor: University of Michigan Press.

Kurath, H. (1972) *Studies in Area Linguistics*. Bloomington: Indiana University Press.

Laberge, S. and Sankoff, G. (1980) Anything *you* can do. In G. Sankoff (ed.), *The Social Life of Language*. Philadelphia: University of Pennsylvania Press, pp. 271–93.

Labov, W. (1963) The social motivation of a sound change. *Word*, 19, 273–309.

Labov, W. (1966) *The Social Stratification of English in New York City*. Washington, DC: Center for Applied Linguistics.

Labov, W. (1969) Contraction, deletion and inherent variability of the English copula. *Language*, 45, 715–62.

Labov, W. (1972a) *Language in the Inner City*. Philadelphia: University of Pennsylvania Press.

Labov, W. (1972b) *Sociolinguistic Patterns*. Philadelphia: University of Pennsylvania Press.

Labov, W. (1973) Where do grammars stop? In R. W. Shuy (ed.), *Sociolinguistics, Current Trends and Perspectives*. Washington, DC: Georgetown University Press, pp. 43–88.

Labov, W. (1975) *What is a Linguistic Fact?* Lisse: Peter de Ridder.

Labov, W. (ed.) (1980) *Locating Language in Time and Space*. New York: Academic Press.

Labov, W. (1981) Resolving the Neogrammarian controversy. *Language*, 57, 267–309.

Labov, W. (1982a) Building on empirical foundations. In W. P. Lehmann and Y. Malkiel (eds.), *Perspectives on Historical Linguistics*. Amsterdam and Philadelphia: Benjamins, pp. 79–92.

Labov, W. (1982b) Objectivity and commitment in linguistic science. *Language in Society*, 11, 165–201.

Labov, W. (1984) Field methods of the project on linguistic change and variation. In J. Baugh, and J. Sherzer (eds.), *Language in Use: Readings in Sociolinguistics*. Englewood Cliffs, NJ: Prentice Hall, pp. 28–66.

Labov, W. (1986) Language structure and social structure. In S. Lindenberg, J. Coleman, and S. Nowak (eds.), *Approaches to Social Theory*. New York: Russell Sage.

Labov, W. (1990) The intersection of sex and social class in the course of linguistic change. *Language Variation and Change*, 2, 205–54.

Labov, W. (1991) The three dialects of English. In P. Eckert (ed.), *New Ways of Analyzing Sound Change*. New York: Academic Press, pp. 1–44.

Labov, W. (1994) *Principles of Linguistic Change, Volume 1: Internal Factors*. Oxford: Blackwell.

Labov, W. (1996) When intuitions fail. In L. McNair, K. Singer, L. Dobrin, and M. Aucoin (eds.), *CLS 32: Papers from the Parasession on Theory and Data in Linguistics*. Chicago: Chicago Linguistics Society, pp. 77–105.

Labov W. (1998) Co-existent systems in African-American Vernacular English. In S. Mufwene, J. Rickford, G. Bailey, and J. Baugh (eds.), *African-American English: Structure, History, and Use*. London: Routledge, pp. 110–53.

Labov, W. (2001a) The anatomy of style-shifting. In P. Eckert and J. Rickford (eds.), *Style and Sociolinguistic Variation*. Cambridge: Cambridge University Press.

Labov, W. (2001b) *Principles of Linguistic Change, Volume 2: Social Factors*. Oxford: Blackwell.

Labov, W., Ash, S., and Boberg, C. (forthcoming) *Atlas of North American English*. Berlin and New York: Mouton de Gruyter.

Labov, W., Cohen, P., Robins, C., and Lewis, J. (1968) *A Study of the Non-Standard English of Negro and Puerto-Rican Speakers in New York City*. Report on Co-operative Research Project 3288. Washington DC: Office of Education.

Labov, W. and Harris, W. (1986) De facto segregation of black and white vernaculars. In Sankoff (ed.), *Diversity and Diachrony*. Amsterdam and Philadelphia: Benjamins, pp. 1–24.

Labov, W., Yaeger, M., and Steiner, R. (1972) *A Quantitative Study of Sound Change in Progress*. Report on NSF Project no. GS-3287. Philadelphia: US Regional Survey.

Labrie, N. (1988a) Comments on Berlin vernacular studies. In N. Ditmarr and P. Schlobinski (eds.), *The Sociolinguistics of Urban Vernaculars*. Berlin: de Gruyter, pp. 191–206.

Labrie, N. (1988b) Social networks and code-switching: A sociolinguistic investigation of Italians in Montreal. In N. Ditmarr and P. Schlobinski (eds.), *The Sociolinguistics of Urban Vernaculars*. Berlin: de Gruyter, pp. 217–32.

Ladefoged, P. (1993) *A Course in Phonetics* (3rd edn.). New York: Harcourt Brace Jovanovich.

Larsen, S. S. (1982) The two sides of the house: Identity and social organisation in Kilbroney, Northern Ireland. In A. P. Cohen (ed.), *Belonging*. Manchester: Manchester University Press, pp. 131–64.

Lass, R. (1997) *Historical Linguistics and Language Change*. Cambridge: Cambridge University Press.

Lass, R. (1999) Phonology and morphology. In R. Lass (ed.), *The Cambridge History of the English Language, Vol. III: 1476–1776*. Cambridge: Cambridge University Press, pp. 56–186.

Lavandera, B. (1975) Linguistic Structure and Sociolinguistic Conditioning in the Use of Verbal Endings in 'si' Clauses (Buenos Aires Spanish). Unpublished doctoral dissertation, University of Pennsylvania.

Lavandera, B. (1978a) The variable component in bilingual performance. In J. Alatis (ed.), *International Dimensions of Bilingual Education*. Washington, DC: Georgetown University Press, pp. 391–411.

Lavandera, B. (1978b) Where does the sociolinguistic variable stop? *Language in Society*, 7, 171–82.

Lavandera, B. (1982) Le principe de réinterpretation dans la théorie de la variation. In N. Dittmar and B. Schlieben-Lange (eds.), *Die Soziolinguistik in Romanischsprachigen Ländern*. Narr: Tübingen, 87–96.

Lavandera, B. (1984) *Variacion y significado*. Buenos Aires: Hachette.

Laver, J. (1981) Linguistic routines and politeness in greeting and parting. In F. Coulmas (ed.), *Conversational Routines*. The Hague: Mouton, pp. 289–318.

Le Page, R. B. (1954) *Linguistic Survey of the British Caribbean: Questionnaire A*. Jamaica: University College of the West Indies.

Le Page, R. B. (1957) General outlines of creole English dialects in the Caribbean. Part 1. *Orbis*, 6, 373–91.

Le Page, R. B. (1958) General outlines of creole English dialects in the Caribbean. Part 2. *Orbis*, 7, 54–64.

Le Page, R. B. and Tabouret-Keller, A. (1985) *Acts of identity*. Cambridge: Cambridge University Press.

Lefkowitz, D. (1997) Intonation, affect, and subaltern dialects. In A. Chu, A.-M. P. Guerra, and C. Tetreault (eds.), *Proceedings of the Fourth Annual Symposium about Language and Society – Austin* (Texas Linguistic Forum 37). University of Texas, Department of Linguistics, pp. 46–58.

Lepschy, G. (1982) *A Survey of Structural Linguistics* (2nd edn.). Oxford: Blackwell.

Levinson, S. (1983) *Pragmatics*. Cambridge: Cambridge University Press.

Linguistic Minorities Project (1985) *The Other Languages of England*. London: Routledge.

Lippi-Green, R. (1989) Social network integration and language change in progress in an alpine rural village. *Language in Society*, 18, 213–34.

Li Wei, (1994) *Three Generations, Two Languages, One Family*. Clevedon: Multilingual Matters.

Li Wei (1995) Variations in patterns of language choice and codeswitching by three groups of Chinese/English speakers in Newcastle upon Tyne. *Multilingua*, 14 (3), 297–323.

Li Wei (1996) Network analysis. In H. Goebl, P. Nelde, S. Zdenek, and W. Woelck (eds.), *Contact Linguistics: A Handbook of Contemporary Research*. Berlin: de Gruyter, pp. 805–12.

Li Wei (1998) The 'why' and 'how' questions in the analysis of conversational code-switching. In P. Auer (ed.), *Code-Switching in Conversation: Language, Interaction and Identity*. London: Routledge, pp. 156–79.

Li Wei (ed.) (2000) *The Bilingualism Reader*. London: Routledge.

Li Wei, Milroy, L., and Pong Sin Ching (2000) A two-step analysis of code-switching and language choice: The example of a bilingual Chinese community in Britain. In Li Wei (ed.), *The Bilingualism Reader*. London: Routledge, pp. 188–209.

Llamas C. (2000) *Variation in the north-east of England*. Paper presented at NWAV 29, Michigan State University, October 5–8.

Lloyd, P. (1979) *Slums of Hope?* Harmondsworth: Penguin.

Local, J. K., Kelly, J., and Wells, W. H. G. (1986) Towards a phonology of conversation: Turntaking in Tyneside. *Journal of Linguistics*, 22, 411–37.

Longacre, R. E. (1964) *Grammar Discovery Procedures*. The Hague: Mouton.

Macafee, C. (1983) *Glasgow*. Amsterdam: Benjamins.

Macafee, C. (1994) *Traditional Dialect in the Modern World: A Glasgow Case Study*. Frankfurt am Main: Lang.

Macaulay, R. K. S. (1977) *Language, Social Class, and Education*. Edinburgh: Edinburgh University Press.

Macaulay, R. K. S. (1978) Variation and consistency in Glaswegian English. In P. Trudgill (ed.), *Sociolinguistic Patterns in British English*. London: Arnold, pp. 132–43.

Maher, J. (1996) Fishermen, farmers, traders: Language and economic history on St. Barthélemy, French West Indies. *Language in Society*, 25 (3), 373–406.

Martin, S. and Wolfram, W. (1998) The sentence in African-American Vernacular English. In S. Mufwene, J. R. Rickford, G. Bailey, and J. Baugh (eds.), *African-American English: Structure, History and Use*. London and New York: Routledge.

Martineau, F. and Mougeon, R. (2001) Sociolinguistic research on the origins of NE deletion in European and Quebec French. Manuscript.

McCafferty, K. (1998) Shared accents, divided speech community? Changes in Northern Ireland English. *Language Variation and Change*, 10 (2), 97–122.

McCafferty, K. (1999) (London)derry: between Ulster and local speech – class, ethnicity and language change. In P. Foulkes and G. J. Docherty (eds.), *Urban Voices*. London: Arnold, pp. 246–64.

McCafferty, K. (2000) *Ethnicity and Language Change: English in (London)Derry, Northern Ireland*. Amsterdam and Philadelphia: Benjamins.

McCawley, J. D. (1971) Tense and time reference in English. In C. J. Filmore and D. T. Langedoen (eds.), *Studies in Linguistic Semantics*. New York: Holt, Rinehart & Winston, pp. 96–103.

McEntegart, D. and Le Page, R. B. (1982) An appraisal of the statistical techniques used in the Sociolinguistic Survey of Multilingual Communities. In S. Romaine (ed.), *Socio-historical Linguistics: Its Status and Methodology*. Cambridge: Cambridge University Press, pp. 105–24.

McIntosh, A. (1952) *An Introduction to a Survey of Scottish Dialects*. Edinburgh: Nelson.

Mees, I. M. (1987) Glottal stop as a prestigious feature in Cardiff English. *English World-Wide*, 8, 25–39.

Mees, I. M. and Collins, B. (1999) Cardiff: A real-time study of glottalization. In P. Foulkes and G. Docherty (eds.), *Urban Voices*. London: Arnold, pp. 185–202.

Mendoza-Denton, N. (1997) Chicana/Mexicana Identity and Linguistic Variation: An Ethnographic and Sociolinguistic Study of Gang Affiliation in an Urban High School. Unpublished doctoral dissertation, Stanford University.

Mendoza-Denton, N. (1999) Sociolinguistics and linguistic anthropology of US Latinos. *Annual Review of Anthropology*, 28, 375–95.

Milardo, R. M. (1988) Families and social networks: An overview of theory and methodology. In R. M. Milardo (ed.), *Families and Social Networks*. Newbury Park, California: Sage, pp. 13–47.

Milroy, J. (1976) Length and height variation in the vowels of Belfast vernacular. *Belfast Working Papers in Language and Linguistics*, 1, Chapter 3 (page numbers not available).

Milroy, J. (1981) *Regional Accents of English: Belfast*. Belfast: Blackstaff.

Milroy, J. (1982) Probing under the tip of the ice-berg: Phonological normalization and the shape of speech communities. In S. Romaine (ed.), *Sociolinguistic Variation in Speech Communities*. London: Arnold, pp. 35–47.

Milroy, J. (1992) *Linguistic Variation and Change*. Oxford: Blackwell.

Milroy, J. (1996) A current change in British English: Variation in (th) in Derby. *Newcastle and Durham Papers in Linguistics*, 4, 213–22.

Milroy, J. and Harris, J. (1980) When is a merger not a merger? The MEAT/ MATE problem in a present-day English vernacular. *English World-Wide*, 1 (2), 199–210.

Milroy, J. and Milroy, L. (1978) Belfast; change and variation in an urban vernacular. In P. Trudgill (ed.), *Sociolinguistic Patterns in British English*. London: Arnold, pp. 19–36.

Milroy, J. and Milroy, L. (1985) Linguistic change, social network and speaker innovation. *Journal of Linguistics*, 21, 339–84.

Milroy, J. and Milroy, L. (1999) *Authority in Language* (3rd edn.). London: Routledge.

Milroy, J., Milroy, L., Hartley, S., and Walshaw, D. (1994) Glottal stops and Tyneside glottalization: Competing patterns of variation and change in British English. *Language Variation and Change*, 6, 327–57.

Milroy, L. (1987) *Language and Social Networks* (2nd edn.). Oxford: Blackwell.

Milroy, L. (1999) Women as innovators and norm-creators: The sociolinguistics of dialect leveling in a northern English city. In S. Wertheim, A. C. Bailey, and M. Corston-Oliver (eds.), *Engendering Communication: Proceedings of the Fifth Berkeley Women and Language Conference*. Berkeley, CA: Berkeley Women and Language Group, pp. 361–76.

Milroy, L. (2001a) Bridging the micro-macro gap: Social change, social networks and bilingual repertoires. In J. Klatter-Folmer and P. Van Avermaet (eds.), *Theories on Maintenance and Loss of Minority Languages: Towards a More Integrated Explanatory Framework*. Münster and New York: Waxmann Verlag, pp. 39–64.

Milroy, L. (2001b) Social networks. In J. Chambers, P. Trudgill, and N. Schilling-Estes (eds.), *Handbook of Variation and Change*. Oxford: Blackwell, pp. 509–72.

Milroy, L. (ed.) (2002) Investigating change and variation through dialect contact. Special issue of *Journal of Sociolinguistics*, 6 (1).

Milroy, L. and Li Wei (1995) A social network approach to code-switching. In L. Milroy and P. Muysken (eds.), *One Speaker, Two Languages*. Cambridge: Cambridge University Press, pp. 136–57.

Milroy, L., Li Wei, and Moffatt, S. (1995) Discourse patterns and fieldwork strategies in urban settings: Some methodological problems for researchers in bilingual communities. In I. Werlen (ed.), *Verbale Kommunikation in der Stadt*. Narr: Tübingen, pp. 277–95.

Milroy, L. and Milroy, J. (1992) Social network and social class: Towards an integrated sociolinguistic model. *Language in Society*, 21, 1–26.

Milroy, L., Milroy, J., Docherty, G. J., Foulkes, P., and Walshaw, D. (1999) Contemporary English: Evidence from Newcastle upon Tyne and Derby. *Cuadernos de Filologia Inglesa*, 8. Departamento de Filologia Inglesa de la Universidad de Murcia, pp. 35–46.

Milroy, L. and Muysken, P. (eds.) (1995) *One Speaker, Two Languages*. Cambridge: Cambridge University Press.

Milroy, L. and Preston, D. R. (1999) Attitudes, perception and linguistic features. *Journal of Language and Social Psychology*, 18 (1), 3–8.

Milroy, L. and Raschka, C. (1996) Varieties of English in contemporary Britain: The grammatical characteristics of ethnic minority speakers in the North East of England. In J. Klemola, M. Kyto, and M. Rissanen (eds.), *Speech Past and Present: Essays in Honour of Ossi Ihilainen*. Frankfurt am Main: P. Lang, pp. 187–212.

Mitchell, J. C. (1986) Network procedures. In D. Frick and H.-W. Hoefert (eds.), *The Quality of Urban Life*. Berlin: de Gruyter, pp. 73–92.

Mithun, M. (1996) The description of the native languages of North America: Boas and after. In I. Goddard (ed.), *Handbook of North American Indians, Vol. 17: Languages*. Washington: Smithsonian, pp. 43–63.

Mithun, M. (2001) Who shapes the record: The speaker and the linguist. In P. Newman and M. Ratliff (eds.), *Linguistic Fieldwork*. Cambridge: Cambridge University Press, pp. 34–54.

Montgomery, M. (1996) Was colonial American a koine? In J. Klemola, M. Kyto, and M. Rissanen (eds.), *Speech Past and Present. Studies in English Dialectology in Memory of Ossi Ihalainen*. New York: P. Lang, pp. 213–35.

Morgan, M. (1994) The African-American speech community: Reality and socio-linguistics. In M. Morgan (ed.), *The Social Construction of Identity in Creole Situations*. Los Angeles: Center for Afro-American Studies, UCLA, pp. 121–48.

Moser, C. A. and Kalton, G. (1971) *Survey Methods in Social Investigation*. London: Heinemann.

Moulton, W. G. (1960) The short vowel systems of northern Switzerland: A study in structural dialectology. *Word*, 16, 155–83.

Mufwene, S., Rickford, J., Bailey, G., and Baugh, J. (1998) *African-American English: Structure, History, and Use*. London: Routledge.

Mugglestone, L. (1995) *Talking Proper: The Rise of Accent as a Social Symbol*. Oxford: Clarendon Press.

Mühlhäusler, P. and Harré, R. (1990) *Pronouns and People*. Oxford: Blackwell.

Murray, J. A. H. (1873) *The Dialect of the Southern Counties of Scotland: Its Pronunciation, Grammar and Historical Relations*. London: Philological Society.

Murray, S. O. (1993) Network determination of linguistic variables. *American Speech*, 68 (2), 161–77.

Murray, T. E. (1986) *The Language of St. Louis, Missouri: Variation in the Gateway City*. New York: P. Lang.

Murray, T. E., Frazer, T. C., and Simon, B. L. (1996) *Need* + past participle in American English. *American Speech*, 71, 255–71.

Murray, T. E. and Murray, C. R. (1992) On the legality and ethics of surreptious recording. *Legal and Ethical Issues in Surreptitious Recording, Essays by Donald W. Larmouth, Thomas E. Murray and Carmen Ross Murray*. Publications of the American Dialect Society, 76. Tuscaloosa: University of Alabama Press.

Murray, T. E. and Murray, C. R. (1996) *Under Cover of Law: More on the Legality of Surreptitious Recording*. Publications of the American Dialect Society, 79. Tuscaloosa: University of Alabama Press.

Murray, T. E. and Simon, B. L. (1999) *Want* + past participle in American English. *American Speech*, 74, 140–64.

Myers-Scotton, C. (1993) *Social Motivations for Code-Switching*. Oxford: Oxford University Press.

Myers-Scotton, C. (ed.) (1998) *Codes and Consequences*. Oxford: Oxford University Press.

Myers-Scotton, C. and Bolonyai, A. (2001) Calculating speakers: Codeswitching in a rational choice model. *Language in Society*, 30 (1), 1–28.

Nagy, N. (2000) What I didn't know about working in an endangered language community: Some fieldwork issues. *International Journal of the Sociology of Language*, 144, 143–60.

Nagy, N. (2001) "Live free or die" as a linguistic principle. *American Speech*, 76, 30–41.

Nagy, N. and Reynolds, B. (1997) Optimality theory and word-final deletion in Faetar. *Language Variation and Change*, 9 (1), 37–55.

Neu, H. (1980) Ranking of constraints on /t, d/ deletion in American English: a statistical analysis. In W. Labov (ed.), *Locating Language in Time and Space*. New York: Academic Press, pp. 37–54.

Neuman, W. L. (1997) *Social Research Methods: Qualitative and Quantitative Approaches* (3rd edn.). Boston: Allyn & Bacon.

Nevalainen, T. (1999) Making the best use of "bad" data: Evidence for sociolinguistic variation in Early modern English. *Neophilologische Mitteilungen*, 4 (C), 499–533.

Nevalainen, T. (2000a) Gender differences in the evolution of standard English. *Journal of English Linguistics*, 28 (1), 38–59.

Nevalainen, T. (2000b) Mobility, social networks and language change in Early Modern England. *European Journal of English Studies*, 4 (3), 253–64.

Nevalainen, T. and Raumolin-Brunberg, H. (1996) *Sociolinguistics and Language History*. Amsterdam and Atlanta: Rodopi.

Newbrook, M. (1999) West Wirral: Norms, self report and usage. In P. Foulkes and G. J. Docherty (eds.), *Urban Voices*. London: Arnold, pp. 90–106.

Nichols, P. C. (1998) Black women in the rural south: Conservative and innovative. In J. Coates (ed.), *Language and Gender: A Reader*. Oxford: Blackwell, pp. 55–63.

Nordberg, B. (1980) *Sociolinguistic Fieldwork Experiences of the Unit for Advanced Studies in Modern Swedish*. FUMS Report no. 90. Uppsala: FUMS.

Ochs, E. (1979) Transcription as theory. In E. Ochs and B. Schieffelin (eds.), *Developmental Pragmatics*. New York: Academic Press, pp. 43–72.

Ohala, J. J. (1992) The segment: Primitive or derived? In G. J. Docherty and D. R. Ladd (eds.), *Papers in Laboratory Phonology II: Gesture, Segment, Prosody*. Cambridge: Cambridge University Press, pp. 166–89.

Ó'Riagáin, P. (1997) *Language Policy and Social Reproduction: Ireland 1893–1993*. Oxford: Oxford University Press.

Orton, H. (1962) *Survey of English Dialects: Introduction*. Leeds: E. J. Arnold.

Parasher, S. N. (1980) Mother-tongue-English diglossia: A case-study of educated Indian bilinguals' language use. *Anthropological Linguistics*, 22 (4), 151–68.

Patterson, D. (1860) *Provincialisms of Belfast*. Belfast: Mayne Boyd.

Payne, A. C. (1980) Factors controlling the acquisition of the Philadelphia dialect by out-of-state children. In W. Labov (ed.), *Locating Language in Time and Space*. New York: Academic Press, pp. 143–78.

Payne, T. E. (1997) *Describing Morphosyntax: A Guide for Field Linguists*. Cambridge: Cambridge University Press.

Pederson, L. A. (1965) *The Pronunciation of English in Metropolitan Chicago*. Publication of the American Dialect Society, 44. Tuscaloosa: University of Alabama Press.

Peterson, G. E. and Barney, H. L. (1952) Control methods used in a study of the vowels. *Journal of the Acoustical Society of America*, 24, 175–84.

Pinzuk, S. and Kroch, A. S. (1989) The rightward movement of complements and adjuncts in the Old English of Beowulf. *Language Variation and Change*, 1 (2), 115–44.

Pitts, A. (1983) Urban Speech in Ulster: A Comparative Study of Two Communities. Unpublished doctoral dissertation, University of Michigan.

Pitts, A. (1985) Urban influence on phonological variation in a Northern Irish speech community. *English World-Wide*, 6 (1), 59–85.

Pollock, J.-Y. (1989) Verb movement, universal grammar, and the structure of IP. *Linguistic Inquiry*, 20, 365–424.

Pomeranz, A. and Fehr, B. J. (1997) Conversation Analysis: An approach to the study of social action as sense making practices. In T. A. van Dijk (ed.), *Discourse as Social Interaction, Discourse Studies: A Multidisciplinary Introduction*, 2. London and Thousand Oaks, CA: Sage, pp. 64–91.

Poplack, S. (1993) Variation theory and language contact: Concept, methods and data. In D. R. Preston (ed.), *American Dialect Research*. Amsterdam: Benjamins, pp. 251–86.

Poplack, S. (ed.) (2000) *The English History of African American English*. Oxford: Blackwell.

Poplack, S. and Meecham M. (1995) Patterns of language mixture: Nominal structure in Wolof-French and Fongbe-French bilingual discourse. In L. Milroy and P. Muysken (eds.), *One Speaker, Two Languages*. Cambridge: Cambridge University Press, pp. 199–232.

Poplack, S. and Meecham, M. (eds.) (1998) Instant loans, easy conditions: The productivity of bilingual borrowing. Special issue of *International Journal of Bilingualism*, 2 (2).

Poplack, S., Sankoff, D., and Miller, C. (1988) The social correlates and linguistic processes of lexical borrowing and assimilation. *Linguistics*, 26, 47–104.

Poplack, S. and Tagliamonte, S. (2001) *African American English in the Diaspora*. Oxford: Blackwell.

Pratt, L. and Denison, D. (2000) The language of the Southey–Coleridge Circle. *Language Sciences*, 22, 401–2.

Preston, D. R. (1989) *Perceptual Dialectology: Nonlinguists' Views of Areal Linguistics*. Dordrecht: Foris.

Preston, D. R. (1996) Where the worst English is spoken. In E. W. Schneider (ed.), *Focus on the USA*. Amsterdam: Benjamins, pp. 297–361.

Preston, D. R. (ed.) (1999) *Handbook of Perceptual Dialectology*, Vol. 1. Amsterdam and Philadelphia: Benjamins.

Prince, E. (1988) Discourse analysis: A part of the study of linguistic competence. In F. Newmeyer (ed.), *Linguistics: The Cambridge Survey: Vol II: Linguistic Theory: Extensions and Implications.* Cambridge: Cambridge University Press, pp. 164–82.

Psathas, G. (1995) *Conversation Analysis: The Study of Talk in Interaction.* Qualitative research methods series, 35. Thousand Oaks, CA: Sage.

Queen, R. (2001) Bilingual intonation patterns: Evidence of language change from Turkish–German bilingual children. *Language in Society*, 30 (4), 55–80.

Rampton, B. (1995) *Crossing: Language and Ethnicity Among Adolescents.* London: Longman.

Rampton, B. (1996) Language crossing and the problematisation of ethnicity and socialisation. *Pragmatics*, 5 (4), 485–513.

Rampton, B. (ed.) (1999) *Styling the Other.* Special Issue of *Journal of Sociolinguistics*, 4 (3).

Reid, E. (1977) *Social Class Differences in Britain.* London: Open Books.

Reid, E. (1978) Social and stylistic variation in the speech of children: Some evidence from Edinburgh. In P. Trudgill (ed.), *Sociolinguistic Patterns in British English.* London: Arnold, pp. 158–72.

Rickford, J. R. (1986) The need for new approaches to social class analysis in sociolinguistics. *Language and Communication*, 6 (3), 215–21.

Rickford, J. R. (1987) The haves and have nots: Sociolinguistic surveys and the assessment of speaker competence. *Language in Society*, 16 (2), 149–78.

Rickford, J. R. (1997a) Suite for ebony and phonics. *Discover*, 18 (12), 82–7.

Rickford, J. R. (1997b) Unequal partnership: Sociolinguistics and the African American community. *Language in Society*, 26, 161–97.

Rickford, J. R. (1999) *African American Vernacular English.* Oxford: Blackwell.

Rickford, J. R., Ball, A., Blake, R., Jackson, R., and Martin, N. (1991) Rappin on the copula coffin: Theoretical and methodological issues in the analysis of copula variation in African American Vernacular English. *Language Variation and Change*, 3 (1), 103–32.

Rickford, J. R. and McNair-Knox, F. (1994) Addressee- and topic-influenced styleshift: A quantitative sociolinguistic study. In D. Biber and E. Finegan (eds.), *Sociolinguistic Perspectives on Register.* Oxford: Oxford University Press, pp. 235–76.

Rickford, J. R., Wasow, T. A., Mendoza-Denton, N., and Espinoza, J. (1995) Syntactic variation and change in progress: Loss of the verbal coda in topic-restricting *as far as* constructions. *Language*, 71 (1), 102–31.

Rimmer, S. (1982) On variability in Birmingham speech. *MALS Journal*, 7, 1–16.

Robins, R. H. (1967) *A Short History of Linguistics.* London: Longman.

Romaine, S. (1978) Post-vocalic /r/ in Scottish English: Sound change in progress. In P. Trudgill (ed.), *Sociolinguistic Patterns in British English.* London: Arnold, pp. 144–57.

Romaine, S. (1980) A critical overview of the methodology of urban British sociolinguistics. *English World-Wide*, 1 (2), 163–98.

Romaine, S. (ed.) (1982) *Socio-historical Linguistics: Its Status and Methodology.* Cambridge: Cambridge University Press.

Romaine, S. (1984) On the problem of syntactic variation and pragmatic meaning in sociolinguistic theory. *Folia Linguistica*, 18 (3–4), 409–37.

Romaine, S. and Lange, D. (1991) The use of *like* as a marker of reported speech and thought: A case of grammaticalization in progress. *American Speech*, 66, 227–79.

Romaine, S. and Reid, E. (1976) Glottal sloppiness: A sociolinguistic view of urban speech in Scotland. *Teaching English*, 9 (3). Edinburgh: CITE.

Rubin, J. (1968) *National Bilingualism in Paraguay*. The Hague: Mouton.

Russell, J. (1982) Networks and sociolinguistic variation in an African urban setting. In S. Romaine (ed.), *Sociolinguistic Studies in the Speech Community*. London, pp. 125–40.

Sampson, G. (1980) *Schools of Linguistics*. Stanford, CA: Stanford University Press.

Sankoff, D. (ed.) (1978) *Linguistic Variation: Models and Methods*. New York: Academic Press.

Sankoff, D., Cedergren, H., Kemp, W., Thibault, P., and Vincent, D. (1989) Montreal French: Language, class and ideology. In W. Fasold and D. Schiffrin (eds.), *Language Change and Variation*. Amsterdam: Benjamins, pp. 107–18.

Sankoff, D. and Laberge, S. (1978) The linguistic market and the statistical explanation of variability. In D. Sankoff (ed.), *Linguistic Variation: Models and Methods*. New York: Academic Press, pp. 239–50.

Sankoff, G. (1980a) A quantitative paradigm for the study of communicative competence. In G. Sankoff (ed.), *The Social Life of Language*. Philadelphia: University of Pennsylvania Press, pp. 47–79.

Sankoff, G. (ed.) (1980b) *The Social Life of Language*. Philadelphia: University of Pennsylvania Press.

Sankoff, G. (1980c) Above and beyond phonology in variable rules. In G. Sankoff (ed.), *The Social Life of Language*. Philadelphia: University of Pennsylvania Press, pp. 81–93.

Sankoff, G. and Vincent, D. (1980) The productive use of *ne* in spoken Montreal French. In G. Sankoff (ed.), *The Social Life of Language*. Philadelphia: University of Pennsylvania Press, pp. 295–310.

Schatz, H. (1986) *Plat Amsterdams in its Social Context*. Amsterdam: P. J. Meertens Institut voor Dialectologie, Volkskunde en Naamkunde.

Schiffrin, D. (1987) *Discourse Markers*. Cambridge: Cambridge University Press.

Schiffrin, D. (1994) *Approaches to Discourse*. Oxford: Blackwell.

Schilling-Estes, N. (1998) Self-conscious speech in Ocracoke English. *Language in Society*, 27 (1), 53–83.

Schilling-Estes, N. (1999) Reshaping economies, reshaping identities: Gender-based patterns of language variation in Ocracoke English. *Engendering Communication: Proceedings of the Fifth Berkeley Women and Language Conference*. Berkeley, CA: Berkeley Women and Language Group, pp. 509–20.

Schilling-Estes, N. (2002) On the nature of insular and post-insular dialects: Innovation, variation and differentiation. *Journal of Sociolinguistics*, 6 (1), 64–85.

Schilling-Estes, N. and Wolfram, W. (1994) Convergent explanation and alternative regularization patterns: *Were/weren't* leveling in a vernacular variety. *Language Variation and Change*, 6, 273–302.

Schmidt, A. (1985) *Young People's Djirbal*. Cambridge: Cambridge University Press.

Schooling, S. (1990) *Language Maintenance in Melanesia*. Dallas: SIL.

Schütze, C. E. (1996) *The Empirical Base of Linguistics: Grammatical Judgments and Linguistic Methodology*. Chicago: University of Chicago Press.

Shin, S. J. (1998) Paibu dollar please! Bilingual Korean American children in New York City. Unpublished doctoral dissertation, University of Michigan.

Shin, S. J. and Milroy, L. (1999) Bilingual language acquisition by Korean school-children in New York City. *Bilingualism: Language and Cognition*, 2, 147–67.

Shin, S. J. and Milroy, L. (2000) Conversational Code-switching among Korean–English bilingual children. *International Journal of Bilingualism*, 4 (3), 351–83.

Shuy, R. W. (1993) Risk, deception, confidentiality, and informed consent. *American Speech*, 68, 103–6.

Shuy, R. W., Wolfram, W. A., and Riley, W. K. (1968) *Field Techniques in an Urban Language Study*. Washington, DC: Center for Applied Linguistics.

Sidnell, J. (2000) Competence. *Journal of Linguistic Anthropology*, 9 (1–2), 39–41.

Silva-Corvalán, C. (1994) *Language Contact and Change: Spanish in Los Angeles*. Oxford: Clarendon Press.

Sivertsen, E. (1960) *Cockney Phonology*. Oslo: Oslo University Press.

Smith, J. (2000) Synchrony and Diachrony in the Evolution of English: Evidence from Scotland. Unpublished doctoral dissertation, University of York, England.

Stuart-Smith, J. (1999) Glasgow: Accent and voice quality. In P. Foulkes and G. Docherty (eds.), *Urban Voices*. London: Arnold, pp. 203–22.

Sugrue, T. (1996) *The Origins of the Urban Crisis: Race and Inequality in Post-War Detroit*. Princeton: Princeton University Press.

Tagliamonte, S. (1998) *Was/were* across the generations: View from the city of York. *Language Variation and Change*, 10 (2), 153–92.

Tagliamonte, S. and Hudson, R. (1999) Be like et al. beyond America: The quotative system in British and Canadian youth. *Journal of Sociolinguistics*, 3 (2), 147–72.

Tagliamonte, S. and Smith, J. (2000) Old *was*, new ecology: Viewing English through the sociolinguistic filter. In S. Poplack (ed.), *The English History of African American English*. Oxford: Blackwell, pp. 141–71.

Tannen, D. (1994) The relativity of linguistic strategies: Rethinking power and solidarity in gender and dominance. In D. Tannen (ed.), *Gender and Discourse*. Oxford: Oxford University Press, pp. 19–52.

Ten Have, P. (1999) *Doing Conversation Analysis: A Practical Guide*. London: Sage.

Thakerer, J. N., Giles, H., and Cheshire, J. (1982) Psychological and linguistic parameters of speech accommodation theory. In C. Fraser and K. R. Scherer (eds.), *Advances in the Social Psychology of Language*. Cambridge: Cambridge University Press, pp. 205–55.

Thomas, E. R. (1997) A rural/metropolitan split in the speech of Texas Anglos. *Language Variation and Change*, 9 (3), 309–32.

Thomas, E. R. (2001) *An Acoustic Analysis of Vowel Variation in New World English*. Publication of the American Dialect Society, 85. Durham, NC: Duke University Press.

Thompson, E. P. (1963) *The Making of the English Working Class*. London: Gollantz.

Tieken-Boon van Ostade, I., Nevalainen, T., and Caon, L. (eds.) (2000) *European Journal of English Studies*: Special issue entitled *Social Network Analysis and the History of English*.

Tillery, J. (2000) The reliability and validity of linguistic self-reports. *Southern Journal of Linguistics*, 24, 55–68.

Tillery, J. and Bailey, G. (1998) Yall in Oklahoma. *American Speech*, 73, 257–78.

Tizard, B. and Hughes, M. (1984) *Young Children Learning*. London: Fontana.

Tollfree, L. (1999) South East London English: Discrete versus continuous modeling of consonantal reduction. In P. Foulkes and G. J. Docherty (eds.), *Urban Voices*. London: Arnold, pp. 163–84.

Tottie, G. and Harvie, D. (2000) It's all relative: Relativization strategies in early African American English. In S. Poplack (ed.), *The English History of African American English*. Oxford: Blackwell, pp. 198–230.

Trudgill, P. (1974) *The Social Differentiation of English in Norwich*. Cambridge: Cambridge University Press.

Trudgill, P. (1983) *On Dialect*. Oxford: Blackwell.

Trudgill, P. (1986) *Dialects in Contact*. Oxford: Blackwell.

Trudgill, P. (1988) Norwich revisited: Recent changes in an English urban dialect. *English World-Wide*, 9 (1), 33–49.

Trudgill, P. (1989) Contact and isolation in linguistic change. In L. E. Breivik and E. H. Jahr (eds.), *Language Change: Contributions to the Study of its Causes*. Trends in Linguistics: Studies and Monographs, 43. Berlin: Mouton de Gruyter, pp. 227–37.

Trudgill, P. (1996) Language contact and inherent variability: The absence of hypercorrection in East Anglian present tense forms. In J. Klemola, M. Kyto, and M. Rissanen (eds.), *Speech Past and Present: Studies in English Dialectology in Memory of Ossi Ihalainen*. Frankfurt am Main: P. Lang, pp. 412–45.

Trudgill, P. (1999) *The Dialects of England* (2nd edn.). Oxford: Blackwell.

Trudgill, P. and Britain, D. (2001) *Dialects in Contact* (2nd edn.). Oxford: Blackwell.

Trudgill, P., Gordon, E., Lewis, G., and Maclagan, M. (2000) Determinism in new-dialect formation and the genesis of New Zealand English. *Journal of Linguistics*, 36 (2), 299–318.

Tuten, D. N. (1998) Koineization in Medieval Spanish. Unpublished doctoral dissertation, University of Wisconsin-Madison.

Upton, C. and Llamas, C. (1999) Two large-scale and long-term language variation surveys: A retrospective and a plan. *Cuadernos de Filología Inglesa*, 8. Departamento de Filologia Inglesa de la Universidad de Murcia, pp. 291–304.

Van de Velde, H., van Hout, R., and Gerritsen, M. (1997) Watching Dutch change: A real time study of variation and change in standard Dutch pronunciation. *Journal of Sociolinguistics*, 1, 361–91.

Viereck, W. (1966) *Phonematische Analyse des Dialekts von Gateshead-upon-Tyne, Co. Durham*. Hamburg: Cram de Gruyter.

Voegelin, C. F. and Harris, Z. S. (1951) Methods for determining intelligibility among dialects of natural languages. *Proceedings of the American Philosophical Society*, 95, 322–9.

von Schneidemesser, L. (1996) Terms used for children's games: Comparing DARE's findings with usage of today's youth. In E. W. Schneider (ed.), *Focus on the USA*. Amsterdam and Philadelphia: Benjamins, pp. 63–80.

Wakelin, M. (1972) *Patterns in the Folk Speech of the British Isles*. London: Athlone.

Walker, J. A. (2000) Rephrasing the copula: Contraction and zero in early African American English. In S. Poplack (ed.), *The English History of African American English*. Oxford: Blackwell, pp. 35–72.

Walters, K. (1991) Women, men and linguistic variation in the Arab world. In B. Comrie and M. Eid (eds.), *Perspectives on Arabic Linguistics III*. Amsterdam and Philadelphia: Benjamins, pp. 199–229.

Walters, K. (1996) Gender, identity and the political economy of language: Anglophone wives in Tunisia. *Language in Society*, 25 (4), 515–55.

Walters, K. (2002) Review of N. Haeri "The Sociolinguistic Market of Cairo." *Journal of Sociolinguistics*, 6 (1), 152–5.

Wang, W. S. (1969) Competing changes as a cause of residue. *Language*, 45, 9–25.

Wardhaugh, R. (1986) *An Introduction to Sociolinguistics*. Oxford: Blackwell.

Watt, D. J. L. (1998) Variation and Change in the Vowel System of Tyneside English. Unpublished doctoral dissertation, University of Newcastle upon Tyne.

Watt, D. J. L. (2002) I don't speak with a Geordie accent, I speak like, the Northern accent. *Journal of Sociolinguistics*, 6, 44–63.

Watt, D. J. L. and Milroy, L. (1999) Patterns of variation and change in three Tyneside vowels: Is this dialect levelling? In P. Foulkes and G. J. Docherty (eds.), *Urban Voices*. London: Arnold, pp. 25–46.

Watt, D. and Tillotson, J. (2002) A spectrographic analysis of vowel fronting in Bradford English. *English World-Wide*, 22 (2), 271–304.

Weiner, E. J. and Labov, W. (1983) Constraints on the agentless passives. *Journal of Linguistics*, 19, 29–58.

Weinreich, U. (1954) Is a structural dialectology possible? *Word*, 10, 388–400. [Reprinted in Fishman, J. (ed.), (1968) *Readings in the Sociology of Language*. The Hague: Mouton.]

Weinreich, U., Labov, W., and Herzog, M. (1968) Empirical foundations for a theory of language change. In W. Lehmann and Y. Malkiel (eds.), *Directions for Historical Linguistics*. Austin: University of Texas Press, pp. 95–188.

Wells, J. (1982) *Accents of English* (3 vols). Cambridge: Cambridge University Press.

Williams, A. and Kerswill, P. (1999) Dialect levelling: Change and continuity in Milton Keynes, Reading and Hull. In P. Foulkes and G. J. Docherty (eds.), *Urban Voices*. London: Arnold, pp. 141–62.

Wilson, J. and Henry, A. (1998) Parameter setting within a socially realistic linguistics. *Language in Society*, 27 (1), 1–21.

Winford, D. (1996) The problem of syntactic variation. In J. Arnold et al. (eds.), *Sociolinguistic Variation: Data, Theory and Analysis*. Selected papers from NWAVE 23 at Stanford. Stanford: Center for the Study of Language and Information, pp. 177–92.

Winford, D. (1998) On the origins of African American Vernacular English – A creolist perspective. Part II: Linguistic features. *Diachronica*, XV (1), 99–154.

Wolfram, W. (1969) *A Sociolinguistic Description of Detroit Negro Speech*. Washington: Center for Applied Linguistics.

Wolfram, W. (1993a) Ethical considerations in language awareness programs. *Issues in Applied Linguistics*, 4, 225–55.

Wolfram, W. (1993b) Identifying and interpreting variables. In D. R. Preston (ed.), *American Dialect Research*. Amsterdam and Philadelphia: Benjamins, pp. 193–221.

Wolfram, W. (1998a) Language ideology and dialect. *Journal of English Linguistics*, 26, 108–21.

Wolfram, W. (1998b) Scrutinizing linguistic gratuity: Issues from the field. *Journal of Sociolinguistics*, 2, 271–9.

Wolfram, W. and Beckett, D. (2000) The role of the individual and the group in Earlier African American English. *American Speech*, 75 (1), 3–33.

Wolfram, W. and Christian, D. (1976) *Appalachian Speech*. Washington, DC: Center for Applied Linguistics.

Wolfram, W., Hazen, K., and Schilling-Estes, N. (1999) *Dialect Change and Maintenance on the Outer Banks*. Publication of the American Dialect Society, 81. Tuscaloosa and London: University of Alabama Press.

Wolfram, W. and Schilling-Estes, N. (1995) Moribund dialects and the endangerment canon: The case of the Ocracoke brogue. *Language*, 71, 696–721.

Wolfram, W. and Schilling-Estes, N. (1996) Dialect change and maintenance in a post-insular community. In E. Schneider (ed.), *Focus on the USA*. Amsterdam: Benjamins, pp. 103–48.

Wolfram, W. and Schilling-Estes, N. (1998) *American English*. Oxford: Blackwell.

Wolfram, W. and Sellers, J. (1999) Ethnolinguistic marking of past *be* in Lumbee vernacular English. *Journal of English Linguistics*, 27, 94–114.

Wolfram, W., Thomas, E. R., and Green, E. W. (2000) The regional context of earlier African American speech: Evidence for reconstructing the development of AAVE. *Language in Society*, 29, 315–55.

Wolfson, N. (1982) *CHP: The Conversational Historic Present in American English Narrative*. Dordrecht: Foris.

Woods, A., Fletcher, P., and Hughes, A. (1986) *Statistics in Language Studies*. Cambridge: Cambridge University Press.

Woolard, K. (1985) Language variation and cultural hegemony: Towards an integration of linguistic and sociolinguistic theory. *American Ethnologist*, 12, 738–48.

Woolard, K. (1997) Between friends: Gender, peer group structure and bilingualism in urban Catalonia. *Language in Society*, 26 (4), 533–60.

Wyngaerd, G. V. (2001) Measuring events. *Language*, 77 (1), 61–90.

Yaeger-Dror, M. (1991) Linguistic evidence for social psychological attitudes: Hyperaccommodation of (r) by singers from a Mizraji background. *Language and Communication*, 11 (4), 309–31.

Yaeger-Dror, M. (1993) Linguistic analysis of dialect "correction" and its interaction with cognitive salience. *Language Variation and Change*, 5 (2), 189–24.

Yaeger-Dror, M. (1996) Intonation and register variation: The case of the English negative. In J. Arnold, R. Blake, B. Davidson, S. Schwenter, and J. Solomon (eds.), *Sociolinguistic Variation: Data, Theory, and Analysis*. Selected Papers from NWAV 23 at Stanford. Stanford: Center for the Study of Language and Information, pp. 243–60.

Young, M. and Wilmott, P. (1962) *Family and Kinship in East London*. Harmonds-
  worth: Penguin.
Zentella, A. C. (1997) *Growing up Bilingual*. Oxford: Blackwell.
Zubritskaya, K. (1997) Mechanism of sound change in optimality theory. *Language
  Variation and Change*, 9 (1), 121–48.

Index